Manchester Museum Mummy Project

Multidisciplinary Research on
Ancient Egyptian Mummified Remains

Edited by A. Rosalie David

Production Editor: J. Forde-Johnston

Published by Manchester Museum

Distributed by Manchester University Press, Oxford Road, Manchester M13 9PL, England

ISBN 0-7190-1293-7

Printed by
W. S. MANEY & SON LTD   LEEDS   ENGLAND

CONTENTS

Acknowledgements

We would like to express our thanks to the following for their support and co-operation: the University of Manchester, the Chairman and members of the Manchester Museum Committee, and the Director of the Museum; Dr A. J. N. W. Prag and other members of the curatorial staff; Mrs C. M. Higginbottom, the Superintendent, and members of the technical staff of the Museum, especially in the areas of photography, conservation, drawing, and joinery; the British Academy for a grant towards our research, and Kodak Ltd for a most generous supply of film; the staff of various departments and institutions of the University, including Dr F. B. Beswick, Executive Dean of the Medical School; Mr F. Silvo and members of the staff of the Medical School; Mr L. Lawler, Director of the Audio-Visual Service; Mr K. Wrench, Producer, and the staff of the department; Mr P. Radcliffe, Head of Communications, and the staff of the Communications Office; Miss R. McGuiness and the staff of the Dental School; Miss E. McCauley, Department of Pharmacy; Dr C. A. Shuttleworth and Mrs J. L. Ward, Department of Medical Biochemistry; Mr M. Ashworth, Department of Medicine; Professor W. S. MacKenzie, Department of Geology; the Department of Zoology for use of transport; the staff of the Departments of Neuro-radiology and Anatomy at Manchester Royal Infirmary and the Director and staff of the Department of Medical Illustration at that hospital; Mr K. Hollins, Senior Chief Technician at Withington Hospital and his team of histology technicians at that hospital; Mr R. White for preliminary radiography at the Museum; Dr O. Amit for an authentic sample of Dead Sea bitumen; Mr G. Irving; Mrs J. Ovenden; the Flinders Petrie Museum, University College, London; Mr P. Jordan and Miss A. Benson Gyles, and members of the BBC Chronicle team. Finally, the team would like to thank Book Club Associates for their encouragement and enthusiasm throughout the production of the popular version of this book, which has helped to contribute towards the cost of publication.

The members of the team who have pursued these aims with me during the past six years include specialists from various departments of the University of Manchester and Manchester Museum, and from several hospitals in the area; experts in certain fields have also joined the team from London. The team includes Dr A. Curry, a zoologist and electron-microscopist at the University Hospital of South Manchester, and his co-worker, Mrs C. Anfield; Dr D. M. Dixon, Lecturer in Egyptology and Curator of the Flinders Petrie Museum at University College, London; Detective Chief Inspector A. Fletcher of the Greater Manchester Police; Mr R. Garner of the Manchester Museum Conservation staff; Professor I. Isherwood, Head of the Department of Diagnostic Radiology at the University of Manchester, and his colleagues, Dr R. A. Fawcitt, Senior Lecturer in that department, and Miss H. Jarvis, Superintendent Radiographer at Manchester Royal Infirmary; Dr F. N. Leach, Director of the Drug Information Centre of St Mary's Hospital, Manchester, and his colleagues, Dr G. G. Benson and Dr Sarah Hemingway, Lecturers in Pharmacy at the University of Manchester; Mr F. F. Leek, a dental surgeon and authority on the study of the teeth of Egyptian mummies; Mr R. A. H. Neave, Assistant Director of the Department of Medical Illustration at Manchester Royal Infirmary; Dr G. W. A. Newton, Lecturer in Chemistry at the University of Manchester; and Dr E. Tapp, Consultant Histo-pathologist at the group laboratory, Preston Royal Infirmary. Other specialists who have advised on and taken part in the project include Dr J. P. Wild of the Department of Archaeology at the University of Manchester, who has contributed the chapter on textiles, and Dr A. Ahmed of the Department of Pathology of the University of Manchester, and Professor W. E. Kershaw, formerly of Salford University, who participated in the unwrapping of No. 1770.

This publication is financed by the University of Manchester and by the advance royalties from the popular book on the same theme, published by Book Club Associates in 1978, which members of the team have donated for this purpose.

A. ROSALIE DAVID
Manchester, 1978

v

Introduction

In 1907, Dr Margaret Murray, Egyptologist at the Manchester Museum, undertook one of the earliest scientific investigations of Egyptian mummies when she unwrapped and dissected the mummies of the Two Brothers at Manchester University. Her experiment was then unique in that she headed an interdisciplinary team whose members were specialists in the fields of anatomy, chemical analysis, and the study of textiles. They all contributed their knowledge to the detailed examination of these mummies, and the results of their investigations were published in the book entitled *The Tomb of the Two Brothers* (1910).

Nearly seventy years later, in 1972, it was decided to undertake a similar investigation, but for this project the whole collection of Egyptian mummified remains at the Museum were examined, and they were subjected to an intensive study using as many modern scientific techniques as possible. The unique situation of the Museum with its ready access to University departments and its physical proximity to hospitals with highly specialized, advanced equipment, ensured that the project had access to considerable resources. A highly specialized team was drawn from various departments and an interdisciplinary approach was achieved; moreover, it was possible to move Museum collections without difficulty to the nearby hospitals for examination under near-ideal conditions. The supportive attitude of the University authorities, and of the Chairman, Committee, and Director of the Museum, was another major factor in enabling the team members to undertake this programme of study and to complete their research. Additional financial aid was granted by the British Academy, and Kodak Ltd most generously supplied much of the x-ray film.

The project had two basic aims. First, the intention was to discover as much information as possible from a specific group of mummies which could be related to existing knowledge of religious and funerary customs, living conditions, the state of physical and dental health, and the process of mummification in ancient Egypt; it was also hoped to identify evidence of disease and, in addition, possible causes of death. The second aim was to establish a methodology, using many different techniques under near-ideal conditions, for the examination of a group of Egyptian mummified remains, which other institutions could adopt and adapt for the investigation of their own collections.

In order to apply as many techniques as possible to one mummy under near-ideal conditions, the decision was eventually taken to perform an autopsy on one of the mummies as part of the overall investigation. For several reasons the mummy known by its museum acquisition number as 1770 was selected for this purpose, and was unwrapped at the Manchester Medical School in June 1975.

The collection in the Manchester Museum includes seventeen human and thirty-one animal mummies; in addition there are a number of mummified human and animal detached heads, limbs and other organs.

The collection spans a period from c.1900 B.C. to c.4th century A.D., at the time of the Roman occupation of Egypt. It has been acquired from a variety of sources; some of the material is provenanced, originating mainly from sites excavated by Sir Flinders Petrie, but also from the excavations of the Egypt Exploration Society and of Professor Garstang. Other material, mostly acquired from private individuals, is unprovenanced. A major part of the mummy collection, and indeed the entire Egyptian collection, came to the Manchester Museum through the generosity of Dr Jesse Haworth, a Manchester businessman and friend of Sir Flinders Petrie. Other mummies have been acquired through the British School of Archaeology in Egypt, the Egyptian Research Account, the Egypt Exploration Society (via the British Museum), various museums and private collections, and from individual donors.

Extensive examination of this collection has recently been undertaken by the team of specialists already listed in the Acknowledgements, and the results of their researches form the basis of this book. The various techniques employed have included a radiological survey and study of all the mummies. This method, being non-destructive, could be applied to all the mummies in the collection, and radiographs were also used, in addition to visual examination, in the survey undertaken of the teeth of the human mummies and the detached heads. Where mummified soft tissue or organs were preserved and available for study, a range of techniques in the field of pathology were applied in an attempt to identify disease in the human mummies. These included the rehydration and processing of mummified tissue to enable satisfactory histological sections to be prepared for examination by light microscopy and electron microscopy. The insects found in the mummies and their wrappings were also examined and identified by means of electron microscopy.

Some techniques were applied specifically to the mummy (1770) on which the autopsy was performed in 1975. Various methods of analysis, especially chromatography, were used in an attempt to identify the natural products employed in mummification; an analysis of the material of the bandages and other related factors were carried out; Carbon-14 dating techniques were brought in to establish the approximate age of the bones and the bandages of this mummy, and to determine whether or not they belonged to the same period.

Another related study involved the investigation of the actual process of mummification as practised by the ancient Egyptians and as described in the writing of

Herodotus. A summary of the history and development of mummification in Egypt is beyond the scope of this publication and is covered fully elsewhere,[1] but the basic facts are mentioned in connection with these experiments.

Other specialists obtained the fingerprints and toe-prints of one of the mummies which had been unwrapped before being acquired by the Museum, and which was particularly well-preserved; this technique assisted in determining the person's age at death, and gave some indication of her lifestyle. It has also been possible to reconstruct the major features of selected mummified human heads from the collection, with some degree of accuracy, thus enabling those viewing the mummified remains to relate more easily to the appearance of these people when alive. Using this technique, it has been possible to produce three-dimensional heads which could serve as models on which to base illustrations for purposes of publication or exhibition.

A. R. DAVID

[1] See *Catalogue of Egyptian Antiquities in the British Museum — Mummies and Human Remains*, pp. vii–xiii, and G. Elliot Smith and W. R. Dawson, *Egyptian Mummies*, pp. 72–132.

A Catalogue of Egyptian Human and Animal Mummified Remains

by
A. ROSALIE DAVID

This catalogue of the Manchester Museum collection includes mummified human bodies (but excludes other skeletal remains and dry skulls), animal remains, and parts of human mummies from Egypt.

A future catalogue will give a detailed description of the coffins and cartonnage cases, including the religious scenes and texts, and this information is therefore omitted here.

Measurements given in the catalogue indicate the approximate length of the unwrapped bodies and the external dimensions of those which are wrapped in bandages, or enclosed in cartonnage cases or a reed cover.

Human Mummies

Middle Kingdom

Nos. 21470 and 21471 These two mummies were discovered together in an unopened tomb at Rifeh. The complete tomb-group is in Manchester Museum, and includes the two bodies, two wooden painted and inscribed rectangular coffins (belonging to Nekht-ankh, 4724a and b, and belonging to Khnum-nakht, 4725a and b), two wooden painted anthropoid coffins (Nekht-ankh, 4739, and Khnum-nakht, 4740), wooden painted and inscribed canopic chest belonging to Nekht-ankh (4726), four canopic jars of Nekht-ankh (4727–4730), pottery vase (4731), pottery bowl (4732), containing leaves and stalks (4733), female servant statuettes (4734 and 4738), wooden statuettes inscribed for Nekht-ankh (4735 and 4736) and for Khnum-nakht (4737), two model boats (4741 and 4742), bandages from both mummies (21472a and b), mummified tissue from Nekht-ankh, including brain, lung, liver, larynx, finger-nails, penis, aortic arch and pericardium and fragmentary tissue (21472c–j).

This group came from the excavation of Sir Flinders Petrie and was donated to the museum by the British School of Archaeology in Egypt. The mummies were unwrapped in 1907 by Dr Margaret Murray at Manchester University.[1] The coffin inscriptions indicate that the men shared a common mother, but their bodies display such physical differences that their relationship has been questioned.[2]

No. 21470 Mummy of an adult male, named Nekht-ankh, son of Aa-Khnum[3]

Date:	XII Dynasty
Provenance:	Rifeh[4]
Length:	161 cm
Date of acquisition:	1906

When unwrapped, the bones were intact, although the body tissue had disintegrated. The dark brown facial skin was partly preserved, the finger- and toe-nails were well-preserved and the dark brown hair was turning grey. Possibly eunochoid, the estimated age at death of this man was about 60 years. Large numbers of beetles were present among the inner bandages. The internal and external organs were mummified and placed in two of his canopic jars. The skull is of the orthognathous or non-negroid type, although the body was found in the body coffin of which the face is painted black. Also, the skull shows a marked resemblance to the head of the wooden statuette inscribed with the name of Khnum-nakht (4737).

No. 21471 Mummy of an adult male, named Khnum-nakht, son of Aa-Khnum, great w'b-priest[5]

Date:	XII Dynasty
Provenance:	Rifeh
Length:	158 cm
Date of acquisition:	1906

When unwrapped the body was in a very dry condition, and the soft tissues dissolved into fine powder. Very little skin tissue now remains. No special attention had been given to the preservation of the finger- and toe-nails, and the soft tissues and internal organs had been reduced to dark brown powder. No beetles were present among the bandages. The man was aged about 40 years at death. The mummy was less well-preserved than that of Nekht-ankh and had not been provided with canopic jars. The skull is of the prognathous or negroid type, although this body was found in the body coffin of which the face is painted yellowish-white. The skull also closely resembles the head of one of the wooden statuettes (4736) inscribed for Nekht-ankh.

New Kingdom

No. 3496 Mummy of a child, name unknown[6]

Date:	XVIII Dynasty
Provenance:	Gurob
Length:	85 cm
Date of acquisition:	1904[7]

The body is wrapped in a reed mat, tied with ropes at either end.

No. 9354 Mummy of an adult male, in a wooden coffin, bearing the name Khary, Divine Father of Amun[8]

Date:	XIX Dynasty
Provenance:	Unrecorded
Length:	161 cm
Date of acquisition:	1935[9]

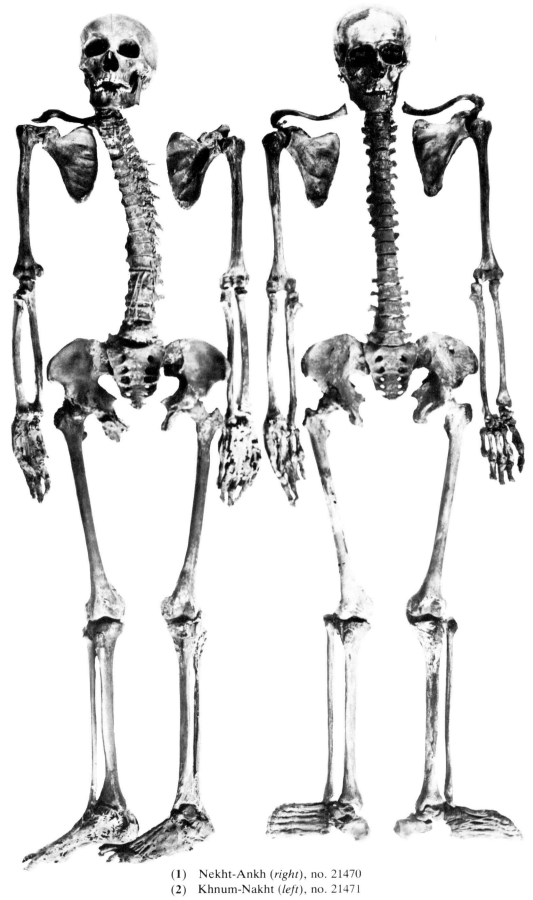

(1) Nekht-Ankh (*right*), no. 21470
(2) Khnum-Nakht (*left*), no. 21471

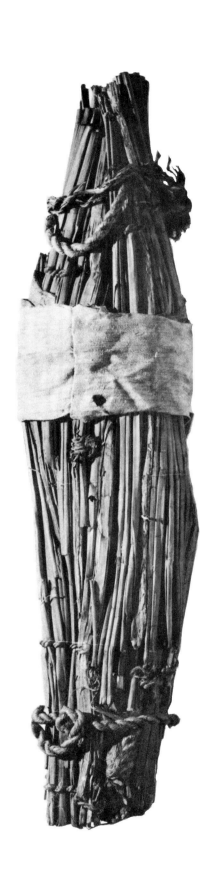

(3)   No. 3496

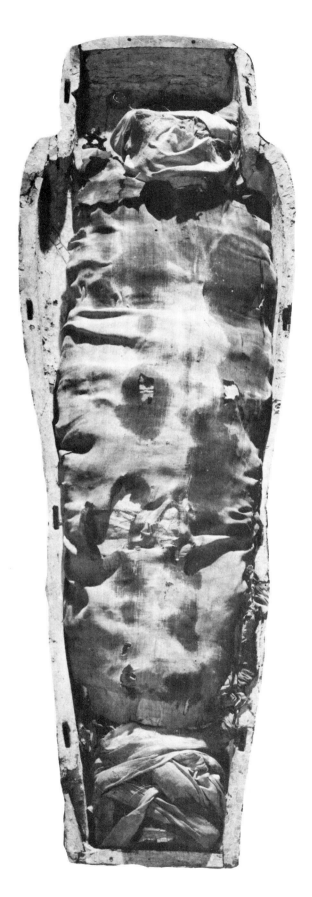

(4)   No. 9354

3

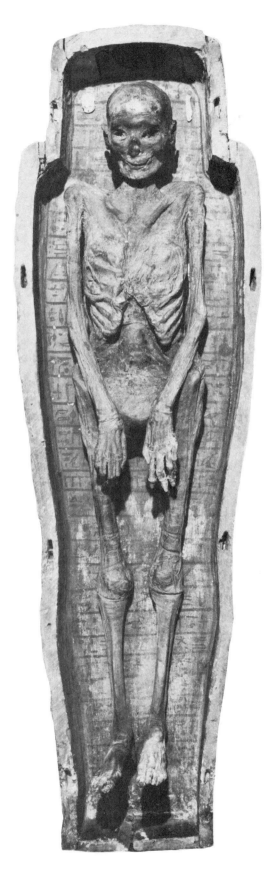

(5) No. 1976 51a   (6) No. 10881   (7) No. 1777

The anthropoid coffin is decorated with painted scenes and inscriptions. The mummy had been partly un-wrapped before entering the Museum collection. One fist is open and the other is clenched.

No. 1976.51a   Mummy of an adult female in a wooden coffin, name unknown.[10]

Date:	Probably XXV Dynasty
Provenance:	Unrecorded, but possibly Luxor[11]
Length:	160 cm
Date of acquisition:	1976[12]

The painted decoration on the anthropoid coffin is indistinct. The mummy had been unwrapped by its owner and was re-examined after arrival at the Museum in July 1976. The body is well-preserved, with fine facial features, and slender hands and feet. The embalmer's incision in the left side of the abdomen is visible.

Late Period (XXI–XXV Dynasties)

No. 10881   Mummy of an adult, possibly female, in a wooden coffin, bearing the name Ta-aath[13]

Date:	XXI–XXV Dynasty
Provenance:	Unrecorded but possibly Luxor[14]
Length:	160 cm
Date of acquisition:	1948[15]

The anthropoid coffin is decorated with painted scenes and inscriptions. The mummy had been unwrapped and loosely re-wrapped before its acquisition by the Manchester Museum.[16]

The Curator of the Hastings Museum is said to have brought in authorities from the British Museum to examine the mummy.[17]

No. 1777   Mummy of an adult female, with two wooden coffins, bearing the name of Asru[18]

Date:	Probably XXV Dynasty
Provenance:	Unrecorded, but possibly Luxor
Length:	150 cm
Date of acquisition:	1825[19]

The inner and outer anthropoid coffins are decorated with painted scenes and inscriptions. The mummy had been unwrapped before entering the Museum collection. It is well-preserved, with fine facial features; the arms and hands are outstretched and extend over the thighs. A package of mummified viscera was placed upon the thighs.

No. 5053a   Mummy of an adult female, in a wooden coffin, bearing the name of Perenbast, Chantress of Amun.[20]

Date:	XXV Dynasty
Provenance:	Qurneh[21]
Length:	167 cm
Date of acquisition:	1909[22]

The anthropoid coffin (5053c) is pitched and decorated with scenes and inscriptions painted in yellow; the eyes and eyebrows are inlaid with glass. Lotus flowers (Sacred Lotus flowers, *Nelumbo nucifera*) were placed in the coffin beneath the mummy. The body is bandaged and covered with a thin coat of pitch. Radiological examination has indicated the presence of amulets between the layers of bandages. Other equipment from this tomb in the Manchester collection includes wooden dowels to fasten the coffin (5053b), a statuette of Ptah-Sokar (5053d), a wooden box to contain ushabti-figures (5053e), another wooden box (5053f) and about 360 ushabti-figures from the above boxes (5053g), in which they were placed on clean sand.

(8)   No. 5053a

The Graeco-Roman Period

No. 1766   Mummy of an adult female, name unknown[23]

Date:	Roman Period (1st/2nd century A.D.)
Provenance:	Fayoum
Length:	166 cm
Date of acquisition:	1895–6[24]

A body enclosed in bandages coated in resin, painted with three horizontal registers of funerary scenes. There is a painted cartonnage cover of separate pieces for the head, breast and feet; the head, breast and feet are gilded and the sole of the foot cover is decorated with painted figures. Imitations of serpent-bracelets, rings, necklaces inlaid with glass to represent semi-precious stones, and a bunch of flowers held in the woman's hand decorate the cartonnage breast cover.

No. 1767   Mummy of an adult male, name unknown[25]

Date:	Roman Period (1st/2nd century A.D.)
Provenance:	Fayoum
Length:	161 cm
Date of acquisition:	Possibly 1888–90[26]

A body enclosed in bandages coated in resin, painted with a red background on which a wsh-collar and five horizontal registers of funerary scenes are depicted. There is a portrait-panel over the face, showing a bearded man, which is encircled by a cartonnage head cover which extends over the breast and imitates a white cloak covering the head and bust. The hands are gilded, and the right one is shown holding the cloak while the left one holds a green loop. A cartonnage foot cover, with gilded toe-nails, protrudes from the bandages.

No. 1768   Mummy of an adolescent boy, name unknown[27]

Date:	Roman Period (1st century B.C.)
Provenance:	Hawara[28]
Length:	168 cm
Date of acquisition:	1888[29]

A body enclosed in elaborate diagonal bandaging, interspersed with gilded studs; a cartonnage piece covers the feet.[30] The fine portrait-panel over the face shows an adolescent boy wearing a laurel wreath.

No. 1769   Mummy of a child, sex uncertain, name unknown[31]

Date:	Roman Period (2nd century A.D.)
Provenance:	Hawara[32]
Length:	99 cm
Date of acquisition:	1888–90

A body enclosed in bandages, coated with resin, painted with three horizontal registers of funerary scenes on a pink background. There is a cartonnage cover of separate pieces for the head, breast and feet. The head, bust and feet are gilded, and on the bust there are imitations of serpent-bracelets and jewellery inlaid with glass to represent semi-precious stones. On the head piece, wavy hair is indicated and the eyes are inlaid.

No. 1770   Mummy of an adolescent, sex uncertain but probably female[33]

Date:	Originally thought to be Ptolemaic, but see results of Carbon-14 dates, p. 146
Provenance:	Unrecorded, but possibly Hawara[34]
Length:	132 cm
Date of acquisition:	1895–6[35]

This body was wrapped in reddish-brown bandages which were in a poor state of preservation. The head was enclosed in a cartonnage cover with a gilded face and inlaid eyes and eyebrows. When it was unwrapped at Manchester in June 1975,[36] a cartonnage breast cover, decorated soles, gilded nipple amulets, a prosthetic phallus, and gilded toe-nail and finger-nail covers were discovered.

No. 1775   Mummy of an adult male, named Artemidorous[37]

Date:	Roman Period (early 2nd century A.D.)
Provenance:	Hawara[38]
Length:	167 cm
Date of acquisition:	1888[39]

The body is enclosed in a cartonnage case, painted red with mythological scenes in gold leaf. A portrait-panel covers the face,[40] showing an elderly man wearing a laurel wreath; on the chest is the inscription 'O, Artemidorous, farewell'.

No. 2109   Mummy of a child, sex uncertain, name unknown[41]

Date:	Roman Period
Provenance:	Hawara
Length:	80 cm
Date of acquisition:	1888–90[42]

The body is enclosed in diagonal bandaging interspersed with gilded studs, and cartonnage pieces to cover the head and the feet. The face piece is gilded and gilded toes are visible protruding from the bandaging.

No. 9319   Mummy of a child, probably male, name unknown[43]

Date:	Roman Period
Provenance:	Hawara
Length:	90 cm
Date of acquisition:	c.1933[44]

The body is enclosed in diagonal bandaging interspersed with gilded studs. The portrait-panel which originally covered the face was taken to the Boulaq Museum, Cairo.[45]

No. 20638   Mummy of an adult female, bearing the name Demetria, wife of Icaious[46]

Date:	Roman Period (c.100 A.D.)
Provenance:	Hawara[47]
Length:	159 cm
Date of acquisition:	1910–11[48]

6

(9)   No. 20638   (10)   No. 1767

7

(**11**)   No. 1768   (**12**)   No. 1769

8

(13) No. 1770

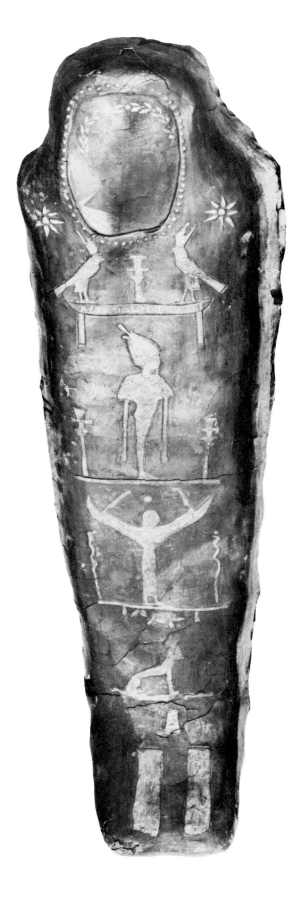

(14) No. 1775

(15)   No. 2109   (16)   No. 9319

10

The body is enclosed in bandages coated in resin; cartonnage pieces cover the head, chest and feet. The resin-coated wrappings are painted red and decorated with four horizontal registers of deities; the face and chest covers are gilded, and the eyes are inlaid. Imitation jewellery is indicated on the chest cover; serpent-bracelets are shown, and the jewellery is inlaid with glass to represent semi-precious stones. The face piece has been repaired and restored. A Greek inscription on the headband gives the name of the deceased.

Mummified Human Parts

No. 5275   Head

Date:	Unknown but said to be Ptolemaic(?) by G. Elliot Smith
Provenance:	Unrecorded
Height:	21.5 cm
Date of acquisition:	Unrecorded, but donated by Miss Wroe of Manchester

The features are well-preserved; the hair, moustache and a few eyelashes are present.

No. 7740   Head

Date:	Unknown
Provenance:	Unrecorded, but stated to be near Cairo
Height:	21 cm
Date of acquisition:	1925[49]

The upper part of the skull has been removed and is now attached by clips. The skull was opened by Mr Crabtree. The brain was extracted in antiquity, but the brain membrane is well-preserved.[50]

No. 21475   Head

Date:	Unknown
Provenance:	Unrecorded
Height:	23.5 cm
Date of acquisition:	Unrecorded. Found in the collection together with the mummified foot (no. 21474)

The head is in a poor state of preservation and areas of the skin tissue are worn away. The skin tissue is dark brown and some small pieces of bandage still adhere to it. The head is shaven, the eye sockets are plugged with packing, the nose is flattened, and the mouth is slightly open, revealing well-preserved teeth.

No. 22940   Head

Date:	Unknown
Provenance:	Unrecorded
Height:	23 cm
Date of acquisition:	Unrecorded

The mid-brown skin tissue is well-preserved, the head is shaven, the eyelids closed, the nose flattened and the imprint of the bandages is still visible on the skin.

(17)   No. 1766

No. 1765   Hand, right

Date: Unknown
Provenance: Unrecorded
Length: 20 cm
Date of acquisition: Unrecorded

The yellowish skin-tissue still remains and the thumb, fingers and nails are all present.

No. 9384   Hand, left

Date: Unknown
Provenance: Unrecorded
Length: 13.5 cm
Date of acquisition: 1936[51]

The hand is wrapped in bandages to which a few glazed beads are attached. The thumb and all the fingers are present.

No. 9428   Hand, right

Date: Unknown
Provenance: Unrecorded
Length: 14 cm
Date of acquisition: 1936[52]

No bandages remain and the thumb is missing. This hand was rehydrated as part of the research undertaken by the Manchester Research Team in July 1976.

No. 1977.1154   Hand, left

Date: Unknown
Provenance: Unrecorded
Length: 19.5 cm
Date of acquisition: 1977[53]

The skin tissue is dark brown, the fingers are complete and bandages still adhere to parts of the hand. Fragments of a blue faience ring remain embedded at the base of the second finger.

No. 1977.1155   Hand, right

Date: Unknown
Provenance: Unrecorded
Length: 17.4 cm
Date of acquisition: 1977[54]

The skin tissue is dark brown. No bandages remain.

No. 1977.1156   Hand, right

Date: Unknown
Provenance: Unrecorded
Length: 11.5 cm
Date of acquisition: 1977[55]

The hand is completely bandaged. The fingers are bent over, and the top phalange of each of the first three fingers is missing; one loose finger-tip is present.

No. 1977.1157   Hand

Date: Unknown
Provenance: Unrecorded
Length: Approx. 16.5 cm
Date of acquisition: 1977[56]

The hand is in a poor state of preservation, and consists of a jumble of bones.

No. 1977.1158   Hand, right

Date: Unknown
Provenance: Possibly Thebes
Length: 17 cm
Date of acquisition: 1977[57]

The hand is in a poor state of preservation.

No. 21476   Hand, left

Date: Unknown
Provenance: Unrecorded, possibly Luxor
Length: 18.5 cm
Date of acquisition: 1905[58]

A well-formed hand, with darkened skin to which some pieces of bandage still adhere. All the fingers and the thumb are present, but the top phalanges of the fingers are missing.

No. 21474   Foot, right

Date: Unknown
Provenance: Unrecorded
Length: 20 cm
Date of acquisition: Unrecorded. Found in the collection together with the mummified head (No. 21475)

The skin tissue is dark brown, and the toes and toe-nails are still present.

No. 21473   Mummified viscera from Asru (Mummy No. 1777)[59]

Date: Probably XXV Dynasty
Provenance: Unrecorded, but probably Luxor
Date of acquisition: 1825

A linen-wrapped package containing viscera, which was placed between the legs of the mummy.[60]

No. 21472a–j   Bandages and viscera from the Two Brothers (Nekht-ankh and Khnum-nakht)[61]

Date: XII Dynasty
Provenance: Rifeh
Date of acquisition: 1906

No. 21472a   Bandages from the mummy of Nekht-ankh.

No. 21472b   Bandages from the mummy of Khnum-nakht.

The following organs are from Nekht-ankh:[62]

No. 21472c   Brain

No. 21472d   Lung tissue

No. 21472e   Liver

No. 21472f   Larynx

No. 21472g   Finger-nails

No. 21472h   Penis

No. 21472i   Aortic arch and pericardium[63]

No. 21472j   Mummified dust

Mummified Animals

No. 563   Young mammal, possibly a puppy
Date: Probably XVIII–XIX Dynasty
Provenance: Gurob
Height: 32 cm
Date of acquisition: 1906[64]
Wrapped in brown bandages.

No. 6293   Cat
Data: XXII Dynasty
Provenance: Beni Hasan[65]
Height: 34.5 cm
Date of acquisition: June 1920[66]
The elaborate bandaging around the mummy is well-preserved, and forms concentric squares.

No. 6842   Young mammal, possibly a kitten, *Felis silvestris libyca*
Date: Unknown
Provenance: Unrecorded
Height: 31 cm
Date of acquisition: August 1922[67]
Wrapped in brown bandages, and the ears are imitated in linen; the eyes are outlined in black on the bandaging, and other details are marked in black and red.

No. 9303   Kitten inside a wooden coffin, *Felis silvestris libyca*
Date: Late period
provenance: Unrecorded
Height (with case):   46 cm
Date of acquisition: 1921[68]
The mummy is inside a case in the form of a cat, which is painted white, with the features carefully carved.

No. 1977.1162   Cat
Date: Unknown
Provenance: Unrecorded
Height: 37 cm
Date of acquisition: 1977[69]
Wrapped in brown bandages.

No. 22947   Cat
Date: Late period
Provenance: Unrecorded
Height: 18 cm
Date of acquisition: Unrecorded
Unwrapped; it has yellowish fur, the teeth and front paws are well-preserved, and part of the spinal column is separate from the body.

No. 11123   Head of a young cat, *Felis silvestris libyca*
Date: Unknown
Provenance: Unrecorded
Height: 8.5 cm
Date of Acquisition: 1959[70]

No. 22948   Head of a cat, *Felis silvestris libyca*
Date: Possibly Middle Kingdom
Provenance: Beni Hasan
Height: 9.5 cm
Date of acquisition: Unrecorded
Unwrapped; well-preserved teeth, ear flaps and whiskers; yellowish fur. An attached label reads 'Felis Maniculata A.45'.

No. 22949   Head of a cat, *Felis silvestris libyca*
Date: Possibly Middle Kingdom
Provenance: Beni Hasan
Height: 11.5 cm
Date of acquisition: Unrecorded
Unwrapped; dark skin with traces of yellow fur; eyelashes are visible. An attached label reads 'Felis Maniculata A.44'.

No. 1772   Crocodile, *Crocodylus niloticus*
Date: Unknown
Provenance: Unrecorded
Length: 64.5 cm
Date of acquisition: 1895–96[71]
Wrapped in brown bandages.

No. 3005   Crocodile, *Crocodylus niloticus*
Date: Roman Period
Provenance: Hawara
Length: 46.5 cm
Date of acquisition: 1887–88[72]
Wrapped in brown bandages.

No. 7892   Crocodile — part of a crocodile, *Crocodylus niloticus*
Date: Possibly Roman Period
Provenance: Unrecorded
Length: 37 cm
Date of acquisition: 1925[73]
Wrapped in bandages of dark and light brown linen, arranged in rectangular patterns.

No. 22941   Crocodile, *Crocodylus niloticus*
Date: Possibly Ptolemaic
Provenance: Unrecorded
Length: 64.5 cm
Date of acquisition: Unrecorded
Wrapped in three sections of simple diagonal bandaging, separated by straight bandaging on top of the mummy. Two protuberances indicate the position of the eyes under the bandages. An attached label reads 'E.G.95'.

No. 22942   Crocodile, *Crocodylus niloticus*

Date: Late Period
Provenance: Unrecorded
Length: 19 cm
Date of acquisition: Unrecorded

In a poor state of preservation, with the outer bandages loosened. An attached label reads 'E.G.7'.

No. 22943   Crocodile, *Crocodylus niloticus*

Date: Late Period
Provenance: Unrecorded
Length: 52.5 cm
Date of acquisition: Unrecorded

Flattened, with a curved tail and wrapped in light brown bandages.

No. 5373a, b, c, d   Four imitations of mummified crocodiles, made of reeds covered with cloth, containing a juvenile crocodile and 2 crushed eggs, *Crocodylus niloticus*

Date: Roman Period
Provenance: Hawara[74]
Length: a — 53 cm   c — 30.5 cm
                             b — 43 cm   d — 23.5 cm
Date of acquisition: 1910–11

No. 6035   Kestrel, *Falco tinnunculus*

Date: Unknown
Provenance: Unrecorded; bought at Aswan
Height: 24.5 cm
Date of acquisition: Unrecorded[75]

No. 9371   Sparrowhawk, *accipiter nisus*

Date: Unknown
Provenance: Unrecorded
Height: 26.5 cm
Date of acquisition: 1934[76]

No. 9248   Hawk

Date: Unknown
Provenance: Unrecorded
Height: 26.5 cm
Date of acquisition: 1936[77]

No. 9429   Hawk

Date: Unknown
Provenance: Unrecorded
Height: 26 cm
Date of acquisition: 1936[77]

No. 11293   Hawk

Date: Late Period
Provenance: Unrecorded
Height: 36.8 cm
Date of acquisition: January 1959[78]

The mummy depicts Osiris; it is enclosed in bandages and has a gilded head-cover and breast-cover.

No. 11294   Kestrel, *Falco tinnunculus*

Date: Late Period
Provenance: Unrecorded
Height: 22 cm
Date of acquisition: January 1959[79]

No. 11295   Hawk

Date: Possibly Ptolemaic Period
Provenance: Unrecorded
Height: 36.5 cm
Date of acquisition: January 1959[80]

No. 22944   Hawk

Date: Late Period
Provenance: Unrecorded
Height: 26 cm
Date of acquisition: Unrecorded

The dark brown outer bandages are still almost intact and the beak and an eye socket are visible.

No. 1971.21   Kestrel, *Falco tinnunculus*

Date: XXVI–XXX Dynasty
Provenance: Sakkara[81]
Height: 44.5 cm
Date of acquisition: 1971[82]

Wrapped in bandages, with ornamental bandaging on the chest; there is painted decoration on the head in black and red; the beak and the right eye are missing.

No. 11296   Sacred Ibis, *Threskiornis aethiopica*

Date: Probably Ptolemaic Period
Provenance: Unrecorded
Height: 29 cm
Date of acquisition: January 1959[83]

Wrapped in elaborate diagonal bandaging.

No. 11501   Sacred Ibis, *Threskiornis aethiopica*

Date: Late Period
Provenance: Sakkara
Height: 45 cm
Date of acquisition: 1969[84]

Wrapped in elaborate diagonal bandaging, decorated with Thoth seated on a throne and surmounted by the Atef-crown.

No. 6098   Sacred Ibis, *Threskiornis aethiopica*

Date: Roman Period
Provenance: Abydos, Ibis cemetery[85]
Height: 66 cm
Date of acquisition: 1913–14[86]

Wrapped in diagonal bandaging of dark and light brown linen; the head is modelled to represent Thoth, and the Atef-crown is supported behind the head.

No. 5923   Three fragments of bird bones, mummified

Date: Unknown
Provenance: Unrecorded
Date of acquisition: 1921[87]

No. 1195   Snake inside a wooden box, species unidentified

Date:	XXVI Dynasty
Provenance:	Hibeh
Length (of box):	14.8 cm
Date of acquisition:	1903[88]

The lid of the wooden box is decorated with the carving
of a snake.

No. 6032   Circular linen bundle containing a shrew,
possibly *Crocidura flavescens olivieri* or *Suncus murinus*

Date:	Unknown
Provenance:	Unrecorded; bought at Aswan
Diameter: .	8.1 cm
Date of acquisition:	Unrecorded[89]

No. 6033a, b   Linen package containing a shrew, with
another package attached to it, possibly *Crocidura
flavescens olivieri* or *Suncus murinus*

Date:	Unknown
Provenance:	Unrecorded; bought at Aswan
Length:	12.3 cm
Date of acquisition:	Unrecorded[90]

A long oval package; the smaller, similar package is
empty.

No. 6034   Linen package

Date:	Unknown
Provenance:	Unrecorded; bought at Aswan
Length:	18.7 cm
Date of acquisition:	Unrecorded[91]

No. 22945   Package containing a mummified animal,
identified as a kitten, *Felis silvestris libyca*

Date:	Late Period
Provenance:	Unrecorded
Length:	23.7 cm
Date of acquisition:	Unrecorded

An attached label reads 'E.G.9'.

No. 22946   Package containing a mummified mammal,
not identified

Date:	Unknown
Provenance:	Unrecorded
Length:	17 cm
Date of acquisition:	Unrecorded

An attached label reads 'E.G.8'.

Not all the animal mummies have been examined and
identified at the time of publication, but will be discussed
in a forthcoming article.

Bibliography

W. R. Dawson and P. H. K. Gray, *Catalogue of the
Human Remains in the Department of Egyptian
Antiquities, British Museum, London* (London, 1968).

G. Elliott Smith, *The Royal Mummies* (Catalogue
général des antiquités Égyptiennes du Musée du
Caire. Cairo, 1912).

C. C. Edgar, *Graeco-Egyptian coffins, masks and
portraits* (Catalogue général des antiquités Égyptiennes
du Musée du Caire. Cairo, 1905).

Cl. Gaillard and G. Daressy, *La Faune Momifiée de
l'Antique Égypte* (Catalogue général des antiquités
Égyptiennes du Musée du Caire. Cairo, 1905).

R. Engelbach and D. E. Derry, 'Mummification' in
Annales du Service des Antiquités de l'Égypte, 41
(1942), 233–65.

A. S. Griffiths, *A Catalogue of Egyptian antiquities of the
XII and XVIII Dynasties from Kahun, Illahun and
Gurob* (Manchester, 1910).

*Catalogue of the Robinow Collection of Egyptian
Antiquities deposited at the Manchester Museum in
1896.*

P. H. K. Gray, *Radiological Aspects of the mummies of
the ancient Egyptians in the Rijksmuseum van
Oudheden, Leiden* (Oudheidkundige mededelingen
uit het Rijksmuseum van Oudheden, Leiden 47,
Leiden, 1966).

W. Hayes, *The Scepter of Egypt*, I (New York, 1953).

A. Lucas, *Ancient Egyptian materals and industries* (4th
edition, London, 1962).

M. A. Murray, *The Tomb of the Two Brothers*
(Manchester, 1910).

T. E. Peet and W. L. S. Loat, *Cemeteries of Abydos III*
(London, 1913).

W. M. F. Petrie, *Gizeh and Rifeh* (London, 1907).

——, *Hawara, Biahmu and Arsinoe* (London, 1889).

——, *Qurneh* (London, 1909).

——, *Roman Portraits and Memphis IV* (London, 1911).

Clare Sheridan, *Nuda Veritas* (Thornton Butterworth
Ltd, 1927).

A. F. Shore, *Portrait Painting from Roman Egypt*
(British Museum, London, 1962).

G. Elliot Smith, 'Egyptian Mummies', in *Journal of
Egyptian Archaeology* (1914), Vol. I, 192.

—— and W. R. Dawson, *Egyptian Mummies* (London,
1924).

——, 'A contribution to the study of mummification in
Egypt, with special reference to the measures adopted
during the time of the Twenty-first Dynasty for
moulding the form of the body', in *Mémoires présentés
à l'Institut Égyptien*, Vol. V, fasc. 1 (Cairo, 1906),
1–53 and pls. 1–19.

Notes
[1] M. A. Murray, *The Tomb of the Two Brothers*; G. Elliot
Smith and W. R. Dawson, *Egyptian Mummies*, pp. 82–83.
[2] See Conclusion, p. 160.
[3] Pl. 1. Since the bodies of Khnum-nakht and Nekht-ankh
are now dismembered, the photographs used here date to
the unwrapping in 1907.
[4] W. M. F. Petrie, *Gizeh and Rifeh*, pp. 12, 27, Pls. Xa–Xe.
[5] Pl. 2.
[6] Pl. 3.
[7] Through the Egyptian Research Account.
[8] Pl. 4.

9 Donated by Lt-Colonel Magnus of Cheadle, Cheshire. The mummy had been brought to England in December 1893.

10 Pl. 5.

11 The mummy was acquired from a London dealer, who gave Luxor as its provenance.

12 The mummy is on loan to the museum from Colonel C. J. H. Parr.

13 Pl. 6.

14 The mummy was brought to England by John Frewen Esq. of Brickwall House, Northiam, Nr Rye, Sussex, who made a journey to the Crimea and Egypt. It was believed that he had acquired the mummy at Luxor. Clare Sheridan in *Nuda Veritas*, gives an account of this.

15 The mummy remained at Brickwall House for many years. It was suspected of bringing ill fortune to the family, and when the house became a school in 1926, it was placed on loan at the Hastings Museum. In 1947, the Hastings Museum wished to concentrate on displaying local history, and Mrs Frewen gave the Curator permission to find alternative accommodation for the mummy. It was subsequently offered to the Manchester Museum.

16 An accompanying set of glass slides dating to May 1907 show the coffin and the body before and after unwrapping.

17 From an extract taken from a notebook in the family archives, written by Louisa Frewen (1925). The authorities are said to have stated that the mummy was female, that she had 'lived and died in the time of the prophet Jeremiah, had been a member of a middle-class family, and had died of arthritis'.

18 Pl. 7.

19 This mummy was received from E. and W. Garratt, and was the earliest Egyptian antiquity of importance in the museum collection.

20 Pl. 8.

21 W. M. F. Petrie, *Qurneh*, p. 15 and Pls. LII, LIII. Found together with a mummy of an adult male in an unopened courtyard tomb.

22 Donated by the British School of Archaeology in Egypt.

23 Pl. 17.

24 From the collection of M. E. Robinow.

25 Pl. 10.

26 Donated by Dr Jesse Haworth.

27 Pl. 11.

28 W. M. F. Petrie, *Hawara, Biahmu and Arsinoe*, frontispiece 4, and p. 43.

29 Donated by Dr Jesse Haworth.

30 Cf. *Catalogue of Egyptian Antiquities in the British Museum: Mummies and Human Remains*, No. 59 (13595), pp. 31–32, and Pl. XVIa. An adolescent boy, name unknown, from Hawara.

31 Pl. 12.

32 W. M. F. Petrie, *Hawara, Biahmu and Arsinoe*, p. 17. Found together with mummies of a woman and two other children, a boy and a girl. The girl has a gilded bust-piece and the boy and the mother have portrait-panels. The boy is in the British Museum collection (no. 21809) (see B.M. Catalogue, No. 60, p. 32 and Pl. XVIb). According to Petrie, op. cit., the group could probably be dated to c. A.D. 130–140, and provides an example of one grave containing two overlapping styles — the gilded cartonnage bust and the portrait-panel. A comparison is also provided by No. 67 in the *B.M. Catalogue* (22108), p. 25 and Pl. XVIIIa, which is a child mummy from Hawara with a gilded cartonnage case.

33 Pl. 13.

34 Examination of the archives at University College London and the correspondence between Sir Flinders Petrie and the Manchester Museum suggests that this mummy may have come from Petrie's excavation at Hawara.

35 From the M. E. Robinow collection.

36 See p. 83 ff.

37 Pl. 14.

38 W. M. F. Petrie, *Hawara, Biahmu and Arsinoe*, p. 18. Discovered in a brick-lined chamber together with two others similarly decorated, belonging to a younger Artemidorous (British Museum collection No. 21810), see *B.M. Catalogue*, No. 66, p. 35 and Pl. XVIId); also W. M. F. Petrie, op. cit., p. 18, W. M. F. Petrie, *Seventy Years in Archaeology*, p. 84, and A. F. Shore, *Portrait Painting from Roman Egypt*, p. 26 and Pl. I) and a woman named Thermoutharin (see Catalogue général des antiquités Égyptiennes du Musée du Caire, C. C. Edgar, *Graeco-Egyptian coffins, masks and portraits*, No. 33221, pp. 81–82 and Pl. XXXII. 0.

39 From the Committee of Ancoats Art Museum, Manchester, from the Jesse Haworth collection, 1887–88.

40 One of the earliest known portrait-panels.

41 Pl. 15.

42 Donated by Dr Jesse Haworth.

43 Pl. 16.

44 Donated by Dr Jesse Haworth.

45 Possibly to be identified in the Catalogue général des antiquités Égyptiennes du Musée du Caire, *Graeco-Egyptian Coffins, Masks and Portraits*, as No. 33240, p. 93 and Pl. XXXVII.

46 Pl. 9.

47 W. M. F. Petrie, *Roman Portraits and Memphis IV*, pp. 9, 15 and Pl. XIII, 5.

48 From Sir Flinders Petrie's excavation. Donated by the British School of Archaeology in Egypt.

49 Donated by H. Victor Crabtree.

50 See p. 35.

51 From the Whitworth Art Gallery, Manchester. Said to have been purchased from an attendant at a museum in Munich.

52 From Mrs C. Thomas.

53 From the National Museum of Wales, Cardiff.

54 From the National Museum of Wales, Cardiff.

55 From the National Museum of Wales, Cardiff.

56 From the National Museum of Wales, Cardiff. Given to the Museum in 1888 by A. E. G. Knight of Tre-groes, Pencoed, Bridgend.

57 From the National Museum of Wales, Cardiff. Given to the Museum by Mrs Henry Lewis of Ty-nant.

58 Presented by 'H.B.M.' Found with a label stating that the hand was taken from the 'tombs at Luxor'.

59 See p. 99.

60 For further details of the investigation, see p. 99.

61 See p. 97.

62 Nos. 21472c–i were found in the Amset-headed and Hapy-headed canopic jars belonging to Nekht-ankh; the other two jars in the set were empty.

63 For full details of Nos. 21472a–i, see M. A. Murray, *The Tomb of the Two Brothers*.

64 From Sir Flinders Petrie's excavation. See A. S. Griffith, *A Catalogue of Egyptian antiquities of the XII and XVIII Dynasties from Kahun, Illahun and Gurob* (Manchester Museum 1910), p. 52. Collection of Jesse Haworth.

65 From Professor Garstang's excavation.

66 Bought from the Liverpool Institute of Archaeology.

67 Donated by Mrs Robinow.

68 Donated by T. A. Coward.

69 From the National Museum of Wales, Cardiff. An attached label states 'March 1898' which may be the date of acquisition.

70 From the Robinow Collection (*Catalogue of the Robinow Collection of Egyptian Antiquities deposited at the Manchester Museum in 1896*, No. 68).

71 Donated by M. E. Robinow.
72 Donated by Jesse Haworth.
73 Donated by W. Sharp Ogden.
74 W. M. F. Petrie, *Hawara, Biahmu and Arsinoe*, p. 10.
75 Donated by J. and A. Williams.
76 Purchased by the Museum.
77 Donated by Mrs E. Thomas.
78 From the Robinow Collection, op. cit., No. 71.
79 From the Robinow Collection, op. cit., No. 70.
80 From the Robinow Collection, op. cit., No. 69.
81 From the Egypt Exploration Society excavations at North Sakkara, seasons 1968/9, 1969/70. Excavation number: H5–2587; inventory number: 4864.
82 From the above excavation, via the British Museum, London.

83 From the Robinow collection, op. cit., No. 67.
84 From the Egypt Exploration Society, via the British Museum, excavation seasons 1966/7, cf. *Journal of Egyptian Archaeology*, 53 (1967), p. 141 ff.
85 See Peet and Loat, *Cemeteries of Abydos*, III, 40, 46; Pl. XX, 6; for type of bandaging, Pl. XXI, G.
86 From the Egypt Exploration Fund.
87 Donated by T. A. Coward.
88 From the Egypt Exploration Fund.
89 Donated by J. and A. Williams.
90 Donated by J. and A. Williams.
91 Donated by J. and A. Williams.

Experimental Mummification

by

R. GARNER

Introduction

This study was carried out in order to investigate mummification as the ancient Egyptians are believed to have performed it. The intention was to study the methods and to examine factors which may have affected them. The ancient Egyptians believed the body of a dead person would be needed by the spirit, which departed at death, on its subsequent return. Therefore, it was important to maintain the body in as lifelike a condition as possible.

Modern science has provided us with three excellent methods of preservation: injection of preserving fluids into the blood vessels, deep freezing, and freeze-drying. As these were not available to the ancient Egyptians they were left with the alternative method of drying the body. They undoubtedly knew that bodies buried in the desert sand were eventually dried by the heat of the sun. Their early burials were in shallow graves, and many would have been disturbed, giving ample evidence of the process. However, the length of time necessary, and the organisational difficulties involved in arranging large 'temporary graveyards' would rule it out as a practical proposition. Drying by artificial heat from a fire would be both difficult to control and unpredictable, apart from its extravagant use of their sparse fuel supplies. No Egyptian mummies have been found which show any real evidence of having been dried in this manner.

The use of a chemical agent for desiccation was thus the only practical method available. Common salt was used in early times for preserving meat and fish, but there is little evidence to show that it was used in mummification other than in a minor role.[1] The overwhelming evidence points to the use of natron as the main agent in the preparation of a mummified body. It has been found in tombs,[1] and Herodotus, writing in the fifth century B.C., specifically named it as the material used. Less certain has been its method of use. Few accounts of mummification have survived from ancient times, and, of those which have, most give very little detail. The account of Herodotus stands out as the clearest and most detailed, but it must be borne in mind that it was written after the art of embalming had passed its peak.

In his account Herodotus detailed three methods of mummification in decreasing order of complexity and cost. The first method involved opening the body, removing some of the organs, cleaning and packing the cavity, and then treating the whole body with natron. The second method called for filling the inside of the body with oil, treating it with natron, and finally removing any remaining oil. The third, and cheapest method involved washing out the body with an un-named fluid — possibly water or a dilute salt solution — and then treating it with natron. Early translation of this account led to a long-held misconception about the form in which natron was used. The words 'soak', 'steep' and 'brine' in these translations seemed to indicate that solutions of natron were used. Evidence from mummies was also thought to indicate the use of a solution. However, re-examination of the original Greek texts and the mummy evidence has shown them to provide no real basis for the belief.[1] Experimental work done by Lucas confirmed the modern thinking that the natron was used in its natural dry state.[2]

Methods

Natron is a mixture of sodium carbonate and bicarbonate which is found in natural deposits. Although sodium chloride and sulphate are also commonly found mixed with these deposits they usually constitute less than half of the total, and may be considered as impurities. Analysis of modern natron samples often shows a higher proportion of the 'true' salts — carbonate and bicarbonate — than is found in samples from tombs. If the ancient samples were used during mummification, chemical reactions would be more likely to affect these salts, thus reducing their relative proportions.

For the experiments carried out in this study 'artificial' natron samples were made up from laboratory chemicals. The proportion of true natron salts was kept high, in excess of 65 per cent; the remainder of the sample was made up of sodium chloride and sulphate 'impurities'. These samples were used in the investigations of the three methods of mummification mentioned by Herodotus. Later tests were designed to study the affect of high levels of impurities, and these used salt mixtures with carbonate and bicarbonate forming less than 40 per cent of the sample. A final series of experiments was carried out to compare the preservative properties of dry natron mixtures with natron solutions.

Laboratory rats and mice were used in the experiments because of their convenient size and availability. For all but the final series of experiments a ventral incision was made and the thoracic and abdominal organs were exposed. In some of the tests the organs were removed and buried separately, the body cavity being packed with salt mixture. If the organs were not removed they were packed round with salt when the animal was buried. Before salt treatment the animals were weighed, the body was then laid on a thick bed of loosely packed salt in a large open container and covered to a similar depth

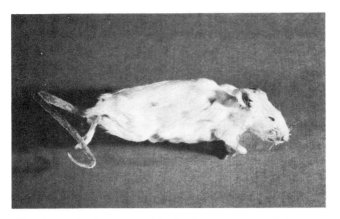

(1) An animal preserved in fresh natron, containing more than 60% sodium carbonate. There is very little shrinkage, and no loss of fur.

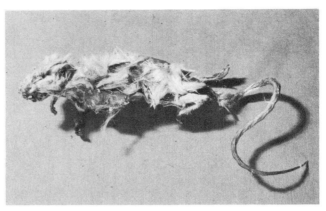

(2) An animal preserved in a re-used mixture containing a high proportion of sodium chloride. There is considerable loss of fur, and marked shrinkage on drying.

(3) An animal preserved in natron after water injection. The general preservation is very poor.

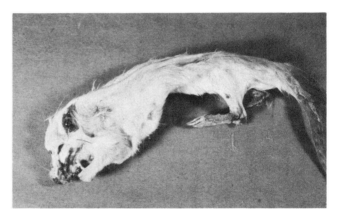

(4) An animal preserved in natron after oil injection. There is considerable shrinkage on drying, but the general preservation is good.

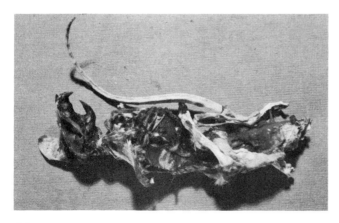

(5) An animal preserved in natron solution. There is considerable tissue loss during treatment due to extensive decay.

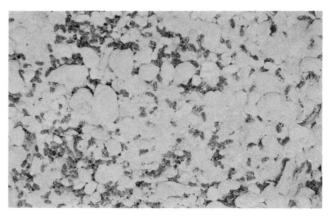

(6) Natron sample, showing large numbers of dead fly larvae.

20

(7) Close-up of rat showing larvae of *Dermestes lardarius*. The pale brown fibrous material is body tissue which has been attacked by the insects.

(8) Samples of natron and salt mixtures showing clumping and staining after use.
Left hand row: (*Top*) Natron some distance from the body — unsoiled. (*Middle*) Natron closer to the body — some soiling and clumping. (*Bottom*) High-chloride mixture, away from the body — some soiling and clumping.
Middle row: (*Top*) High-chloride mixture close to the body — some clumping, heavy soiling. (*Middle*) High-sulphate mixture, away from the body — slight soiling, some clumping. (*Bottom*) High-sulphate mixture close to the body — some clumping, heavy soiling.
Right hand row: Natron samples from close to the body — large hard lumps.

with more salt. Initially ten animals were buried, then individually removed from the natron at approximately weekly intervals. On removal the excess salt was brushed off and the condition of the body was noted. It was then weighed and left exposed to the atmosphere, its condition and weight were checked periodically. In this way it was possible to obtain an approximate figure for the minimum time required for natron treatment. Shorter times resulted in noticeable decay after removal, while longer times gave little improvement in subsequent preservation. Repeated experiments confirmed this time.

For the second series of tests the salt mixtures contained over 60 per cent sodium chloride or sulphate. The animals were then buried and checked as in the first series. After the completion of the treatments two samples were taken from each mixture, one close to the body, the other several inches away. These were checked to determine the amount of moisture they had taken up during the treatment. Some of the mixtures were then re-used up to four times in order to compare their effectiveness with fresh mixtures.

To investigate the possibility of fluids being used for preservation a series of solutions were made. They were of the same composition as those used in the first series of tests, with the salts dissolved in water to give 3 per cent or 10 per cent solutions.

To study the second method mentioned by Herodotus, rats were injected, through the rectum, with a mixture of turpentine and cedar-wood oils. For Herodotus's third method the intestines were washed out with water. Both of these operations were difficult to carry out and several animals had oil or water injected into their body cavities. After injection the animals were buried in natron. A few rats were also opened and buried in dry sand. This was done in order to compare the effectiveness of an inert drying medium with a chemical one such as natron.

Results

Animals buried in natron showed little sign of reaching a stable condition in less than twenty days. If they were removed before that time the tissue was still very soft and moist, and they continued to decay. As treatment was extended beyond twenty days the amount of subsequent decay decreased. In general, animals which were dry and free from strong odour when they were removed from natron were found to be stable. No absolute time could be found for treatment, after which further decay would be minimal, but the time usually fell within the range of thirty to forty days. One of the main factors appeared to be the amount of fat in the body. Large amounts of fat not only increased the treatment time, they also gave the body a greater degree of flexibility when it was finally removed from the natron. As has been mentioned there was often a noticeable smell, particularly while the animals were being treated. It was impossible to quantify this, but it was rarely very strong and was usually tolerable.

The results obtained with salt mixtures containing large amounts of sodium chloride or sulphate showed considerable differences. Where the chloride was used the bodies often remained moist, soft and flexible after

21

forty days. After any given time they usually showed more decay than those treated with natron for a comparable period. In general they reached a stable condition after forty-five to fifty days. On removal they dried slowly for the first few days, and then began to harden. The most obvious sign of decay, the smell of putrefaction, was not noticeably different from that of the earlier tests. In the tests carried out with mixtures containing large amounts of sodium sulphate the bodies dried out more slowly than those in natron, but faster than those in high-chloride mixtures; they were usually stable in forty to forty-five days. The greatest difference was that in these tests there was usually a very strong unpleasant smell of decay.

Apart from the condition of the bodies, there was a marked difference between all three salt mixtures after they had been used. The natron tended to form large, very hard, clumps close to the body after about twenty days. These clumps were dry to the touch and often stained brown. Further from the body, or where there was no clumping on a large scale, there were small firm lumps in the natron. Beyond these the salt was clean, dry and apparently unaffected. High-sulphate mixtures also showed some staining and clumping, although the clumps were smaller and not as hard as those in the natron. The clumps were often moist, and this dampness often extended quite a distance from the body, but the salt was not always stained. Salt mixtures containing large amounts of chloride rarely clumped, but they were usually extensively stained and, except where large quantities were used, all of the mixture was damp.

When salt mixtures were re-used their effectiveness reflected the degree of soiling caused by earlier use. As soiling increased so did the time required for the body to become stable, consequently there was more decay. Natron which had been used four times took up to forty-five days to mummify satisfactorily. Re-used mixtures containing high proportions of sulphate extended the treatment time to at least fifty-five days. However, high chloride mixtures which had been re-used four times showed no sign of working effectively even after seventy days.

Within a few days of the beginning of the tests with solutions it became clear that it was unlikely to be a satisfactory method of preservation. The fluid became very dark and there was a very strong smell of decay. Although some of the rats were left in the solution for seventy days none of them were satisfactorily preserved. The worst cases were almost unrecognizable on removal, having lost most of the fur and muscle to leave discoloured skin, bones and fat. Others had decayed to varying extents, but they were all soft and pulpy. It was difficult to remove them from the solutions, and several disintegrated while they were being moved. Those which were removed reasonably intact were washed carefully and allowed to dry. As they dried they all shrank and distorted, and many continued to decay.

After forty days in natron the oil-injected rats were still slightly soft and flexible. They had all shrunk slightly and, in two cases, there was a soft mass in the abdomen. When they were opened this was found to be an oily fluid, and in all cases the organs were dark and soft, but

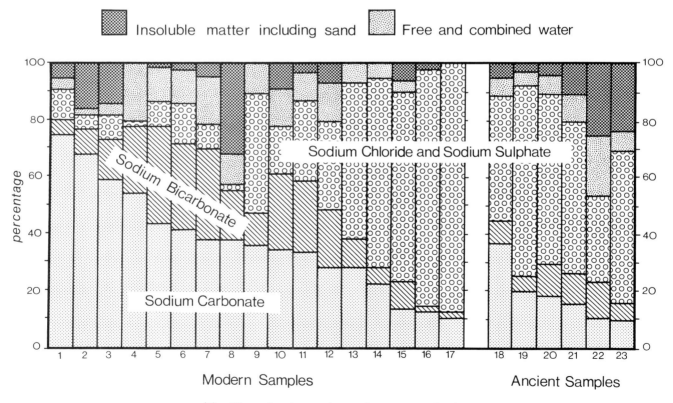

(9) Chart showing analyses of natron samples.[3]

22

still intact and recognizable. Although there was some smell during treatment it was never strong. After removal from the natron the animals dried slowly and shrank a little, but they showed no signs of further decay and did not become completely hard. In contrast, the animals injected with water gave off a strong smell during treatment and while they were drying after removal. After the treatment they had shrunk considerably and had started to harden. No fluid was found in the abdomen, but the organs were shrunken, almost unrecognizable, dark green and clay-like in consistency.

When animals were buried in sand it was usually between fifty and fifty-five days before they became stable, many took up to seventy days. In all cases there was a strong unpleasant smell of decay, and, after treatment, most of the sand was damp.

The early experiments in the study were carried out in the laboratory, and there was no sign of insect attack. Later experiments allowed free access of insects to the containers after the animals were buried, and to the bodies when they were removed. After burial large numbers of flies were attracted to the containers. When treatment was completed some dead larvae were found near several of the rats; they were identified as bluebottle larvae (*Calliphora erythrocephala*). These were found more frequently when the animal was buried in soiled material. After removal most of the bodies were attacked by the Larder beetle (*Dermestes lardarius*) and its larvae; two *Dermestes peruvianus* larvae were also found.

In order to discover how well insects might be able to survive on an animal buried in natron, two rats were opened with a ventral incision and left exposed for several hours; during that time large numbers of flies alighted on them. One of the rats was then buried, the other being left until larvae hatched out. When the rats were removed from the natron, after thirty days, no live insects were found, but it was clear that many had survived for a long period. In the natron around the rat which was buried first there were several larvae and pupae close to the body. There were also two flies which had just emerged from pupae; these were identified as bluebottles. In the other case some larvae had travelled several inches from the body, their progress being clearly indicated by 'tunnels' in the natron. There were also large numbers of pupae and many empty cases; the adult flies, still with partly folded wings, had often travelled a few inches from the pupal case. One fully formed adult was found on the natron surface, and as this was covered with a fine mesh it could only have emerged from the natron. As before, most of these flies were identified as bluebottles, although one was a flesh-fly (*Sarcophaga sp.*).

Conclusion

Several factors make it difficult to attempt any direct comparison between the experiments in this study and ancient Egyptian mummification. The most obvious of these would seem to be the relatively hairless state of the human body when compared with that of a rat or mouse. However, early parallel tests with normal and shaved

rats showed little difference in drying times. There is also the influence of body size and such related factors as the thickness of skin, muscle and fat layers. Within the limitations of the study this was less easy to investigate, but, in general, the use of animals ranging from young mice to large adult rats gave comparable results. A further point is that no attempt was made to simulate the temperature and humidity of the Egyptian climate. A few experiments were carried out at temperatures between 5°C and 8°C higher than the others; this usually resulted in the drying time dropping by two or three days. Despite these reservations the study did highlight several factors which could influence the final condition of the body and its subsequent stability. The most important of these are the composition of the natron, and the way it was used. Obviously the use of too little would either allow considerable decay before the body dried, or make satisfactory drying impossible. There is no way of knowing how much natron the Egyptians used for each body. During the course of this study, it was found that a salt volume at least ten times the volume of the body was necessary to ensure adequate drying. If the natron contained large amounts of sodium chloride or sulphate they would influence the mummification in two ways. When the salt mixture was used for the first time it would probably be necessary to use at least 50 per cent more than would be required if 'pure' natron was used. However, it is when the possibility of re-use occurs that real differences arise. The experiments carried out with 'pure' natron indicated that much of the soiled material formed compact clumps around the body. This would make it easy to remove the worst affected salt before another body was buried. If it was not removed it would form at least a partial barrier between the rest of the natron and the next body. Similar considerations apply to natron mixtures which contain large proportions of sodium sulphate. As the clumps tend to be smaller and not as form they would be more difficult to remove, conversely they would be less of a barrier if they were left. The greatest problem with re-used material occurs when there is a high proportion of sodium chloride. Such mixtures quickly become soiled, and, more importantly, the soiling is extensive which makes it almost impossible to remove without replacing the whole salt bed.

A few of the rats used in the early experiments had started to decay before they were buried in natron, and this appeared to influence the action of the salt. In fresh natron they took two or three days longer before decay was arrested and drying began, but in soiled material the time was extended by over a week.

As has been indicated, many factors may prevent perfect mummification whereby the body is dried and rendered stable as quickly as possible, with the minimum of decay. That 'ideal' conditions could be achieved is shown by the many fine mummies still in existence. However, more late period Egyptian mummies show signs of poor preservation than might otherwise be expected. It is possible that changes in the social and religious aspects of life, after the peak of the Egyptian empire, were reflected in a decline in demand for the embalmer's work at its best. This may have led to a lowering of their standards, which allowed factors influencing mummification to assume a greater significance than before.

References
[1] For a broader consideration of these points, see A. Lucas, *Ancient Egyptian Materials and Industries*, 1962, Chapter XII.
[2] A. Lucas, *Preservative Materials*, pp. 9–10. A Lucas, *J.E.A.*, xviii (1932), 133–34, 137–38.
[3] Compiled from data in A. Lucas, *Ancient Egyptian Materials and Industries*, 1962, pp. 493–4.

Comparison of Weight Loss during Drying with Different Materials

	Main Constituent of Drying Mixture						
	Sodium[1] Carbonate	Sodium[2] Carbonate	Sodium[1,3] Carbonate	Sodium[1,4] Carbonate	Sodium[1] Sulphate	Sodium[1] Chloride	Sand[1]
Weight loss of body during treatment (%)	50	16	34[7]	55[7]	44	38	38
Total weight loss (%)[5]	64	61	63[8]	64[8]	62	61	63
Moisture gain by drying mixture during treatment (% weight)[6]	35	23	10	14	23	2	4

The figures given are averages

[1] Fresh salt
[2] Re-used salt
[3] Rat injected with oil
[4] Rat injected with water
[5] Includes loss during treatment and while exposed to the atmosphere after removal
[6] Close to the body
[7] Taken as a percentage of the weight of the body plus injected fluid
[8] Percentage of original body weight

Radiology of the Manchester Mummies

by

I. Isherwood, H. Jarvis and R. A. Fawcitt

Introduction

Despite the ready acceptance in medical diagnosis of Roentgen's discovery in 1895, little scientific investigation into the value of x-ray technology in Egyptology has been made until recent years. The problems of relatively immobile, dense and heavy objects together with the low-powered equipment and indifferent processing units available for field study seem to have provided significant disincentives.

The first radiographs of mummified material (a child and a cat) were obtained by W. Konig in the Senckenberg Museum in Frankfurt in March 1896.[1] Amongst 261 various x-rays obtained during 1896 by the English pioneer Thurstan Holland[2] in Liverpool is recorded a mummified bird. The author comments on the picture, dated 22 October 1896, that the 'advantage of this class of subject is that there is no movement'. In 1898, Petrie[3] made use of x-rays in the investigation of human mummified remains and shortly afterwards, in 1904, Elliot Smith, assisted by Howard Carter, x-rayed the mummy of Tuthmosis IV[4] (18th Dynasty — c.1575–1308 B.C.). The condition of the epiphyses enabled the age of the King at the time of his death to be estimated with precision.

Moodie,[5] in one of the earliest comprehensive radiological studies, surveyed the Egyptian and Peruvian mummies of the Chicago Field Museum in 1931 and commented that 'Roentgenology supplements all other methods of learning of physical troubles in early times'. Gray,[6] together with various co-workers, has, in a series of systematic radiological surveys at sites in the United Kingdom and Europe since 1960, documented some 193 ancient Egyptian mummies. These include the important collections at the Rijksmuseum, Leiden,[7] The British Museum[8] and the City of Liverpool Museums.[9]

The University of Michigan School of Dentistry over a five-year period in the late 1960s conducted a radiological analysis of the mummies housed in the Egyptian Museum in Cairo.[10] This survey revealed anomalies in the recorded ages at which various Pharoahs died and raised doubts about the genetic relationships amongst members of the ruling families. Detailed radiological studies may contribute significantly to the identification of historical figures[11] and some of the techniques are now well-established in forensic practice.

Most recorded specimens, even in recent years, have been radiographed on site, either in museums or at archaeological sites. The investigation in these circumstances is then significantly limited by the need for mobile compact equipment capable of being attached to local electricity supplies or associated with suitable isotope sources. Special constraints result from the heavy and dense casing in which specimens are frequently housed combined with the problems of varying density artefacts in the complex wrappings. Neither situation is conducive to accurate reproducibility or comparison with modern material. Such comparative studies will only be feasible if standardized conditions prevail. Even with high-powered equipment, overlying artefacts, wrappings and casings may render detailed analysis difficult.

To investigate radiologically the entire collection of the Manchester University Museum in the near-ideal conditions of a modern hospital Department of Diagnostic Radiology containing orbiting, fluoroscopic and tomographic equipment, presented a unique challenge and an unparalleled scientific opportunity. One mummy (1770) was examined before and after unwrapping, enabling the validity of the methods and results to be established.

This report presents the radiological findings on all the human mummified remains currently housed in the University of Manchester Museum together with an account of the techniques employed.

Material and Methods

The ancient Egyptian mummified remains at present in the possession of the Department of Egyptology in the University of Manchester consist of 17 complete human mummies and a number of loose human appendages, including five heads and a number of animals and birds.

All specimens were transported individually from the University Museum to the Department of Neuro-radiology, Manchester Royal Infirmary, where appropriate specialized radiological equipment is available (1). This equipment included the Elema Schonander Mimer III radiological unit equipped with a 0.3 mm focal spot x-ray tube capable of orbiting the subject, of fluoroscopy by means of a 7 in. image intensifier and television and of varying sectional thickness tomography at any angle of orbit. An associated high-power generator made it possible to employ fine grain industrial film (Kodak Industrex C) in order to improve image detail. High-speed (90 seconds) and controlled film processing was immediately available. The investigations were carried out at weekends and at night to avoid interference with patient investigation.

Two specimens (Asru and Khary) were also investigated in the University Department of Diagnostic Radiology, Medical School, University of Manchester, by computed tomography (EMI CT5005) — a technique designed to obtain transverse body sections 5 to 13 mm in thickness.

In the particular case of mummy 1770 a further radiological survey was conducted after unwrapping. This survey enabled detailed radiological observations including macroradiography to be obtained on some of the dissected parts.

Fluoroscopy was carried out on each subject as a first procedure to evaluate the nature of the contents and their disposition. External modelling and decoration on the cartonnage, no matter how elaborate, has no positional relationship to the anatomical remains within (**42**). Under television control during orbiting manœuvres, markers were placed on the outer casing to identify anatomical planes, for example coronal and sagittal, of the human remains within. Particular landmarks, such as the anthropological base line of the skull and the level of the nasion were also located and indicated.

As a routine procedure, a radiographic survey was then obtained in two planes, using overlapping films to include the entire subject (**8**). These radiographs, together with the observations of fluoroscopy, were then studied to devise a logical and more detailed investigation employing thin section tomography or stereoscopy. The radiographic factors are recorded in Table I.

(For explanation of radiological terminology, see Appendix).

TABLE I
(All radiographs were obtained on Kodak Industrial C film)

Mummy		mAs	kVp	Tomo (Angle°)	f.f.d. (cm)	Tube focus (mm)
21470	Skeleton	250	65–76		228	1.0
(NA)	Skull + Tomos	64 – 100		16/31	110	0.3
21471	Skeleton	80 – 250	65–75		110/228	0.3
(KN)	Skull + Tomos	64 – 100		16	110	0.3
3496	AP/Lat	250	65–75		228	1.0
(Reed Coffin)	Tomos	100 – 130		31	110	0.3
9354	AP	130 – 250			183	1.0
(Khary)	Lat	200 × 2 – 250 × 3	65–70		183	1.0
	Skull	100 × 3 – 200 × 4			110	0.3
	Tomos	40 × 3 – 160 × 2		10/31	110	0.3
1976.51a	AP	100 – 250			183	1.0
	Lat	250 × 2 – 250 × 4			183	1.0
	Skull	200	65–70		110	0.3
	Tomos	130 – 130 × 2		10/16	110	0.3
10881	AP	130			183	1.0
(Ta-Aath)	Lat	250 × 3 – 250 × 6			183	1.0
	Skull	100 × 2 – 100 × 3	65–70		110	0.3
	Tomos	200		10/16	110	1.0
1777	AP/Lat	120			183	1.0
(Asru)	Hands + Feet	100			183	1.0
	Skull	100 × 2 – 100 × 3	65		110	0.3
	Tomos	80 – 100 × 4		16	110	1.0
5053	AP	200 × 3 – 200 × 5			183	1.0
(Per-en-bast)	Lat	250 × 12 – 250 × 18			183	1.0
	Skull	100 × 4 – 100 × 10	65–75		110	0.3
	Tomos	200 × 3 – 200 × 8		10/16	110	1.0
	Teeth	200 × 12		31	110	1.0
	Face	200 × 6			110	1.0

Table I — *continued*

Mummy		mAs	kVp	Tomo (Angle°)	f.f.d. (cm)	Tube focus (mm)
1768	AP	600			183	1.0
	Lat	200 × 15			110	0.3
	Skull	100 × 4 − .100 × 6	65–75		110	1.0
	Tomos	200 × 2 − 200 × 6		12/16	110	1.0
1770 (Wrapped)	AP/Lat	250 − 400 × 2	75		228	1.0
	Tomos	100 − 250 × 2		16	110	0.3
(Unwrapped)	Calcif'n + Bone detail	25 − 50	40–75		110	0.3
	Tomos	25 − 64	65–70	31	110–152	0.3
9319	AP/Lat	250 − 320 × 2			183	1.0
	Skull	100 − 260	45–65		110	0.3
	Tomos	100 − 160 × 3		10/16	110	0.3–1.0
2109	AP/Lat	130 − 400 × 2			152–228	1.0
	Skull	160 × 2	65–75		110	0.3
	Tomos	200 − 400		16/31	110	1.0
1769	AP/Lat	400 − 400 × 6			183	1.0
	Skull	360 − 100 × 4	65–75		110	0.3
	Tomos	320 − 250 × 2		10/31	110	1.0
20638 (Demetria)	AP	200 × 3 − 200 × 5			183	1.0
	Lat	200 × 5 − 200 × 16	65–75		183	1.0
	Skull	100 × 5 − 100 × 12			110	0.3
	Tomos	200 × 2 − 200 × 4		10/16	110	1.0
1767	AP	350 − 800			152	1.0
	Lat	200 × 6 − 200 × 12			183	1.0
	Skull	100 × 4 − 100 × 6	65–75		110	0.3
	Tomos	250 × 2 − 320 × 3		10/16	110	1.0
	Teeth	64 × 2 − 200 × 8			110	1.0
1766	AP	300 × 2 − 400 × 2			183	1.0
	Lat	400 × 2 − 200 × 15	65–75		183	1.0
	Skull	200 × 2 − 200 × 3			110	0.3
	Tomos	250 − 400 × 2		16	110	1.0
1775 (Artemidorous)	AP	400			183	1.0
	Lat	200 × 4 − 200 × 14	65–75		183	1.0
	Skull	200 × 2 − 250 × 2			110	0.3
	Tomos	400 − 250 × 2		16	110	1.0
5275 Ptolemaic Head	Skull	160			110	0.3
	Soft tissue	50	65–80		110	0.3
	Tomo	130		16/31	110	0.3
7740 (Head)	Skull	130	70–75		110	0.3
	Tomos	80 × 3		10	110	1.0
21475	Skull	130			110	0.3
	Tomos	130	65–75	16/31	110	0.3
21474	Foot	80			110	0.3
22940	Skull	130	65–75		110	0.3
	Tomos	100 − 80 × 3		10/31	110	0.3
21476	Left Hand ⎫					
9384	Left Hand ⎬	80	65	110	110	0.3
9428	Right Hand ⎭					

TABLE II

Mummy No.	Period	Provenance	Age	Sex	Arms and Hands	PACKING				THORACIC STRUCTURES PRESENT				Evidence of Brain Removal	Opacif'n of IV Disc Spaces	Costal Cartilage Calcif'n	Knee Joint Articular Calcif'n	Vascular Calcif'n	Bladder Calcif'n	OSTEOARTHRITIS			
						Orbits	Upper Resp'y	Thorax	Abdo	Lungs	Pleura	Heart	Pericard'm							CXS	DS	LS	Joints
21470 (NA)	XII Dyn 1900 B.C.	Rifeh	Adult	M	Ext-OT	R		Yes	Yes					Yes						Yes	Yes	Yes	
21471 (KN)	XV Dyn 1900 B.C.	Rifeh	Adult	M	Ext-OT											++				Yes	Yes	Yes	TIP Feet
3496 (Reed Coffin)	XVIII Dyn 1400 B.C.	Gurob	3/12	?	Ext-AT										Yes								
9354 (Khary)	XIX Dyn 1300 B.C.	Unknown	Adult	M	C.P. (L. hand clenched)	R+L			Yes	Yes		Yes	Yes	Yes	Yes		Yes				Yes	Yes	Knees Hips
1976.51a	XXI Dyn	Unknown	Adult	F	Ext-IT	R+L			Yes						Yes	+				Yes	Yes	Yes	
10881a (Ta-Aath)	XXI-XXV Dyn 1087-656 B.C.	Luxor	Adult	F	Ext-AT									Yes	Yes								
1777 (Asru)	XXV Dyn 751-656 B.C.	Thebes	Adult	F	Ext-IT		OP		Yes	Yes	Yes		Yes	Yes	Yes	+++	Yes	Yes		Yes		Yes	TIP
5053 (Per-en-bast)	XXV Dyn 751-656 B.C.	Quernah	Adult	F	Ext-IT		OP	Yes							Yes	+		Yes			Yes	Yes	
1768	100 B.C.	Hawara	20	M	Ext-AT				Yes														Yes (Schmorl's) Knees
1770	Ptolemaic	Hawara	14	F	C.P.	R+L									Yes (resin)								
9319	Roman	Hawara	2	?	Ext-OT	L			Yes	Yes	Yes		Yes		Yes	++	Yes						
2109	Roman	Hawara	2	?	Ext-OT			Yes	Yes					Yes	Yes								
1769	A.D. 130-140	Hawara	3-4	F	Ext-AT	R+L		Yes	Yes	Yes					Yes	+	Yes						
20638 (Demetria)	A.D. 100	Hawara	Adult	F	Ext-OT				Yes	Yes			Yes	Yes		+	Yes			Yes	Yes	Yes	R Knee
1767	A.D. 100-200	Fayoum	Adult	M	Ext-P	R+L	NP		Yes													Yes	
1766	A.D. 100-200	Fayoum	Adult	F	Ext-OT	?			Yes	Yes			Yes		Yes	++	Yes		Yes	Yes	Yes	Yes	MTPs
1775	A.D. 200	Hawara	Adult	M	Ext-P	R+L		Yes	Yes	Yes	Yes		Yes	Yes		++		Yes	Yes	Yes	Yes	Yes	Hips

KEY:
Ext — extended
CP — crossed pectoral — arms folded
P — palms cover genital area
AT — palms on anterior thighs
IT — palms on inner thighs
OT — palms on outer thighs
OP — oropharynx

+ — faint
++ — generalized
+++ — extensive
R — right
L — left
TIP — terminal interphalangeal
NP — nasopharynx

28

Results

A summary of the results is presented in Table II.

No. 21470 (Nekht-Ankh) (2 and 3)

Mummy of man, Nekht-Ankh, son of Aa-Khnum, brother of 2147 (Khnum-Nakht), unwrapped in 1907 by Dr Margaret Murray. Possibly an eunuch and aged 60 at time of death. Non-negroid skull. Contents of canopic jars and other material belonging to this brother include brain, larynx, aortic arch and penis.

General Incomplete, mainly disarticulated skeleton of adult male. Only a little soft tissue adherent to bones.

Skull Vault intact but dorsum sella and right middle turbinate missing (2). No brain tissue remaining. Petrous bone tomography normal. Packing, possibly linen material, in right orbit. Teeth show attrition.

Upper Limbs Right hand and part of left hand missing. Residual soft tissue at head of right humerus and left distal radio-ulnar joint. All epiphyses fused.

Lower Limbs Both distal tibial shafts contain small sclerotic areas. There is a small cystic lesion in left distal fibula with local bone compaction (3). Of the tarsal bones, on the left only a loose os calcis and talus remain. On the right, these bones are also loose but the remainder, minus the navicular which is missing, are attached to the left forefoot. Both sets of metatarsals and phalanges are complete. There are early degenerative changes at both first metatarsophalangeal joints. Soft tissue remnants are present over both feet, with skin thickening. All epiphyses fused.

Thorax Only scapulae, clavicles, body of sternum and manubrium remain. None show abnormality.

Spine and Pelvis Only the sacrum and pelvis remain. The pelvis is android in shape and has an acute subpubic arch. The iliac crest apophysis is fused.

Comment Remains are incomplete but of an adult male with little residual soft tissue. The missing dorsum sella and right middle turbinate are evidence of brain removal. Sclerotic areas in the lower tibial shafts may represent areas of bone infarction. A detailed discussion of the bony skeleton has been documented elsewhere.[17]

No. 21471 (Khnum-Nakht) (5–7)

Mummy of a man, Khnum-Nakht, half-brother of Nekht-Ankh (see above), unwrapped in 1907 by Dr Margaret Murray. Possibly early middle-age at death. Negroid skull. Soft tissue in poor condition; less carefully preserved mummy. Well-marked kypho-scoliosis. Two left incisor teeth of the upper jaw are fused. No canopic jars.

General Incomplete adult male skeleton, with reconstructed thorax.

Skull Skull vault and base intact. Fractures through left zygomatic arch and left mandible are post-mortem. No evidence of brain removal but no intracranial contents identifiable.

Upper Limbs Post-morten fracture of left fifth metacarpal and degenerative changes of the distal interphalangeal joints.

Lower Limbs Growth arrest lines are present in the distal tibiae and proximal fibulae. Both feet and ankles are fully articulated, inverted and have some remaining soft tissue. The left foot has a superficial appearance of a 'club-foot' (talipes equinovarus) but only minor degenerative changes are present in the talonavicular and first metartarso-phalangeal joints (5).

Thorax The thoracic cage has been reconstructed with modern prostheses of the right fourth rib and anterior ends of other ribs on right side. Healed fracture of right tenth rib posteriorly and further fracture (? PM) of left eighth rib.

Spine Cervical — Vertebral body C5 missing. Partial fusion of neural arches of C2 and C3 on left with degenerative changes affecting neurocentral and apophyseal joints from C3 caudally.

 Thoracic and Lumbar — Lumbar spine scoliotic concave to right. Degenerative changes with osteophyte formation present in mid thoracic and lumbar spine.

Pelvis Pelvis android with acute subpubic arch.

Comment Incomplete skeleton of adult male. Advanced degenerative changes in cervical and lumbar spine present with healed fracture through right tenth rib. The previously described[17] left club foot (talipes equinovarus) is not supported by present normal bony appearances. A detailed discussion of the bony skeleton has been documented elsewhere.[17]

No. 3496 (Reed Coffin) (6–8)

Mummy of a child, wrapped in reed mat tied with ropes at each end.

General Infant in fair state of preservation apart from disruption of head, neck and upper thorax. Infant wrapped in opaque material or bandaging within reeds. Arms extended with hands pronated over iliac fossae.

Skull Skull disarticulated and separated from upper thorax. Mandible lies adjacent to thoracic inlet. Deciduous teeth calcifying but not erupted.

Upper Limbs Left shoulder disorganized with scapula lying loose and head of left humerus missing. Capitellum at elbow not calcified. Only capitate in carpus calcified.

Lower Limbs Legs slightly flexed at hips and knees. Neither femoral capital epiphysis is calcified. In right knee epiphyses well formed but with growth arrest lines in upper and lower tibiae. Feet together and internally rotated.

Thorax Upper thorax disrupted with left ribs 1–4 missing. Sternum and costal cartilages not present.

Abdomen No packing evident.

Spine Cervical spine missing together with vertebral bodies T1–4. Appearances otherwise normal.

 Lumbar Spine and pelvis — disc spaces opaque adjacent to end plates.

Comment Infant just under three months of age. Evidence of illness in this short life indicated by growth arrest lines.

No. 9354 (Khary) (9–11)

Mummy of a man, with a coffin.

General Partially unwrapped mummy in excellent condition lying supine. Arms crossed over thorax, right over left. Hands pronated, left hand clenched.

Skull Skull in alignment with trunk, neck extended. Vault shows biparietel thinning and defect in right squamous temporal bone. Midline bone defect in jugum sphenoidale. Falx cerebri and tentorium cerebelli remain. Opaque material possibly resin in posterior fossa would, in the erect position, in part form a 'fluid level'. Calcification in petroclinoid ligament. Teeth show attrition and extensive caries. Rounded well-defined packs in both orbits.

Upper Limbs Small, cortical cyst on lateral aspect of midshaft of right humerus.

Lower Limbs Legs extended with feet together. Small exostosis on left lower femur. Articular cartilages visible in both hips and knees with good visualization of soft tissues.

Thorax Bony cage intact with healed fractures of right eighth and ninth ribs posteriorly and left eighth and ninth ribs in mid axillary line. Pericardium distinctly seen with cardiac remains within. Both lungs present but collapsed. Small, dense opacities between left elbow and chest wall are in wrappings.

Abdomen Diaphragm clearly identified with collection of packing material layered peripherally in abdominal cavity. No organs detectable. Linear prevertebral opacity on lateral projections could be aorta and hollow thin-walled structure in pelvis the remains of rectum.

Spine Cervical — Neck extended and intervertebral discs opaque.

Thoracic — Upper thoracic kyphosis with minor degenerative changes in mid-thoracic spine. Disc spaces opacified throughout.

Lumbar — Degenerative changes at L1/2 and L4/5 with disc space narrowing. All discs opacified. Increased density is within annulus fibrosus, the nucleus pulposus is spared. Protrusion of annulus into spinal canal is visible at L3/4.

Pelvis No evidence of disease. Iliac crest apophyses fused.

Comment Well-preserved, partly wrapped male. Early signs of degenerative disease in thoracic and lumbar spine. Biparietal thinning suggests an elderly man. Horizontal layering of cranial contents might indicate mummified body had been erect for some time after embalming. Clarity of heart and lungs remarkable and demonstration of a herniated intervertebral disc in lumbar spine unique.

No. 1976.51a (12–14)

Mummy of a woman, wrapped in modern gauze bandages, together with painted wooden coffin.

General Adult female in good condition. Arms extended with hands pronated over inner aspect of thighs. One detached digit within abdominal cavity.

Skull Skull straight, neck extended. Vault and base intact. Irregular, rounded opacity within cranial cavity posteriorly suggests residual brain material. Right frontal sinus and both maxillary antra opaque. Teeth show attrition, extensive caries and periapical infection. Maxilla edentulous. Ring opacities, suggesting prosthetic globes, in both orbits.

Upper Limbs Left third and fourth fingers and second and fifth middle and terminal phalanges missing. Osteoarthritic changes present in remaining distal interphalangeal joints. Epiphyseal closure complete. Thin layer of soft tissue present over hands.

Lower Limbs Legs extended, feet plantar flexed. Left foot internally rotated.

Thorax Bony cage intact, costal cartilages faintly opacified. Thoracic cavity filled with homogeneous semi-opaque material. Large, lobulated midline lucency along long axis. No normal tissues identifiable.

Abdomen Semi-opaque substance has layered posteriorly in abdomen and pelvis. In the midline is an air-filled tubular structure. No organ packages, and no evidence of incision site. Displaced digit in epigastrium to right of midline.

Spine Cervical — Neutral position with disc space narrowing and osteophytosis C4–C7. Intervertebral joints show osteoarthritic changes. Disc spaces not opaque.

Thoracic — Spine straight with anterior osteophyte formation at T10/11 almost bridging disc space. All disc spaces opaque.

Lumbar — Lateral osteophytes present at L3/4 and L4/5 but disc spaces not unduly reduced in height. Intervertebral discs opaque due to calcification in annulus, nucleus pulposus spared.

Pelvis Pelvis gynacoid; sacro-iliac margins sclerotic.

Comment Adult female with spinal degenerative disease suggesting advancing age. Features for comment are residual brain tissue, well-defined eye globes probably prosthetic, layering of resinous material in abdomen and pelvis, and extensive intervertebral disc calcification.

No. 10881 (Ta-Aath) (15–16)

Mummy of a woman, with a coffin.

General Adult mummy in poor, disorganized condition due to previous unwrapping. Arms disarticulated, right flexed and left extended. Both hands disarticulated at wrists and pronated over iliac fossae. Long package present between thighs.

Skull Fracture present through sphenoid air sinus, tuberculum sellae on left and base of dorsum sellae. Latter lies in sphenoidal air sinus. Cranial cavity empty. Many teeth missing from maxilla. Left upper canine unerupted and crown directed mesially. Marked dental attrition. Mandible lies separate from skull.

Upper Limbs Upper limbs disarticulated at shoulders, elbows and wrists. Humeri lie parallel to chest walls. Right elbow flexed with ulna parallel to humerus. Right radius parallel to left humerus. Fracture through distal right ulna shaft with distal fragment missing. Both hands separated at wrist joints. Only thumbs complete, the intermediate and distal phalanges of other digits missing. A finger stall is present on right thumb.

Lower Limbs Bones disorganized but all approximately in correct position, except left talus which is adjacent to right knee joint. Epiphyseal development complete.

Thorax Rib cage jumbled. No contents visible.

Abdomen No soft tissue detail.

Spine Cervical — Vertebrae jumbled. No disease.

Thoracic — Two vertebrae missing. Upper thoracic vertebrae jumbled. No disc opacification.

Lumbar — Lumbar vertebrae rotated. Horizontal fracture (? PM) through L5 and disc space narrowing at L1/2. Intervertebral discs throughout show irregular opacification.

Comment Adult — sex uncertain. Evidence of brain removal through sphenoid in midline. General disorganization and loss of some bones consistent with previous unwrapping.

No. 1777 (Asru) (17–20)

Mummy of a woman, with two wooden coffins. The mummy, well-preserved, was already unwrapped when it arrived at the Museum.

General Complete, unwrapped, female mummy; excellent state of preservation. Both arms extended with hands pronated over inner thighs. Widespread, dense, particulate matter throughout soft tissues.

Skull Discrete lytic defect approximately 1 cm in diameter in right posterior parietal bone. Skull base intact except for detached dorsum sella lying to left and behind its normal position. Convoluted density in occipital region is probably brain. Dural remains present in left middle fossa. Acellularity of right mastoid, suggesting previous infection. Remaining teeth show attrition, with abnormal palated angulation of upper central incisors. Pack in posterior nasopharynx. No orbital contents.

Upper Limbs Left third digit shows ankylosis of proximal interphalangeal joint with distal ulnar deviation. Osteoarthritic changes in distal interphalingeal joints. Arterial calcification present. Opacity in left axilla is in wrappings of chest wall.

Lower Limbs Feet together. Lines of arrested growth present in right upper tibia. Reduction in height of medial compartment of right knee with opacification of menisci. Right femoral artery calcified. Soft tissues of feet well preserved with plantar fascia readily visible.

Thorax Intact with normal rib cage. Costal cartilages completely opacified. Pericardial remains identifiable together with mediastinal pleura on left but no cardiac or pulmonary tissue identified. Upper mediastinum rotated to left; within it are opaque cartilaginous rings of trachea and bronchi together with aortic arch calcification. Opaque mass present in left thorax.

Abdomen Diaphragm intact posteriorly. No packaging present in abdomen and no incision site detectable. Elevated peritoneum in right paravertebral gutter detectable. No kidneys visible.

Spine Cervical — Spondylosis marked with generalized disc space narrowing. Osteophyte formation anteriorly and posteriorly with degenerative changes in apophyseal joints. Occipito-atlantal fusion present bilaterally. All disc spaces opaque.

Thoracic — No degenerative changes present. All disc spaces opaque.

Lumbar — Sacralization of L5 with partial collapse of upper border of L3 anteriorly associated with osteophytosis. Extensive disc opacification present. Herniation of annulus posteriorly at L2/3.

Pelvis Pelvis gynaecoid and normal.

Comment Elderly female with marked cervical and lumbar spondylosis and herniated L3/4 lumbar disc following old trauma to L3 vertebra. Abnormal spinal segmentation at both ends of neural axis. Fracture through dorsum sella indicates removal of cranial contents. Calcification of aorta, tracheo-bronchial cartilages, femoral and ulnar arteries, indicate an advanced age at death. Changes in left third digit probably the result of previous septic arthritis. Defect in right parietal bone could be a metastatic tumour deposit.

No. 5053 (Per-en-bast) (21–23)

Mummy of a woman in coffin.

General Well-preserved adult, probably female. No evidence of disturbance. Arms extended with hands pronated over inner thighs. Metallic Horus present over mid thorax and metallic incision plate over left lower abdomen with less dense ceramis scarabs in midline above Horus. Metal objects probably gold.

Skull Skull straight and aligned with no evidence of brain removal. Opaque falx and tentorium remain. Bilateral carotid arterial calcification at level of pituitary fossa. Dental state poor with attrition, caries and peridontal abscess formation. Dense pack in oropharynx. Opacities in orbits may be packs or prosthetic globes.

Upper Limbs No abnormality.

Lower Limbs. Right second metatarsal head flattened and left fourth and fifth proximal phalanges shorter and wider than those on right with osteoarthritic changes in both first metatarso-phalangeal joints. Calcification in left femoral and right dorsalis pedis arteries. Soft tissues of feet well outlined.

Thorax Rib cage intact and thoracic cavity filled with extensive packing containing speckled, high density material. No normal structures visible. Some of lower costal cartilages calcified.

Abdomen Metal plate over left flank indicates embalmer's incision site. Dense packing material in abdominal cavity with at least four separate packs identifiable.

Spine Cervical — No abnormality. No opaque disc material present.

Thoracic — Degenerative changes with osteophyte formation in mid thoracic region. Disc spaces not opaque.

Lumbar — Partial collapse of vertebral bodies L1, L4 and L5 with anterior wedging of body of L1. Disc spaces increased relative to vertebral height with extensive osteophyte formation. Intervertebral discs calcified.

Pelvis Gynaecoid in shape. No bony abnormality.

Comment An elderly female. Carotid artery calcification is evidence of ageing but there is remarkably little degenerative disease in cervical spine. Lumbar spine shows degenerative change and vertebral body collapse suggesting senile osteoporosis or, less probably, metastatic bone malignancy. Flattening of second right metatarsal head could be result of avascular necrosis or stress fracture. Packing in oropharynx, thorax and abdomen dense and may contain mud. Per-en-bast is the only mummy with metal or ceramic artefacts, i.e. flank incision plate and pectoral Horus.

No. 1768 (24–25)

Mummy of a boy.

General Poor state of preservation with disorganization of contents. Arms extended with hands pronated over anterior thighs. Packaging present in left loin. Stiffening board incorporated in wrappings along length of mummy posteriorly with a 'tongued and grooved' joint behind knees.

Skull No evidence of brain removal. Irregular dense material in occipital region probably brain tissue. One of mid cervical vertebrae lies in oropharynx and posterior nasopharynx. Pack in anterior nares. Teeth in excellent condition but wisdom teeth all absent.

Upper Limbs Both humeral and radial heads dislocated (PM). All epiphyses fused.

Lower Limbs Early osteoarthritic changes in both knee joints with sclerosis of tibial plateaux. Cartilage opacification present in knee joints. Upper tibial epiphyses fused.

Thorax Bony thorax collapsed. All ribs present although a number are dislocated at costo-vertebral joints.

Abdomen Diaphragm present on right. Folded material in left flank indicates incision site. Packing present in left loin.

Spine Cervical and Thoracic — Jumbled. No evidence of disease.

Lumbar — Disorganized with disc space narrowing at L1/2 where there is a small Schmorl's node indicating vertebral end plate disease and internal disc herniation.

Pelvis Pelvis android with sacroiliac joints dislocated. Iliac crest apophyses partially fused.

Comment Young adult male aged 20 in poor state of preservation at embalming though possibly disturbed later. Jointed stiffening board incorporated in wrappings posteriorly. Brain tissue present in cranial cavity. Dental state excellent but third molars absent. Early osteoarthritic changes present in knee joints, unusually so in someone so young. No cause of death demonstrated.

No. 1770 (26–32)

Mummy of an adolescent girl.

PRE-UNWRAPPING

General Body in poor condition. Arms folded across chest, right over left with hands pronated. Prosthetic lower legs and feet.

Skull Totally disarticulated but no bone abnormalities. No evidence of brain removal. Spheno-occipital synchondrosis separated. Good dental state with no attrition or decay.

Upper Limbs Both shoulders dislocated. Left humeral head missing, both elbows dislocated. Olecranon epiphysis fused but radial head epiphysis unfused. Carpal bones all present.

Lower Limbs Right leg amputated 10 cm above knee, remainder of leg missing. Left leg amputated below left knee, 10 cm from upper end of tibia. Left lower femoral epiphysis displaced and left patella missing. Lower legs represented by short prosthetic limbs with prosthetic feet. Canine tooth present by right knee.

Thorax Rib cage collapsed with some ribs disarticulated at costo-vertebral joints. Multiple fractures in lower ribs. No thoracic contents detected.

Abdomen No evidence of incision site. Diaphragm not visible. Abdomen full of amorphous opaque material with two distinct opacities, one to the right of L3/4 and one to the left of L4/5 in the abdominal wall. Opacity on right has serpiginous structure. False phallus seen at unwrapping evident on review of radiography.

Spine Cervical — Spine completely disorganized; vertebral bodies loose in wrappings.

Thoracic and Lumbar — Normal alignment apart from T1/3 segments which are displaced. Linear densities present throughout spine in intervertebral disc spaces.

Pelvis Pelvis disorganized with disruption through all synchondroses.

POST-UNWRAPPING

Skull Maxillary block re-radiographed. Left antrum hypoplastic and left inferior and middle turbinates missing. Mud packs present in both orbits. Teeth show no evidence of attrition. Upper molars unerupted with fracture through right upper incisor.

Lower Limbs Irregular bone ends at amputation sites contain compacted mud giving rise to appearance of bone regeneration.

Abdomen The two opacities in abdominal wall were subjected to macroradiography. The right-hand one demonstrates the serpiginous outline of a calcified guinea worm.

Spine Linear densities of intervertebral disc spaces were confirmed and shown to be resinous material.

Sandals No evidence of radio-opaque pigment in paint of the sandals which are therefore assumed to contain vegetable pigment.

Comment Poorly preserved 14-year-old female with evidence of skeletal disturbance. Legs have been amputated either at or shortly after death and there is no bone repair or reaction. Hypoplastic left antrum and missing turbinates together with normal teeth might be evidence of chronic upper respiratory tract infection and a prolonged fluid diet. Only evidence of disease is presence of calcified guinea worm in abdominal wall.

No. 9319 (33–35)
Mummy of a child.

General Mummy of a child, possibly male, in excellent state of preservation. 92 cm crown-heel length. Arms extended with hands pronated on outer thighs. Some longitudinal support present in wrappings behind head and body.

Skull Apart from subluxation at spheno-occipital synchondrosis, the skull is intact and slightly rotated to left. Opaque material present in cranial cavity and layered in occipital region suggests resin. No other evidence of brain removal. All deciduous teeth present; first molars erupted, second molars unerupted.

Upper Limbs Ossification of capitate, hamate, distal radial epiphysis and bases of proximal phalanges; remaining wrist bones still cartilagenous.

Lower Limbs Legs extended, feet together deviating slightly to left. Lines of arrested growth present in lower femur and lower and upper tibiae. In the hip, both femoral heads and greater trochanters ossified. Cartilage in knees has opacified. Upper fibular epiphysis present in cartilage.

Thorax Bony case intact and costal cartilages opaque. All ossification centres in sternum present. Pericardium and pleura visible with some lung tissue on left. Unidentifiable tissue remains in upper mediastinum.

Abdomen Abdominal cavity packed, probably with linen though a more dense and more solid package is present in left loin. No evidence of incision site. Diaphragm easily identified.

Spine Complete and intact. Acute flexion at C2/3 and C3/4. Odontoid process not yet fused to body of C2. Intervertebral disc spaces partially opaque due to increased density and detachment of end plate cartilages.

Pelvis Opacification of acetabular cartilage present. Opaque material present between thighs.

Comment Well-preserved child, probably male, aged about two years. (Bone age two years — two years eight months. Dental age 15–24 months.) There is evidence of previous ill-health — cause of death not known. Extensive cartilaginous opacification noted.

No. 2109 (36)
Mummy of a child.

General Body of child aged about two years. Sex not known. Crown-heel length 83 cm. Spine and ribs disorganized, suggesting disturbance. Arms extended with hands pronated over outer thighs.

Skull Subluxation of spheno-occipital synchondrosis with anterior bone defect through ethmoidal air cells in midline. No intracranial contents remain. Deciduous teeth all present. Dental age just over two years.

Upper Limbs Radial head epiphysis not ossified. Appearance of distal radial epiphysis and carpal bones suggest bone age of about two years. Faint opacification of cartilage in joints of upper limb.

Lower Limbs Legs extended. Hips show no calcification of greater trochanter epiphysis. Patella not yet calcified nor has the proximal fibular epiphysis. Ankle dorsiflexed and appearance of feet suggests pes cavus.

Thorax Ribs markedly disorganized with fracture through right eighth rib. Costal cartilages not opaque. Heterogeneous packing opacities present in right thoracic cavity but no anatomical structures identified.

Abdomen Detail of left hemidiaphragm remains, with packing in left flank and pelvic cavity.

Spine Cervical — Subluxation at atlanto-occipital articulation with defect of atlas anteriorly. Loss of disc space at C3/4. Spine dislocated (PM) at C7/T1 with neural arch of C7 missing.

Thoracic and Lumbar — Dislocation and lateral angulation at T4/5 and T11/12. Disc spaces partially opaque due to cartilage detachment.

Pelvis Apart from lateral compression no other abnormality demonstrated.

Comment Disrupted young child. Both bone and dental age suggest two years. Only suspicion of disease is presence of pes cavus bilaterally.

No. 1769 (37 and 38)
Mummy of a child.

General Mummy of child age three to four years in good state of preservation. No evidence of disturbance. Arms extended and pronated over anterior aspects of thighs.

Skull Subluxation at spheno-occipital synchondrosis and loose bone fragments present in nasopharynx. Left ethmoid sinus partly destroyed but no anterior fossa defect demonstrated. Falx cerebri present in anterior cranial cavity and well-defined packing in orbits. The posterior oropharynx contains a loose molar tooth. Dental age, three to four and a half years.

Upper Limbs Lines of arrested growth present in distal humeri. Epiphyseal development at elbow and hands indicates bone age of three years. Cartilagenous structures notably opaque.

Lower Limbs Legs straight with feet together. Bones normal except for dense epiphyseal margins in femoral heads and upper tibiae. Cartilage opacification prominent. Suspicion of soft tissue packing in legs.

Thorax Thorax compressed with costo-vertebral dislocation on right. Left first rib straightened anteriorly. Costal cartilages faintly calcified. Bilateral lung remains but no evidence of cardiac remains. Well-defined package present in right hemithorax.

Abdomen Soft tissue packing in abdominal cavity but no evidence of incision site.

Spine Intervertebral disc spaces increased in density in both thoracic and lumbar spine due to detached end plate cartilages. Subluxation of vertebral body C5 on C6.

Pelvis Bony pelvis compressed bilaterally.

Comment Well-preserved child aged three years, deformed by tight wrappings. No indication of sex. Dense epiphyseal margins and lines of arrested growth suggest previous illnesses. Packings present in chest and abdomen with evidence of removal of cranial contents through left nostril.

No. 20638 (Demetria) (**39** and **40**)
Mummy and mummy-case of female.

General Adult female in good state of preservation. Arms extended with hands semi-pronated, palms to outer thighs. No artefacts or loose packings.

Skull Skull rotated to left. Vault and base intact except for defect in right supra-orbital fissure. Hyperostosis frontalis interna and non-development of frontal sinuses with large ethmoidal air cells. Teeth show attrition and caries. No orbital contents detectable.

Upper Limbs No abnormality detected. Epiphyseal fusion complete.

Lower Limbs Osteoarthritic changes present in right knee with early lateral osteophyte formation. Meniscal cartilage opacification present on left. Feet reveal claw toes on right fourth and fifth toes and a left pes cavus.

Thorax Rib case compressed with right lower ribs disarticulated posteriorly. Lower articular ends of rib cartilages opacified. Remains of right lung identifiable.

Abdomen Diaphragm identifiable with heterogeneous opaque material packing abdomen. No evidence of incision site.

Spine Cervical — Disc space narrowing C5/6 and C6/7 with subluxation. No osteophytes.
Thoracic — Disarticulation at T7/8 (probably PM). Generalized disc space narrowing with anterior osteophytic lipping from T8–T12.
Lumber — Scoliosis concave to right with generalized disc space narrowing especially L3/4 on left. No osteophytic lipping.

Pelvis Pelvis gynaecoid. Symphysis pubis disarticulated and sacro-iliac joints subluxed.

Comment Middle-aged female with evidence of degenerative disease in thoracic spine. Right knee shows early osteoarthritic change with cartilage calcification.

No. 1767 (**41–43**)
Mummy of a man, in a cartonnage case.

General Poorly preserved elderly male with axial skeleton and rib cage disorganized. Arms extended with hands pronated over genitalia, left hand over right.

Skull Vault and skull base intact with no defect to indicate brain removal. No intracranial contents visible. Orbits and nasopharynx contain packing material. Mandible disarticulated and displaced posteriorly. Left upper central incisor has been reinserted into right lower incisor socket during embalming.

Upper Limbs Post-mortem subluxation of humeral heads. All epiphyses fused.

Lower Limbs Legs straight with feet together and left foot internally rotated. Both feet plantar flexed.

Thorax Bony cage collapsed with some ribs disarticulated at costo-vertebral joints. Costal cartilages opacified. No thoracic contents present.

Abdomen One package present within abdominal cavity but no evidence of incision site.

Spine Cervical — Neck acutely flexed and cervical spine disorganized.
Thoracic — Bony spine disorganized especially upper segments. Osteophytes present in mid-thoracic region. Several disc spaces partially opaque due to resin.
Lumbar — Lower lumbar spine rotated with acute lordosis at L5/S1. Degenerative changes at L4/5 on left. No disc opacification.

Pelvis Pelvis is android. Sacro-iliac joints subluxed.

Comment Poorly preserved mummy of adult male, despite the embalmer's attention to detail represented by the attempted tooth replacement; lumbar spine deformity is ante-mortem.

No. 1766 (**44** and **45**)
Mummy of a woman.

General Supine adult mummy in good state of preservation. Arms extended with hands over outer aspects of thighs. Large package present in sub-pubic region.

Skull Skull rotated to left but no bone defect detected. Cranial cavity empty. Linen wrapping present in orbits.

Upper Limbs All epiphyses fused.

Lower Limbs Legs extended with feet together deviated to left; left foot inverted. Left lateral femoral condyle flattened and articular cartilages in both knee joints faintly opacified. Evidence of pes planum (flat feet) with early degenerative changes of first metatarsophalangeal joints.

Thorax Bony thorax complete with dislocation of right ninth to eleventh costo-vertebral joints. Costal cartilages opaque. Pericardium but no cardiac tissue identified. Right lung present.

Abdomen Diaphragm present but no incision site identifiable. No discrete organ packages but upper abdomen filled with packing material, probably linen. Discrete opacity in packing to right of L3/4. A linear triangular density in pelvis could represent bladder calcification.

Spine Cervical — Subluxation at atlanto-occipital and C5/6 levels. No degenerative changes. Disc material not opaque.
Thoracic — Loss of normal kyphos with an unusually straight back. Minimal anterior osteophytosis in lower thoracic spine.
Lumbar — Mild scoliosis concave to right. Disc spaces generally reduced with forward slip of L1 on L2. A lateral osteophyte present on left at L4/5. Intervertebral disc spaces partially opaque but with preservation of nucleus pulposus at L3/4.

Pelvis Fractures through left superior and inferior pubic rami together with dislocation of left sacro-iliac joint. Pelvis gynacoid. Osteophytic lipping superiorly at symphysis pubis.

Comment Mummy of an adult female. Fractures through pelvis show no evidence of healing and could have occurred immediately before, or after, death. Loss of thoracic kyphos is unusual.

No. 1775 (Artemidorous) (46–48)
Mummy of a man.

General Supine male adult with evidence of disturbance. Several ribs, including the right first rib, are in the lower thoracic cavity. Arms are extended with hands over genitalia. One opaque pack present in lower thorax.

Skull Skull rotated to right. Vault normal but fracture through left frontal sinus. Evidence of brain removal with defect in right ethmoid. Layered opaque material, probably resin, in occipital region. Teeth show attrition except |678. Edentulous mandible eroded on left by continual impact of upper teeth. Eye packs containing flecks of dense material present bilaterally. Facial profile shows a 'hook nose'.

Upper Limbs All epiphyses fused.

Lower Limbs Both legs extended with left foot externally rotated. Early osteoarthritic change present in both hip and knee joints. Menisci in knee joints opaque.

Thorax Fractures of right 2–6 and left 3–4 ribs. Right first rib lies in lower right thorax. Costal cartilages opaque and fragmented lying in lower thorax with rib fragments. Pericardium and pleura present with remains of left lung. Dense, well-defined pack present in right hemithorax.

Abdomen Diaphragm present. No evidence of incision site or packing. Curvilinear pelvic calcification above symphysis pubis probably in bladder. Ante-mortem fracture through right acetabulum extending on to pelvic brim.

Spine Cervical — Neck extended with osteoarthritis of apophyseal joints.
   Thorax — Kypho-scoliosis and post-mortem distraction at T8/9 with marginal osteophyte on right. Disc space between T9/10 narrowed.
   Lumbo-Sacral — Scoliosis with rotation at thoracolumbar junction. Generalized degenerative changes present with disc space narrowing of L3/4, osteophytosis at L1/2 and L2/3 and forward slip of L5 on L4.

Comment Adult male with pelvic fracture resulting from severe trauma. Degenerative changes in spine and hips indicate ageing. Bladder calcification could be due either to schistosomiasis or tuberculosis.

No. 5275 (Ptolemaic Head) (49 and 50)

General Loose head with soft tissues over skull, face and back of neck.

Skull Skull vault intact but defects in base. Dorsum sella fractured at the base and displaced above right petrous bone. Bone defects in left tuberculum sella, anterior pituitary fossa and mid-line cribiform plate. Nasal septum and turbinates missing. During examination a radio-opaque catheter was introduced through the cribiform plate defect. No orbital contents present. Teeth show attrition.

Cervical Spine Only C1–C6 vertebral bodies present but lower two intervertebral disc spaces show signs of degenerative disease with posterior osteophytic lipping. Hyoid bone still in situ.

Comment Skull and cervical spine with soft tissue residue demonstrating anterior fossa defects indicative of brain removal. The dorsum sella fracture and displacement due to embalming technique.

No. 7740 (Head (opened) and upper cervical vertebrae)

Head flexed at cranio-vertebral junction and cut cleanly circumferentially around the vault. Skull base intact. Falx visible together with tentorium and dura in parietal region. Brain remnants present in parieto-occipital region. Orbital packs present. Dental state poor with extensive caries, periodontal disease and missing teeth. Heads of mandibles show marked degenerative change with left temporo-mandibular joint dislocation.

Cervical spine extended with degenerative changes in apophyseal joints from C3 to C5. Spine below this level is missing.

Nos. 21475 and 21474 (Head, upper cervical spine and foot)

Skull vault intact. Left frontal sinus hypoplastic. Defect in left anterior clinoid process and dorsum sella. Bone fragment in posterior fossa on left side. There are no dural remains but opaque material present in the parieto-occipital region. Packs present in orbits, oropharynx and nasopharynx. A loose, careous tooth is situated in the hypopharynx.

Upper cervical spine to C3 present and apparently normal.

Foot disarticulated through tibiotalar joint. Acute dorsiflexion of fifth proximal phalanx with fracture through its base. Degenerative changes present in the first metatarsophalyngeal joint.

No. 22940 (Head and cervical spine)

Head flexed at craniovertebral junction. Skull vault and base intact. There are remains of the tentorium and interclinoid ligaments. Opaque tissue, probably brain, present in right parietal region. Horizontal fractures through three of the upper incisors and caries in both upper 7s.

There is evidence of petromastoid inflammatory disease. The air cells are small and with surrounding bone sclerosis.

Cervical spine extended and scoliotic (concave to right). Neural arch of C7 missing. Degenerative disease evidenced by apophyseal joint sclerosis from C4–6.

No. 21476 (Hand)

Left hand and incomplete wrist (lunate, triquetrum and part of scaphoid missing) of an adult. Thumb adducted and little finger dorsiflexed. Part of terminal tuft of third terminal phalanx missing, probably post-mortem. Small round opacity noted on palmar aspect of fifth metacarpophalyngeal joint.

No. 9384 (Hand)

Complete left hand from radiocarpal joint with fingers in slight flexion. No degenerative changes. Epiphyses closed with closure lines still visible. The bones are well developed and suggest the hand of a young adult male.

No. 9428 (Hand)

Complete right hand from radiocarpal joint with fingers slightly flexed. Post-mortem fracture through head of second metacarpal. Proximal phalanx of thumb fractured with distal fragments missing. Mid portion of second proximal phalanx also missing. Osteoarthritic changes with osteophyte formation present at distal interphalangeal joints. Hand probably of an older male.

Discussion

There are two main categories of interest in the radiological investigation of ancient human remains. One is concerned with the archaeology and preservation of the specimen and their relationship to the time scale of cultural development, the other with the scientific study of morbidity and mortality in ancient civilization. The term palaeopathology is employed for the study of disease in ancient human remains.[12]

Evaluation of Egyptological collections in museums presents difficulties since material is usually drawn from such an extended time scale. Comment in individual specimens is therefore frequently anecdotal and dependent upon comparison with slowly accumulating data from parallel studies. The 17 complete human mummies in Manchester cover a time scale from 1900 B.C. to c.4th Century A.D. and have a reported provenance from Hawara to Thebes.

Age Radiology presents a unique opportunity to evaluate skeletal maturity and development. Ossification of bone begins at certain main centres about the eighth intrauterine week and progresses at some sites into adult life. After birth, bony epiphyses develop at one or both of the cartilagenous ends of long bone. When growing bones have reached adult length the epiphyses fuse with the remainder of the bone. The time scale for bony development varies in different parts of the body. Fusion of skull bones may not take place until adult life. The skull of a child may therefore readily collapse after death. Some 100 ossification centres could be considered in skeletal assessment but as a basis, six body sites are important — hands, feet, elbows, knees, shoulders and hips. Due to overlying structures and varying posture much detailed tomographic study may

be necessary to ensure a proper evaluation of bony development (**7, 8, 28, 34, 35**).

Well-documented European and North American radiological standards exist[13,14] and have been used in the present studies to define bone age. There are, however, significant racial differences related to genetic and nutritional influences with a general tendency towards earlier skeletal maturation in ancient Egyptians. To be truly accurate radiological studies should be from the same ethnic group and from a contemporary population.

Tooth calcification and development, though subject to the same variations and constraints of interpretation, also offer significant information about individual age.[15,16] Tomography in specially contrived planes calculated from the skull radiographs has been necessary to render such data accessible.

It was possible in the present studies to assess skeletal and dental maturity with reasonable accuracy in all six of the mummies where death had occurred during active growth. The calculated age in this sub-group ranged from three months to 20 years (Table II). The age of the remaining adult mummies could only be assessed subjectively, based on various ageing processes, for example osteoarthritis and arterial calcification (**12, 17, 19, 23**).

Sex In some mummies it was possible to determine sex by direct visualization of the genitalia. In others it was necessary to evaluate the size and shape of the pelvis, skull and appendicular skeleton. No discrepancies from the available descriptions were observed. A direct skeletal study of the remains of the two brothers KN (21471) and NA (21470) in 1907[17] had drawn attention to the eunuchoid features of NA (21470). These observations were confirmed by the present re-examination.

Embalming The process of mummification developed over the centuries from pre-dynastic dessication in hot sand to elaborate, stylized, ceremonial in the later dynasties, reaching a peak at the XXIst Dynasty with a subsequent decline towards the Roman period. As a generalization, the later the period after the XXIst Dynasty, the more the attention given by embalmers to the exterior wrapping and less to the treatment of the body within. It might be anticipated that the current study would reveal a wide variety of skeletal and soft tissue changes.

Position of the arms and hands may, together with the general disposition and organization of the other remains, be significant in assessing chronology. The position of the arms and hands on radiographs of 111 mummies were reviewed and evaluated by Gray in 1972.[18] The corresponding information in the Manchester mummies is given in Table II. Most mummies from the XXIst to the XXVth Dynasties have extended arms. The crossed pectoral position of one arm in 10881 is unusual. The remaining arm positions are all consistent with the descriptive dates and the known embalming procedures.

The essential process of mummification consisted of dehydration and desiccation. The abdomen was opened usually by a left flank incision and the abdominal viscera and lungs then removed. Before the XXIst Dynasty the viscera were often placed in four canopic jars. After this period the viscera might be returned to the body cavity in at least four separate packs. The body and viscera up to the XXVth Dynasty were treated with natron (a mixture of sodium bicarbonate and sodium carbonate) as a dehydrating agent.[19] Later more reliance was placed on the use of resin applied in a molten state when, in the words of Dawson, it might 'invade every crevice of the cavity and even the cancellous structure of bone'.[20] In Roman times, Natron was often used again. Body cavity packing materials varied from sawdust to linen and mud. In the present series by the use of tomography it has been possible to distinguish parcels and packing material of heterogeneous and varying density in the abdominal cavity in ten specimens and in the thoracic cavity of five. Resinous material was clearly identified in the body cavity of 1976.51 (14) and the skulls of 9354, 9319, and 1775.

Restorations The soft tissues of the face, trunk and limbs from the XXIst to the XXVIth Dynasty were on occasion restored by subcutaneous packing via small incisions.[8] This type of packing is present in mummy 1769. No definite radio-opaque artificial eyes[21] have been identified in the present series but some form of packing has certainly been identified in nine, possibly ten, specimens. A ring-like opacity revealed by tomography in the orbits of two mummies (1976.51 and 5053) suggests that these particular restorations may be material other than mud or linen, perhaps ceramic, though unusual objects including 'small onions'[4] have been employed (13).

A number of more spectacular embalmers' restorations have been recorded by Elliot Smith and Wood Jones[22] and in the Durham mummy by Gray[23] and again by Gray in Leiden mummy number 24.[7] In mummy 1770 here recorded and the subject of the Manchester unwrapping in 1975, in addition to orbital packs extensive restorations had been undertaken by the embalmer to provide prosthetic lower legs and feet with decorative sandals and gold toe stalls (28, 32). A false phallus was also present.

A simple if inaccurate restoration has been attempted in mummy 1767 by the replacement of an upper incisor tooth in the empty socket of a lower incisor (42). A supporting wooden board is identifiable in 1768, contained within the wrappings. A similar board was noted in Leiden mummy No. 22.[7] In the present specimen a form of tongued and grooved joint is visible.

In brain removal during embalming as described by Herodotus,[24] instrumentation was carried out through the nostrils to avoid disfigurement. Details of the instrumentation and technique have been described by Leek.[25] Evidence of brain removal was sought in the present investigations by detailed thin section tomography together with stereoscopy of the thin ethmoidal plates separating the nasal cavity from the anterior cranial fossa. Such indisputable evidence was obtained in seven of the intact mummies and in one of the decapitated heads. The presence of such characteristic bone defects was detected in mummies ranging from the XIIth Dynasty to the Roman Period (Table II). The dorsum sella was detached in three (21470, 1777 and 5275) (2, 50). A modern radio-opaque Kifa catheter was introduced

through the defect in 5275 in an attempt to dislodge the detached dorsum adherent in resin (50). The attempt recorded radiologically recalls the similarity of modern neurosurgical approaches to the pituitary fossa by the Chiari approach.

Tissue considered to be residual brain has been demonstrated in several mummies (1976.51, 1777, 1768, 7740, 1764), though tissue characterization cannot be certain (12). Evidence that brain tissue can be preserved is afforded by a recent computed tomographic examination of a shrunken ancient Egyptian brain.[26] This examination revealed ventricular cavities together with grey and white matter discrimination in a 3200-year-old mummy.

Intervertebral Disc Opacification Controversy surrounds the aetiology of intervertebral disc opacification in Egyptian mummies. The radiological observation was first recorded by Simon and Zorab[27] in 1961 and a further case added in 1962 by Wells and Maxwell.[28] The changes were attributed by both groups to Alkaptonuria. Alkaptonuria is a rare, inborn error of tyrosine intermediary metabolism in which the enzyme homogentisic acid oxidase is absent. The inability to metabolize homogentisic acid is an autosomal recessively inherited defect which gives rise to the accumulation of homogentisic acid in the urine, which becomes dark on standing, and also to the accumulation of a dark ochre pigment, both intra and extra cellularly, in a variety of connective tissues. The condition is sometimes described as Ochronosis. Joints become arthritic and calcification occurs in intervertebral discs and articular cartilages. In 1967, Gray[29] reviewed 64 mummies from British museums with specific reference to the radiological appearances of the intervertebral disc spaces. Calcification was observed in 18, an incidence of less than one in four. Because of this unexpected frequency together with the absence of any associated osteoarthritic lipping, the appearances were attributed to artefacts of embalming technique. The appearances also coincided closely to the use of natron as an embalming procedure. Attention has been drawn earlier to the changing use of natron and resin in embalming materials. In the present series, ten mummies (six adults and four children) out of seventeen showed evidence of disc space opacification (11, 18, 20, 22). A further two specimens exhibit linear opacification considered to be due to resin within the disc space (29). This last observation was confirmed in one specimen (1770), following unwrapping. Calcification was also observed in the articular cartilage of the knee joints of six mummies (Table II). The remarkable incidence of disc opacification (12 out of 17) adds further doubt to the role of Alkaptonuria as an aetiological factor. Recent biochemical observations, however, have contributed further to the controversy.[30] Ochronotic pigment has been identified from bone biopsy specimens retrieved from Harwa, a 3500-year-old Egyptian mummy which radiologically exhibits calcified intervertebral discs and is presently housed in the Field Museum in Chicago. Furthermore, recent biochemical and clinical surveys of infants in Slovakia (Eastern Czechoslovakia)[31] and in Wales[32] have revealed a much higher incidence of Alkaptonuria (1 in

25,000 and 1 in 44,800 respectively) than the 1 in 5 million previously anticipated. It is our intention to carry out biochemistry of bone biopsy material from the Manchester mummies in a further attempt to elucidate this problem.

Arthritis Degenerative arthritis in both axial and appendicular skeleton as a manifestation of ageing is evident to some extent in almost all the mature adult mummies in the Manchester collection (**12, 19**). Evidence of degenerative disc disease is present in seven with osteophytic lipping. A Schmorl's node was detected in the lumbar vertebral body of one (1768). Sagittal tomography of the spine in mummies 9354 and 1777 revealed herniation of the calcified annulus at L3/4 (**11,18**) — surely the first direct evidence of disc herniation from an ancient civilization. No evidence of ankylosing spondylitis has been detected in the spine or sacro-iliac joints of the 17 mummies examined and we are inclined to support the view[33] that previous descriptions of ankylosing spondylitis have included osteoarthritis.

Trauma Post-mortem trauma can often be inferred readily by the site and character of bone damage (2109) (**36**). Other fractures have classical ante-mortem features Two specimens (1766 and 1775) here recorded exhibit the typical features associated with a pelvic fracture involving the acetabulum (**45, 48, 54**). The absence of any radiological features of healing suggest that both were terminal events. Several healed rib fractures have been demonstrated but no other skeletal sites investigated revealed any evidence of healed fractures. The cut surfaces of the amputated lower limbs in mummy 1770 were denser than normal, raising the possibility of new bone formation but the appearances were demonstrated at tomography and confirmed at unwrapping to be the result of impacted mud (**28**). The mechanism of amputations in 1770 and the time relationship of the events to death remain in doubt. In view of the possibility that the mummy had been immersed in water and the probability of later rewrapping together with the embalmer's attention to detail, crocodile, hippopotamus and shark bites have all been considered. The first is improbable since disarticulation is more likely from crocodile bites; the last two remain possibilities — particularly if sea-water immersion is considered.

Generalized Disease Evidence of generalized disease is frequently reflected in the skeleton. Demineralization of the axial skeleton in mummy 5053 together with the partial collapse of vertebral body L1 (**22**) suggests a menopausal or senile osteoporosis. The absence of localized lesions elsewhere whilst not totally excluding metastatic deposits or myeloma certainly does not support either diagnosis.

Lines of arrested growth, or Harris lines,[34] as seen in 21471, 3496 and 1777 (**4, 7**), are the result of calcium continuing to be laid down close to the growing ends of bone when bone growth has been temporarily arrested by generalized illness. Although some absorption of Harris lines may occur during childhood, their presence is some indication of morbidity during growth.[35]

Arterial calcification is usually associated with degenerative vascular disease and the ageing process. It is well-displayed in 9354, 1777 and 5053 (**17, 23**). There is no definite radiological evidence in these three specimens to suggest any abnormality of calcium metabolism though the calcification in 5053 is particularly widespread and dense. Similar calcification is well-described in other Egyptological specimens.[36, 37]

Biparietal Thinning Thinning of the parietal bones of the skull vault observed in mummy 9354 (**9**) is uncommon but not rare. Loss of bone from the outer table of the skull vault has occurred. The radiological appearances are characteristic of the condition. A number of examples have been described in the skulls of ancient Egyptians.[4, 38, 39] The exact aetiology of the condition is unknown but the condition is most frequently associated with ageing. The possible relationship with the wearing of heavy wigs or carrying of heavy water jars has been largely discounted.[39]

Congenital Anomalies The presence of a left-sided club foot — talipes equinovarus — in 21471 (KN) was suggested in 1910[17] but the radiological normality (**5**) noted by Brothwell[40] and confirmed in this study does not support the diagnosis.

Infection The only residual evidence of bacterial infection in the present radiological study is in the bony ankylosis of the interphalangeal joint of the left third finger in mummy 1777 (**19**). There is, however, strong radiological evidence of pathogenic parasites in three specimens. Characteristic serpiginous calcification in the abdominal wall of 1770 is diagnostic of guinea worm (Dracunculus Medinensis) infestation (**30**). The male guinea worm dies and calcifies frequently in this fashion. The female guinea worm is very long (up to 1.5 m) and works its way through the tissues to the skin surface, usually on the foot, in order to discharge the larvae into water. The worm is classically removed by winding on a stick. The 'fiery serpent' which afflicted the Children of Israel in the flight from Egypt and the 'brass rod' of Moses[41] are considered to be a contemporary, if allegorical, description of this infestation and its cure.

Infection with Bilharzia haematobium (Schistoma haematobium) is widespread in present-day Egypt with the water snail acting as an intermediary host. The adult female worm migrates to the pelvic veins where the ova are laid in the wall of the bladder. The sharp spines of the ova give rise to chronic irritation and calcification in the bladder wall is a frequently-observed radiological feature. The linear calcification in residual bladder tissue observed in 1775 and 1766 is strong evidence of this parasitic infestation (**45, 48**).

Acknowledgements

The authors wish to acknowledge the support and encouragement of Dr Rosalie David and the Manchester Museum Committee in enabling this radiological survey to be carried out. They would also like to thank Kodak Ltd for generous financial support.

Thanks are also conveyed to Mrs M. Tipton and Mrs K. Hale for expert secretarial assistance.

Appendix

X-Rays X-rays belong to the electro-magnetic spectrum, as do light, radio, and television waves. They have the same properties as physical light and obey the same physical laws but their wavelength is much shorter rendering them invisible to the eye. X-rays are produced when a stream of electrons from a heated filament strike a suitable target material. A high-tension electric current attracts the electrons from one to the other. Variation of the speed and quantity of electrons will in turn affect the quantity and penetrative quality of the x-ray beam produced. The region of the target where x-rays, and incidentally heat, are produced is called the focal spot and since sharp shadows are needed this spot must be as small as possible, preferably less than 1 mm square. This is particularly so when any degree of magnification is present in the image.

When an x-ray passes through an object it is differentially absorbed or attenuated by the varying materials making up the object. The degree to which the absorption takes place is dependent on the density and atomic number of the material The higher the atomic number, the greater the absorption. Bone or metal, therefore, absorb more x-rays than soft tissue or air. Those x-rays ultimately transmitted through an object may be recorded on special photographic film. The resultant radiograph represents; therefore, a 'shadowgram' related to the different absorption characteristics of the materials making up the object. Dense materials appear white, less dense materials varying shades of grey to black.

Fluoroscopy If a beam of transmitted x-rays is allowed to reach a fluorescent screen then an immediate and dynamic view of events by the observer is possible. Such a fluoroscopic image is usually amplified in brightness by an image intensifier which in turn may be linked to a closed-circuit television system. It is then possible either to view moving parts in the living or to obtain a conceptual, three-dimensional image of a stationary object by moving it in the x-ray beam. Cine or video recordings of the TV image are standard practice in modern hospital departments.

Orbiting Equipment Detailed investigation of brain disorders in the living have led to the development of specialized radiological equipment capable of orbiting the subject. Complex engineering has enabled a fine focal spot (0.3 mm square) x-ray source together with a suitable imaging device to be placed at opposite points on the surface of an imaginary sphere of known radius at the centre of which a region of interest can be placed. The observer is then enabled to view the x-ray image by TV link from an infinite number of aspects without moving the subject. Particular radiographic projections to display detailed features on film may be selected by this method.

Tomography The 'shadowgram' nature of the conventional radiograph, no matter how it is obtained, may result in features of interest being partially or completely obscured by under- or over-lying structures. Tomography is a method of obtaining x-rays of a section or slice of tissue in a plane of interest. The result may be achieved by blurring out unwanted shadows above and below the plane of interest, the image of which is then left sharply defined. Selected blurring of this sort is carried out by controlled movement of the x-ray tube and film in equal and opposite directions about the fulcrum. Structures in the plane of the fulcrum will remain unblurred by the movement. The extent of movement which may be very complex governs the thickness of the unblurred or focal plane. Slices of tissue 1–2 mm in depth may be achieved in this way.

Such tomographic facilities if combined with orbiting apparatus and television viewing afford a variable and sophisticated method of conducting a radiological examination. Units with these capabilities are expensive and usually only located in highly specialized departments of Diagnostic Radiology.

Computed Tomography Computed Tomography is an x-ray transmission technique where the x-ray beam is highly collimated and the radiographic film replaced by scintillation or ionisation detectors. The system enables cross-sections of an object to be calculated from precise measurements of transmitted radiation intensity. The transmission data is processed by a computer and presented as a numerical print-out. Digital to analog conversion and appropriate grey-scaling enables the large amount of numerical data to be presented as a pictorial display on a television monitor.

Computed Tomography not only eliminates the problem of superimposition but also enables quantitative interrogation of both normal and abnormal structures which may not be visualized by plain radiography or conventional tomography.

References

[1] König, W., 14 photographien mit Röntgen-Strahlen, aufgenommen im *Physikalischen Verein, Frankfurt a M.* Leipzig, J. A. Barth, 1896.

[2] Thurston Holland, X-Rays in 1896, *The Liverpool Medico-Chirurgical Journal*, 1937, 45, 61.

[3] Petrie, W. M. F., Deshashesh 1897, *Fifteenth Memoir of the Egypt Exploration Fund*, Egypt Exploration Fund, London 1898, Plate xxxvii.

[4] Elliot Smith, G., *The Royal Mummies. Catalogue Général des Antiquités du Egyptiennes du Musée du Caire*, No. 61051–61100, Service des Antiquités de l'Egypte, Cairo, 1912, pp. iii–iv.

[5] Moodie, R. L., *Roentgenological Studies of Egyptian Peruvian Mummies*, Field Museum of Natural History, Chicago, Illinois, 1931.

[6] Gray, P. H. K., The Radiography of Mummies of Ancient Egyptians, *Journal of Human Evolution*, 1973, 2, 51–53.

[7] Gray, P. H. K., Radiological Aspects of the Mummies of Ancient Egyptians in the Rijksmuseum van Oudheden, Leiden. Reprinted from *Oudheidkundige mededelingen uit het Rijksmuseum van Oudheden*, Leiden, 47, Leiden, 1966.

[8] Dawson, W. R. Gray, P. H. K., *Catalogue of Egyptian Antiquities in the British Museum (1): Mummies and Human Remains*, Oxford University Press, 1968.

9 Gray, P. H. K., Slow, D., *Egyptian Mummies in the City of Liverpool Museums*, Liverpool Corporation, 1968.

10 Harris, J. E., Weeks, K. R., *X-Raying the Pharoahs*, Charles Scribner & Sons, New York, 1973.

11 Harrison, R. G., An Anatomical Examination of the Pharaonic Remains purported to be Akhenaten, *Journal of Egyptian Archaeology*, 1966, 95, 119.

12 Ruffer, M. A., Studies in Palaeopathology in Egypt, *Journal of Path. and Bact.*, 1913, 18, 149.

13 Francis, C. C., Wesle, P. P., Behm, A., Method of Girdany and Gollen and Method of Francis, *American Journal of Physical Anthropology*, 1939, 24, 273.
(From *Atlas of Roentgenographic Measurement*, Lusted, L. B. and Keats, T. E. Year Book Medical Publishers Inc., Chicago 1972, 3rd edition, pp. 70–72).

14 Greulich, W. W., Pyle, S. I., *Radiographic Atlas of Skeletal Development of the Hand and Wrist* (2nd Edition), Oxford University Press, 1964.

15 Schom, I., Poncheo, H., *Development of Teeth*, Mead, Johnson & Co., 1940, 1945.

16 Prendergass, E. P., Schaeffer, J. P., Hodes, P., *The Head and Neck in Roentgen Diagnosis*, Vol. I, Charles C. Thomas, Illinois, 1956, 442.

17 Murray, M. A., *The Tomb of Two Brothers*, Manchester Museum Publications, 68, Sherratt & Hughes, Manchester, 1910.

18 Gray, P. H. K., Notes concerning the position of Arms and Hands of Mummies with a view to possible dating of the specimen, *Journal of Egyptian Archaeology*, 1972, 58, 200–04.

19 Sandison, A. T., The Use of Natron in mummification in ancient Egypt, *Journal of Near Eastern Studies*, 1963, 22, 259.

20 Dawson, W. R., quoted in *Diseases in Antiquity*, ed. D. Brothwell and A. T. Sandison, C. C. Thomas, Illinois, 1967, p. 25.

21 Gray, P. H. K., Artificial Eyes in Mummies, *Journal of Egyptian Archaeology*, 1971, 57, 125–26.

22 Smith, G. E., Wood Jones, F., *Archaeological Survey Nubia (Human Remains), Report for 1907–08*, Cairo, 1910, p. 124.

23 Gray, P. H. K., Embalmers' Restorations, *Journal of Egyptian Archaeology*, 1967, 52, 138.

24 *Herodotus II*, 86 (translated A. D. Godley in Loeb Classical Library).

25 Leek, F. F., The problem of Brain Removal during Embalming by the Ancient Egyptians, *Journal of Egyptian Archaeology, 1969*, 55, 112–16.

26 Lewin, P. K., and Harwood Nash, D. C., X-Ray Computed Axial Tomography of an Ancient Egyptian Brain, *RCS Medical Science: Anatomy, Human Biology, Biomedical Technology, Nervous System*, 1977, 5, 78.

27 Simon, G., Zorab, P. A., The Radiographic changes in Alkaptonuric Arthritis. A report on three cases (one an Egyptian Mummy), *British Journal of Radiology*, 1961, 34, 384–86.

28 Wells, C., Maxwell, B. M., Alkaptonuria in an Egyptian mummy, *British Journal of Radiology*, 1962, 35, 679–82.

29 Gray, P. H. K., Calcinosis Intervertebralis with special reference to similar changes found in mummies of ancient Egyptians, in *Diseases in Antiquity*, ed. D. Brothwell, A. T. Sandison, C. C. Thomas, Illinois, 1967, pp. 20–30.

30 Lee, S. L., Stenn, F. F., Characterization of Mummy Bone Ochronotic Pigment, *Journal of the American Medical Association*, 1978, 240, 136–38.

31 Srsen, S., Varga, F., Alkaptonuria, *Lancet*, 1978, 2, 576.

32 Harper, P. S., Bradley, D. M., Alkaptonuria, *Lancet*, 1978, 2, 576–77.

33 Zorab, P. A., The Historical and Prehistorical Background of Ankylosis Spondylitis, *PRSM*, 1961, 54, 415–520.

34 Harris, H. A., *Bone Growth in Health and Disease*, Oxford University Press, 1933.

35 Schwager, G. P., The frequency of appearance of transverse lines in the tibia in relation to childhood illnesses, *American Journal of Physical Anthropology*, 1969, 31, 17–22.

36 Ruffer, M. A., On arterial lesions found in Egyptian Mummies, *Studies in the Palaeopathology of Egypt*, ed. R. L. Moodie, University of Chicago Press, Chicago, 1921, pp. 20–31.

37 Sandison, A. T., Degenerative Vascular Disease in the Egyptian Mummy, *Medical History*, 1962, 6, 77–81.

38 Elliot Smith, G., The causation of the symmetricak thinning of the parietal bones in ancient Egyptians, *Journal of Anatomy and Physiology*, London, 1907, 41, 232.

39 Lodge, T., Thinning of the Parietal Bones in early Egyptian populations and its aetiology in the light of modern observations, in *Disease in Antiquity*, ed. D. Brothwell, A. T. Sandison, C. C. Thomas, Illinois, 1967, pp. 405–12.

40 Brothwell, D., Major congenital anomalies of the skeleton. Evidence from earlier populations, in *Diseases in Antiquity*, ed. Brothwell, D., Sandison, A. T., C. C. Thomas, Illinois, 1967, pp. 423–43.

41 *Numbers*, Ch. 21, verses 6–9.

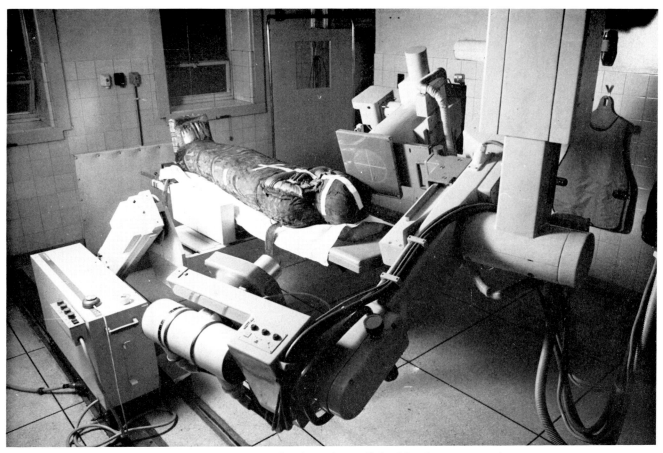

(**1**) (*Above*) Specialized radiological equipment used to investigate all the Manchester mummies in the Department of Neuro-radiology

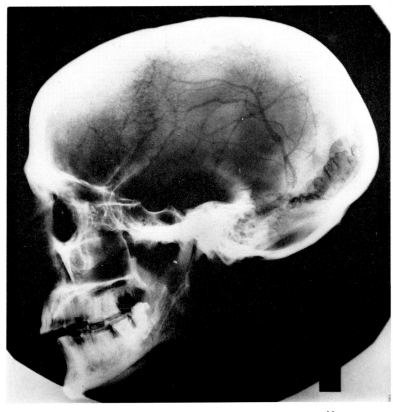

(**2**) 21470 (NA). Lateral skull. Dorsum sella missing. Note attrition of teeth.

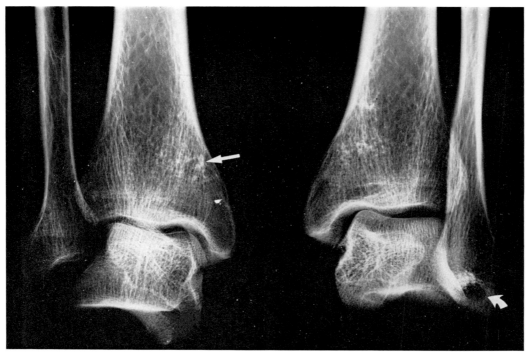

(3) 21470 (NA). Ankles. Sclerotic
zones distal tibiae? bone infarction
(straight arrow). Cystic lesion distal
left fibula (curved arrow).

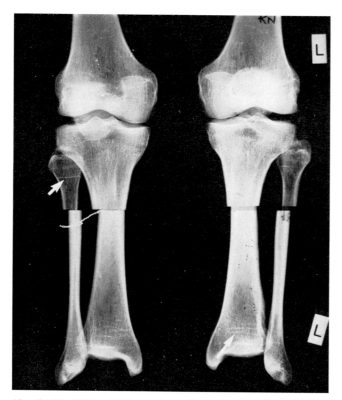

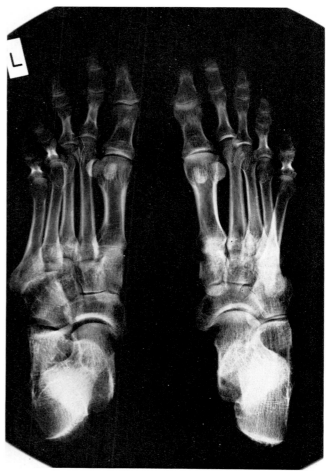

(4) 21471 (KN). AP lower legs. Growth arrest lines (arrow)
distal tibiae and proximal fibulae.

(5) 21471 (KN). AP feet. Club foot deformity was suspected.
No radiological abnormality. Appearances due to tight
bandaging.

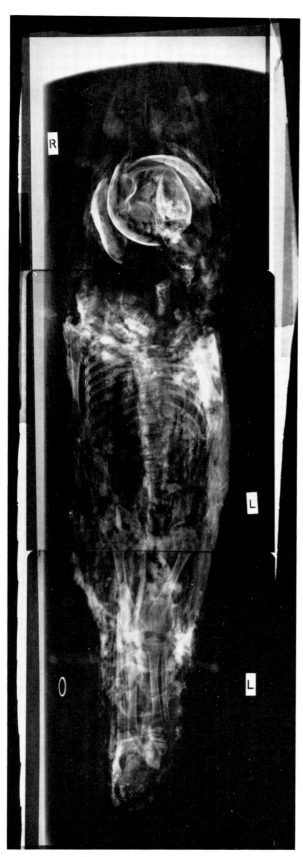

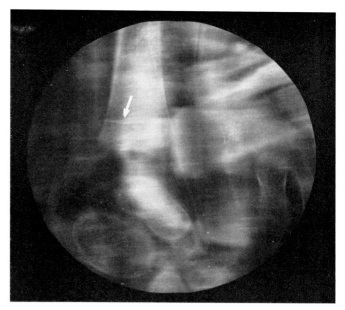

(7) 3496. Lateral tomography ankle and foot demonstrating bone development and lines of arrested growth (arrow).

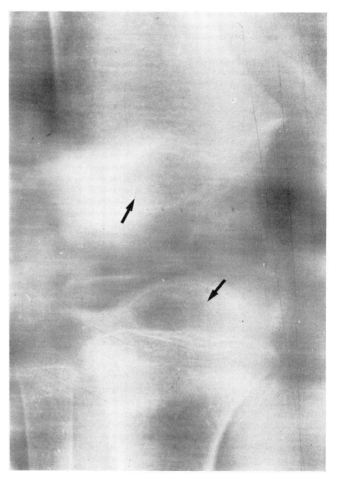

(6) 3496. Preliminary radiographic survey with overlapping films.

(8) 3496. AP right knee demonstrating epiphyseal development at distal femur and proximal tibia (arrow). Age just under three months.

43

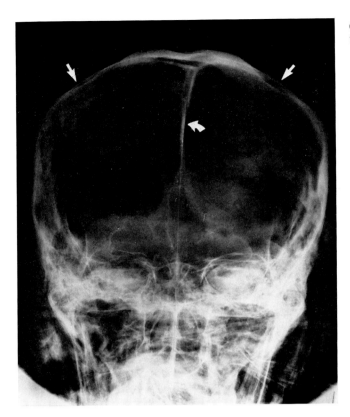

(9) 9354 (Khary). Skull. Biparietal thinning. Note calcification of falx.

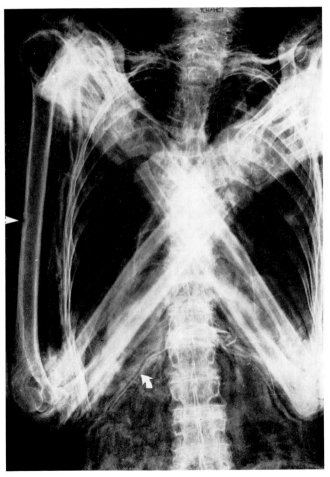

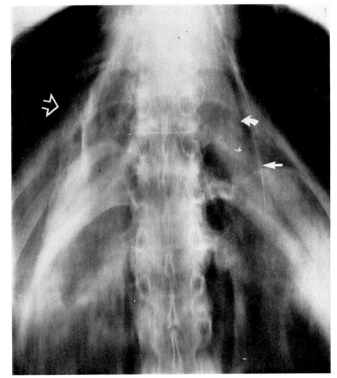

(10) 9354 (Khary). Chest. (*Left*) AP. Arms crossed, left hand clenched. Small cortical cyst on lateral aspect of right humerus (straight arrow). Note diaphragm (curved arrow).

(*Above*) AP tomography. Pericardium (straight arrow), heart (curved arrow) and right lung (open arrow) demonstrated. This area otherwise obscured by crossed arms.

44

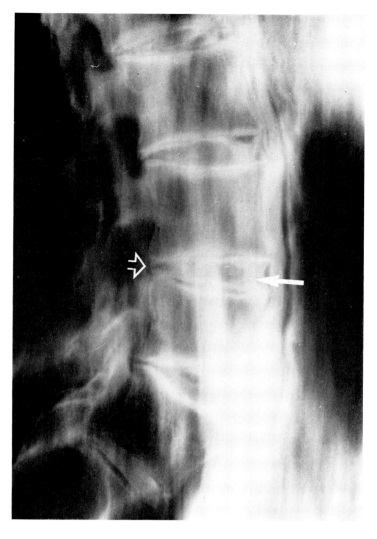

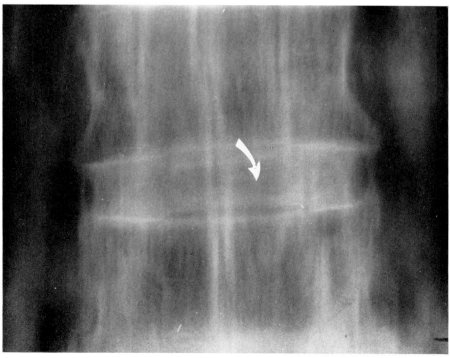

(11) 9354. Lumbar spine
(*Above*) Lateral tomography.
(*Below*) AP tomography.
Peripheral annulus of intervertebral
discs calcified (straight arrow),
nucleus spared (curved arrow).
Note protrusion of annulus at L3/4
(open arrow).

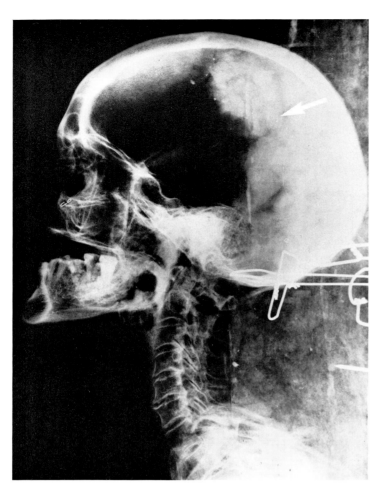

(12) 1976.51. Lateral skull and cervical spine. Residual brain material (arrow). Degenerative change and osteoarthritis in cervical spine. Note attrition of teeth.

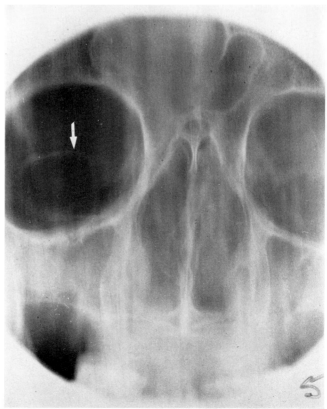

(13) 1976.51. AP tomography face. Right frontal sinus and maxillary antra opaque. Ring opacity in right orbit (arrow) ? prosthetic globe.

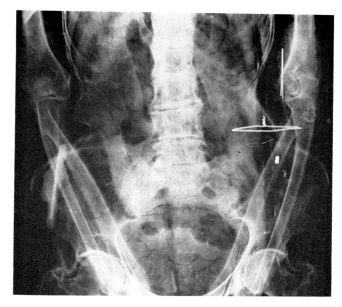

(**14**) 1976.51
(*Above*) AP abdomen.
(*Right*) Ap tomography abdomen.
Air-filled tubular structure in mid-line. Note opacification of
lumbar intervertebral discs and lateral osteophyte formation.

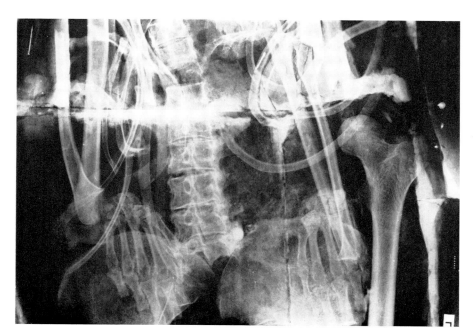

(**15**) 10881 (Ta-Aath). AP
abdomen. Axial and appendicular
skeleton jumbled.

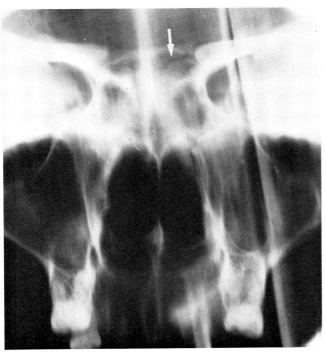

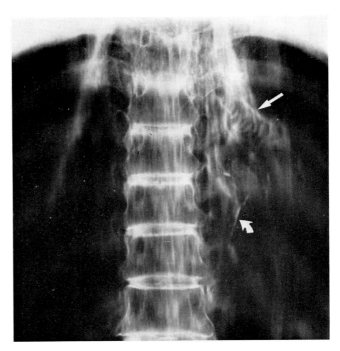

(16) 10881 (Ta-Aath). AP tomography skull. Fracture of tuberculum sellae (arrow) due to brain removal.

(17) 1777 (Asru). Upper thorax and skull.
(*Left*) AP.
(*Above*) Ap tomography.
(*Below*) Computed tomography.
Opaque cartilaginous rings of trachea and bronchi (straight arrow) and aortic arch calcification (curved arrow). Note lytic lesion in right parietal bone (open arrow) and intervertebral disc calcification.

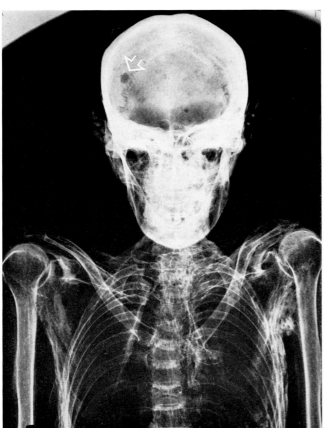

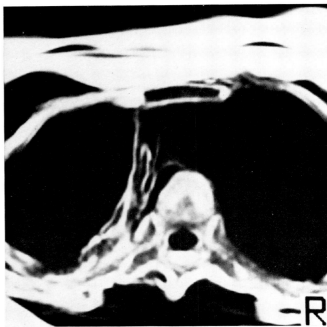

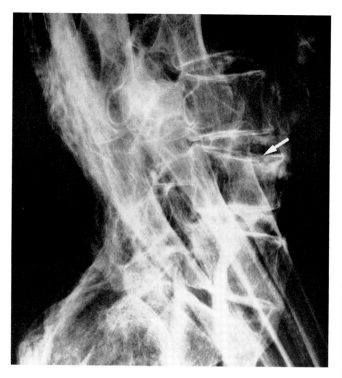

(**18**) 1777 (Asru). Lumbar spine.
(*Above*) Lateral.
(*Below*) Lateral tomography.
Partial collapse of L3 anteriorly due to old trauma (straight arrow). Extensive intervertebral disc calcification with herniation of L3/4 disc posteriorly (curved arrow).

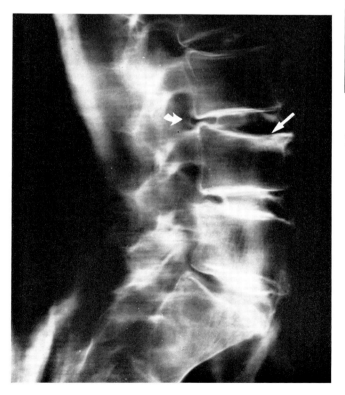

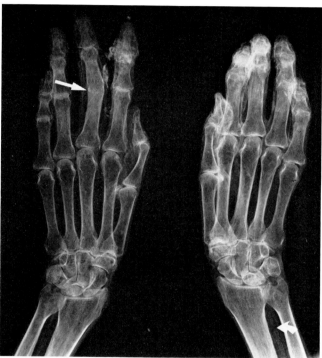

(**19**) 1777 (Asru). AP hands. Osteoarthritis distal interphalangeal joints. Ankylosis of third proximal interphalangeal joint probably following infection (straight arrow). Note arterial calcification (curved arrow).

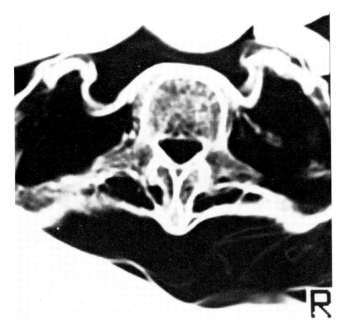

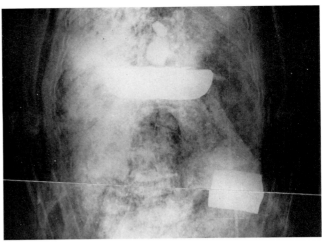

(21) 5053 (Per-en-bast). AP abdomen and thorax. Metallis Horus over mid-thorax and incision plate over left lower abdomen. Less dense scarabs above Horus.

(20) 1777 (Asru). CT spine.
(*Above*) Mid-vertebral body.
(*Below*) Intervertebral disc level.
Calcification in intervertebral disc confined to annulus fibrosis (straight arrow). Nucleus spared (curved arrow).

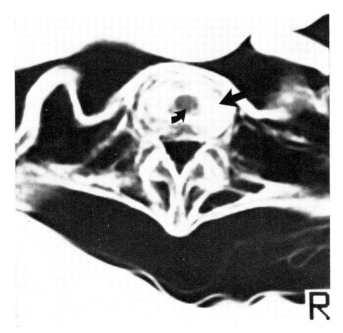

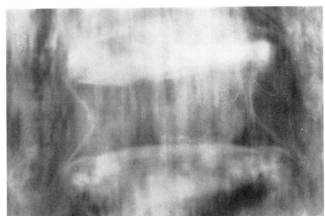

(22) 5053 (Per-en-bast). AP tomography lumbar spine. Partial collapse of Ll vertebra due to osteoporosis with osteophyte formation. Intervertebral disc material calcified.

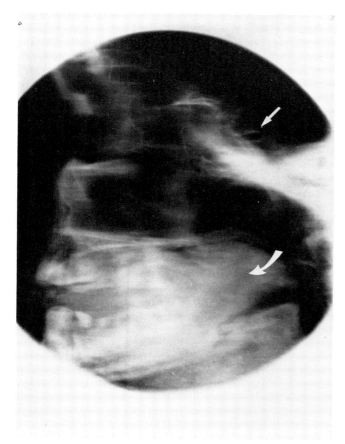

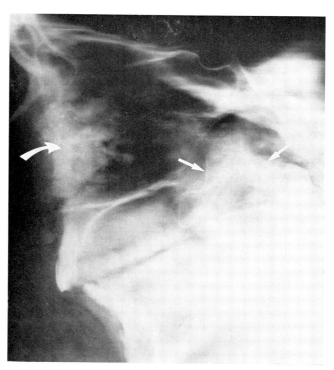

(24) 1768. Lateral tomography face and base of skull. Mid-cervical vertebral body in oropharynx (straight arrow); pack in anterior nares (curved arrow).

(23) 5053 (Per-en-bast).
Tomography face and base of skull.
(*Above*) Lateral.
(*Below*) AP.
Bilateral carotid calcification
(straight arrow). Pack in
oropharynx (curved arrow).

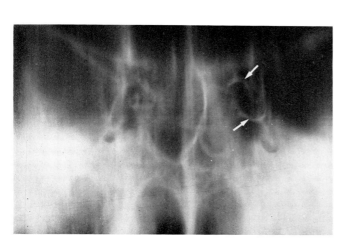

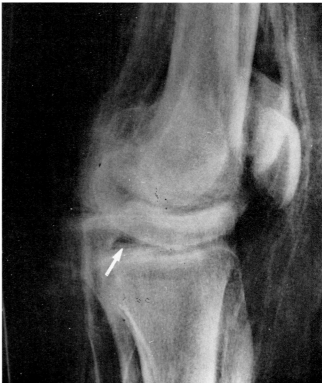

(25) 1768. Lateral knee. Osteoarthritis. Note calcification in meniscus (arrow).

51

(26) 1770. Lateral radiograph of cartonnage. Skull collapsed within.

(27) 1770. AP thorax. Pre-unwrapping. Arms crossed. Note discrete densities in abdominal wall, especially on mummy's right (arrow).

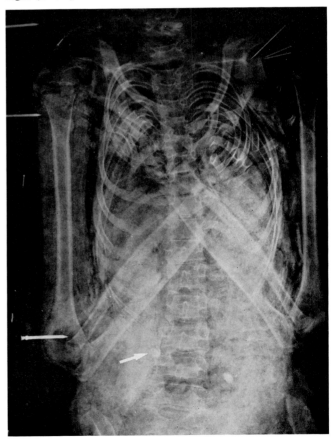

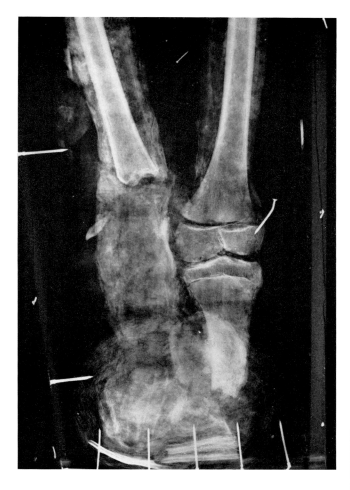

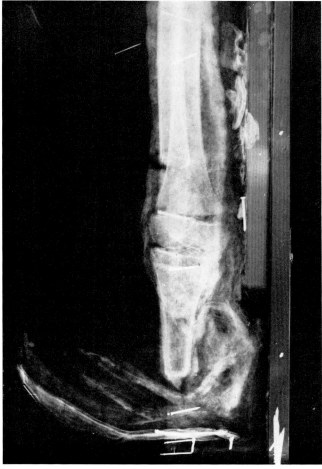

(**28**) 1770. Lower legs.
(*Above*) AP.
(*Right*) Lateral.
Amputations affecting both legs with prosthetic limbs added
including feet. Epiphyseal development of a 14-year-old.
Note displaced tooth.

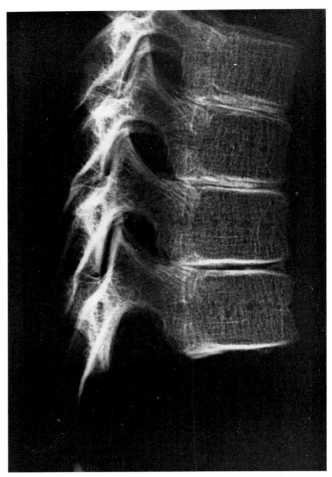

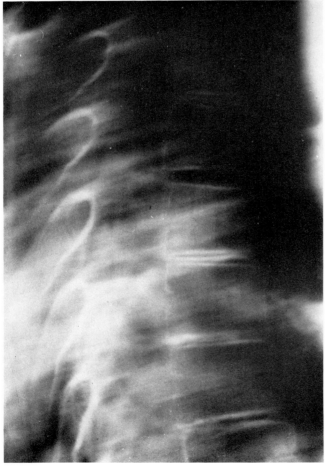

(29) 1770. Lateral spine.
(*Left*) Pre-unwrapping.
(*Above*) Post unwrapping.
Calcification in discs due to resin.

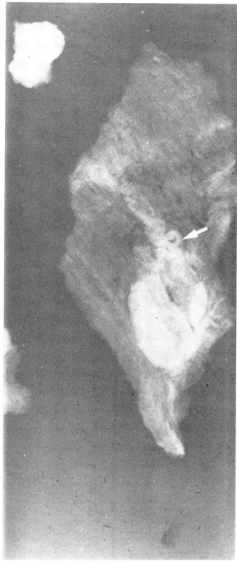

(30) 1770. Macroradiography of abdominal wall density. Serpiginous outline of guinea worm (arrow).

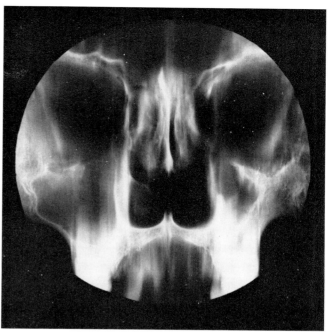

(31) 1770. AP tomography facial bones. Hypoplastic left maxillary antrum.

(32) 1770. Radiography of sandals. No opaque material. Pigment presumed vegetable rather than mineral.

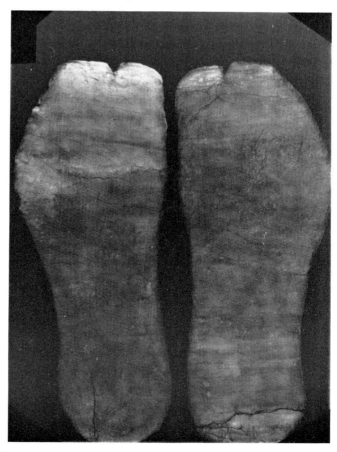

55

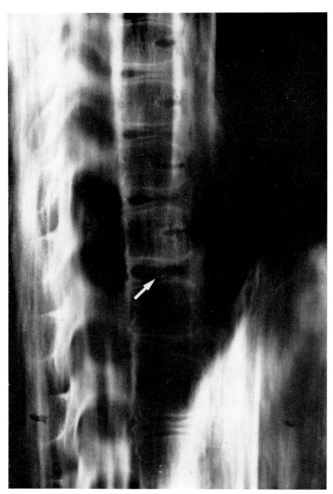

(33) 9319. Lateral tomography spine. Calcification of cartilaginous end plates in intervertebral disc spaces (arrow).

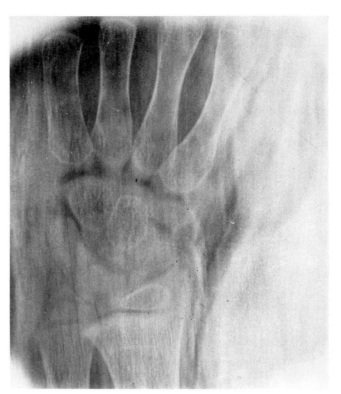

(34) 9319. AP left wrist. Capitate, hamate and distal radial epiphysis ossified. Bone age two years.

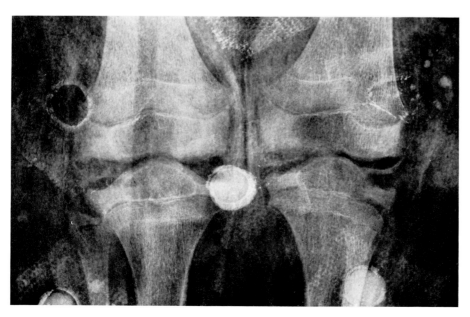

(35) 9319. AP knees. Lines of arrested growth in lower femora and upper tibiae. Calcification present in articular cartilage (arrow).

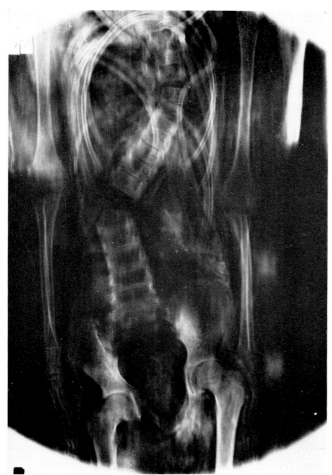

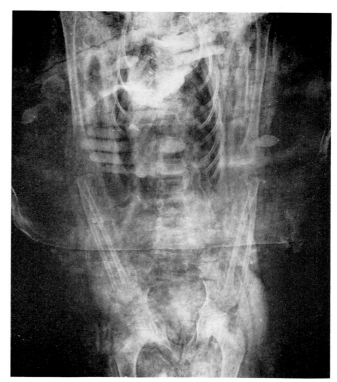

(38) 1769. Abdomen.
(*Above*) AP. (*Below*) AP tomography. Note package in right hemithorax obscured by overlying cartonnage.

(36) 2109. AP thorax and abdomen. Skeleton disorganized with post-mortem fractures at T4/5 and T10/11.
Note epiphyseal development of two-year-old.

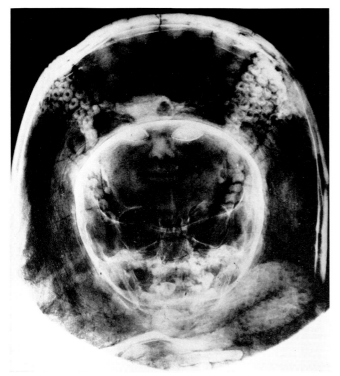

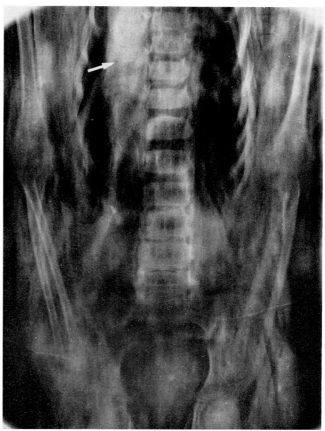

(37) (*Left*) 1769. AP skull. Skull position unrelated to cartonnage.

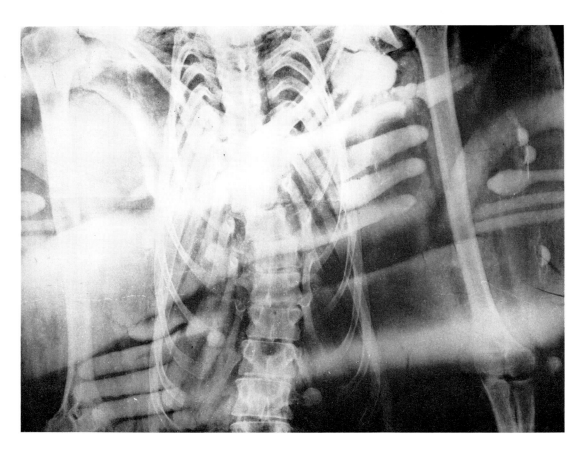

(39) 20638. (Demetria).
(*Above*) Thorax.
(*Below*) Abdomen.
Scoliosis convex to right in lumbar spine.

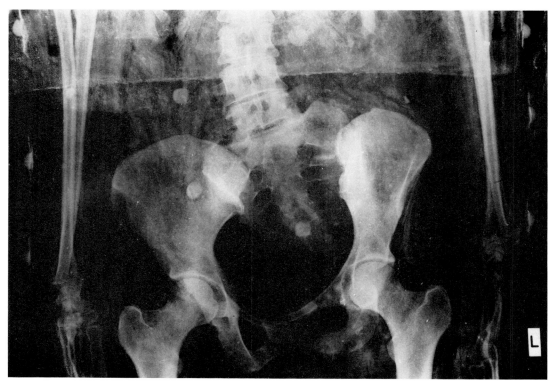

58

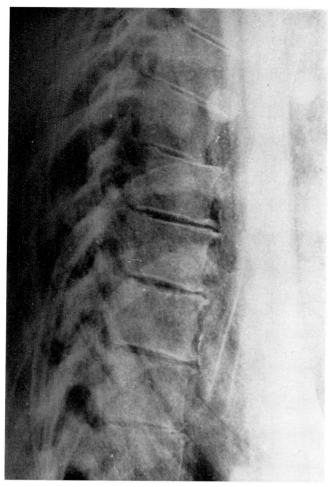

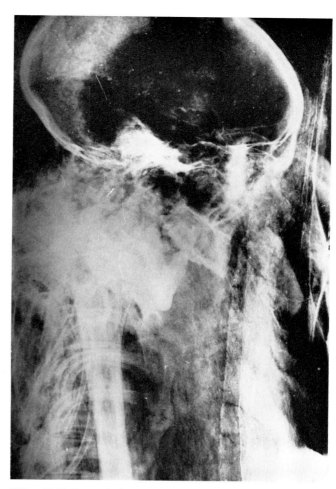

(40) 20638. Lateral thoracic spine. Post-mortem dislocation at T7/8. Anterior osteophytic lipping T8–12.

(41) 1767. Lateral skull. Facial bones. Mandible dislocated posteriorly.

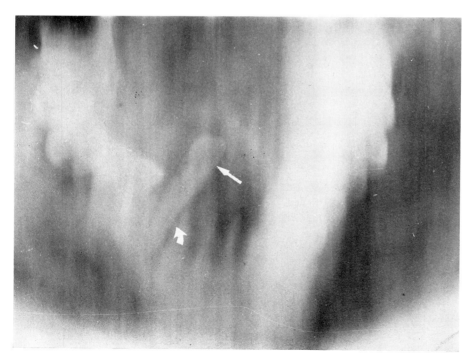

(42) 1767. AP tomography upper and lower jaws. Left upper central incisor (straight arrow) reinserted by embalmer into right lower incisor socket (curved arrow).

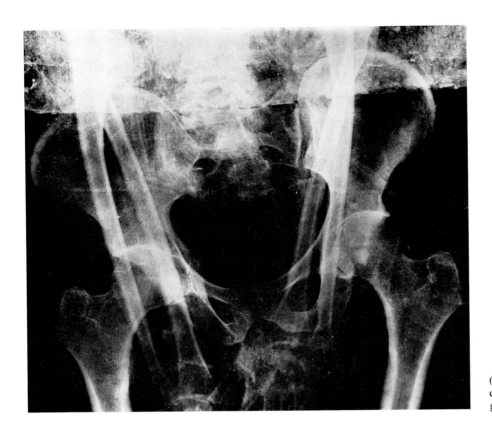

(**43**) 1767. AP pelvis. Arms extended and hands pronated over genitalia. Left hand over right.

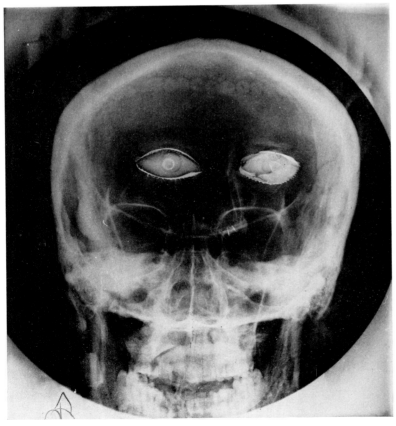

(**44**) 1766. AP skull. No bony abnormality. Jewelled eyes in cartonnage.

60

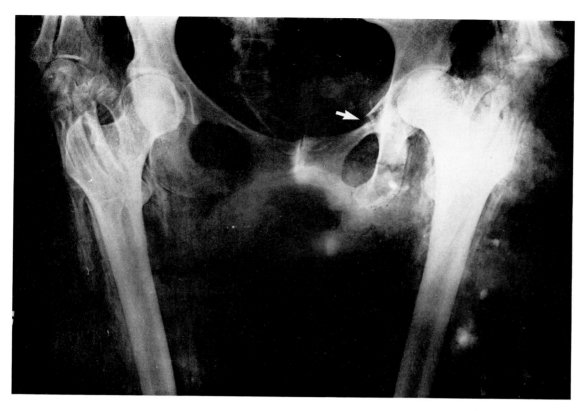

(45) 1766. Lower pelvis.
(*Above*) AP

(*Below*) AP tomography.
Ante-mortem fracture through left
superior and inferior pubic rami
(straight arrow). Calcification in
bladder (curved arrow) possibly
schistomiasis rather than tuberculosis

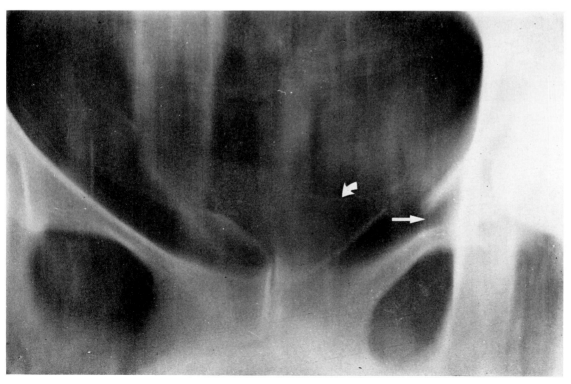

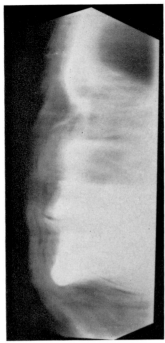 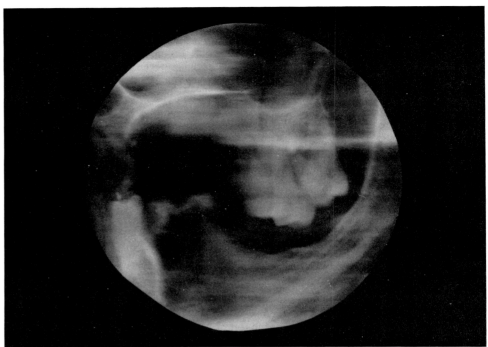

(**46**)   1775.
(*Left*) Lateral facial profile.
(*Right*) Lateral tomography.
Jaws demonstrate erosion of edentulous mandible by residual
teeth.

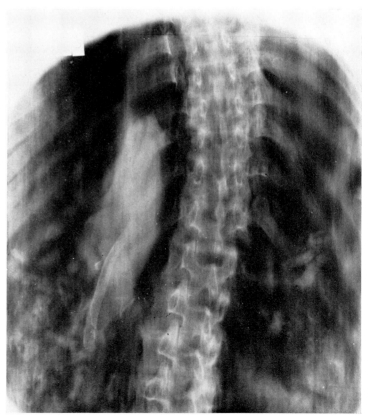

(**47**)   1775. AP thorax. Well-defined package in
right hemithorax.

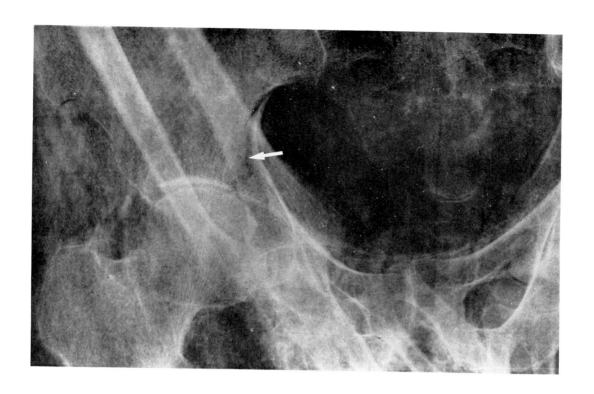

(**48**) 1775. Pelvis.
(*Above*) AP.

(*Below*) AP tomography.
Ante-mortem fracture through right
acetabulum into pelvic brim
(straight arrow). Calcification in
bladder (curved arrow). Probably
schistomiasis rather than
tuberculosis.

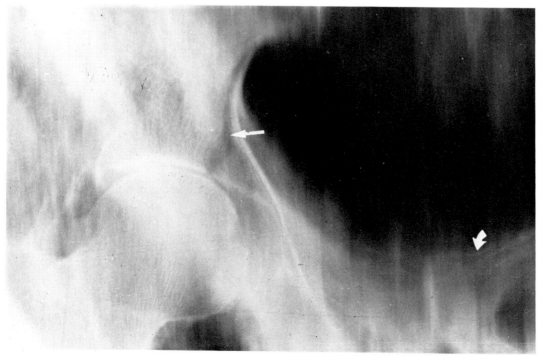

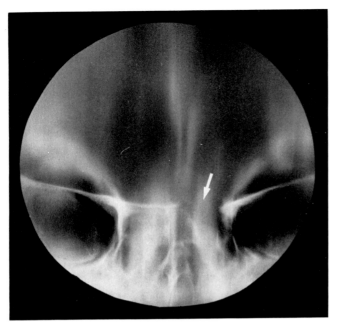

(49) 5275. Ptolemaic head. AP tomography. Defect in left ethmoidal roof produced by instrumentation for brain removal.

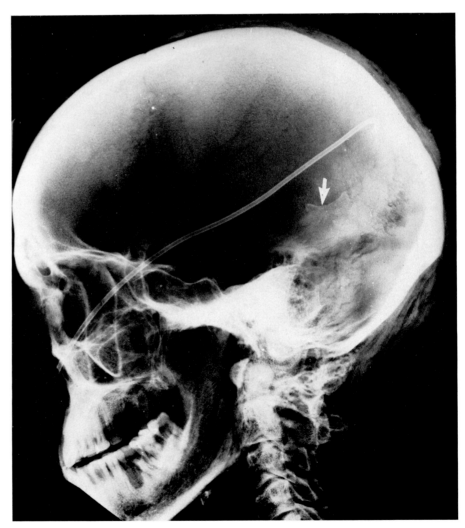

(50) 5275. Ptolemaic head. Lateral skull. Modern radio-opaque catheter inserted through nose into skull demonstrating route of brain removal. Note detached dorsum sella (arrow).

The Dental History of the Manchester Mummies

by

F. FILCE LEEK

In present-day dental practice, in order to establish the well-being of an individual, it is customary to augment a visual examination with a radiological survey of the teeth and their supporting structures. The combination of the findings provides a complete record from which an assessment can be made. If ever it should happen that it became essential to sacrifice one of these surveys, it would be the visual one, as almost all the abnormalities except those of the gingivae and mucosa, would be clearly revealed in the x-rays. This is indeed fortunate, because as will be seen, radiology is the only method by which it is possible to evaluate by non-destructive means, the dental condition of mummified remains.

The radiological examination of the human dentition is common but not simple. Because of the involved shapes and angles of the palate and mandible, some fourteen intra-oral films are required to cover the essential areas. Extra-oral techniques are used for some selected parts, but the unavoidable super-imposition of tissues limits their applications. A recent development has been the Orthopantomograph Unit, a system that provides an ideal panoramic picture of all the teeth and their supporting structures. Unfortunately, the machine is not portable nor is it freely available and, it demands the active co-operation of the patient.

Human mummified remains come from Egypt in a variety of forms, a mummified body, a linen wrapped mummified body, a linen wrapped mummified body confined within a coffin, and sometimes, quite simply, a detached mummified head. Reviewing even the most uncomplicated of these instances, the bony tissues of the face are covered by hard, unyielding leather-like tissue, which effectively prevents the opening of the mouth so that only extra-oral radiographs can be taken. The details in the resulting pictures are frequently blurred, indistinct, and sometimes completely obliterated because of the super-imposition of calcified tissue and other radio-opaque material.

It is indeed fortunate that there exists large collections of dry skulls in various museums and universities, the examination of which, has provided a knowledge of the many pathological and non-pathological abnormalities commonly seen in the dentitions of the ancient Egyptians. It is this knowledge that can sometimes aid the interpretation of a radiograph, the details of which are obscured not only by the super-imposition of calcified tissues but also by the results of the preparation of the body by the embalmers for the life in the hereafter.

During the x-raying of the Manchester mummies, it was most fortunate, that as well as using normal projections, Professor Ian Isherwood was able in selected cases, to use tomographic techniques which provided unique and very much desired records of sections of tissues. This valuable information would not be obtainable by any other means. I am indeed grateful for his ever ready co-operation, as some of the diagnoses would not have been possible without this additional information. I also owe a debt of gratitude to the Radiological Department of the Manchester Dental School, who provided excellent orthopantomograms of some of the detached mummy heads.

The following records of the dentitions and the comments on the dental health of each mummy have been made unless otherwise stated, from radiographs from these two sources.

Mummy No. 21470 (Nekht-Ankh)

Teeth present 8 7 6 5 4 3   1 | 1 2 3 4 5 6 7 8
                 8 7 6 5 4 3 2 1 | 1 2 3 4 5 6 7 8

Attrition   Class III

Comments With the exception of the upper right lateral incisor, all the teeth were present during life (a number have fallen from their sockets post mortem). All the teeth show extensive attrition and only because the deposition of secondary dentine kept pace with the wear of the cusps, no pulp chambers were exposed. There is a small carious pit in the occlusal surface of the lower right third molar and the corresponding tooth on the left side is represented only by its roots. The extensive loss of the buccal plate around the erstwhile socket of the upper right lateral incisor and its adjacent teeth, suggests that its premature loss was the result of some form of violence.

Mummy No. 21471 (Khnum-Nakht)

Teeth present 8 7 6 5 4 3 2 1 | 1 2 3 4 5 6 7 8
                 8 7 6 5 4 3 2 1 | 1 2 3 4 5 6 7 8

Caries   Nil
Attrition   Class II

Comments The two upper central teeth are abnormally large, and the left one has a vertical groove extending from the occlusal edge to the root tip. These represent a rare example of double gemination. Gemination or fusion of teeth can occur between teeth of different dentitions, but more usually between teeth of the same dentition. The most common is between an upper central incisor and a supernumary tooth. It can result in one of two forms:

65

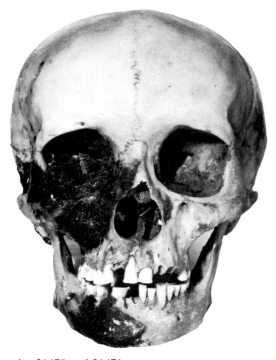

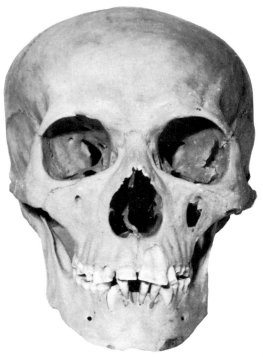

Mummies 21470 and 21471.
Nekht-Ankh and Khnum-Nakht.
Amongst the anatomical differences to be seen are: size and shape of calvarium, size of malar bone, orbits, nasal cavities and mandibles.

Nekht-Ankh: Persistence of metopic suture and supra-orbital foramen.
Khnum-Nakht: Geminated upper central incisors and supra-orbital notch.

(a) The concresed dental units have a common pulp chamber and may have a common pulp canal. The external sign is an enlarged tooth.
(b) The teeth are fused together and each unit has a distinct and separate pulp and pulp canal. It is characterized by a vertical groove between the two elements. The central incisors of Khnum-Nakht exhibit examples of both types.
Note The maxilla, mandible and the dentitions of Nekht-Ankh and Khnum-Nakht could not be more dissimilar. This complete lack of resemblance or similarity also applies to many anatomical features to be seen in the skulls. So much so, that the conclusion must be in accord with that of Dr John Cameron, who together with Dr Margaret Murray, made the first skeletal investigation of 'The Two Brothers'. He wrote: 'The differences are so pronounced that it is almost impossible to convince oneself that they belong to the same race, far less to the same family'.

Mummy No. 5053 (Per-en-bast)

Comment The lower third of the face has an almost radio-opaque covering which, whilst not completely obliterating the underlying structures, effectively prevents their interpretation. Thinking perhaps censoriously, it may be that during life her facial appearances marred her beauty, but if that had been so, all such thoughts were obliterated before her burial, as her coffin was lined with Sacred Lotus flowers (*Nelumbo nucifera*).

Mummy No. 1766

Comment Because of the large size of the teeth and the dental arches, the mummy is probably an adult male, the dentition appears to be intact, but a radio-opaque area beneath the roots of the lower right first molar tooth suggests that there is an apical abscess. It is not possible to discuss the cause because of the unavoidable lack of detail in the radiographs.

Mummy No. 1767

Comments Apart from an absent lower right first molar there is a full compliment of teeth, but the dentition has suffered considerable post-mortem damage. Some of the teeth are extruded from their sockets and the mandible is no longer in normal articulation with the maxilla. There is evidence of Class I+ attrition on some of the molar cusps.

Mummy No. 1768

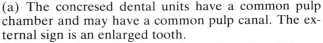

Teeth present	7 6 5 4 3 2 1	1 2 3 4 5 6 7
	7 6 5 4 3 2 1	1 2 3 4 5 6 7
Teeth unerupted	8	8
	8	8

Comments There is considerable fragmentation of both maxilla and mandible, the result of post-mortem damage. The dentition appears to be normal. The first and second molars have erupted, but the roots of the second molars are not fully developed. The partially calcified crowns of the third molars are lying in their crypts. Dental age approximately 13 years.

Mummy No. 1769

Teeth present
$$\frac{\text{e d c b a} \mid \text{a b c d e}}{\text{e d c b a} \mid \text{a b c d e}}$$

Comments The eruption sequence of the teeth appears to· be normal, although the picture is marred by the considerable post-mortem damage suffered by the maxilla and mandible. The cusps of the first permanent molars are calcified and lying in their crypts, the crowns of the premolars are beginning to calcify thus giving a dental age of between three and four years.

Mummy No. 1770

Teeth present
$$\frac{\text{7 6 5 4 3 2 1} \mid \text{1 2 3 4 5 6 7}}{\text{7 6 5 4 3 2 1} \mid \text{1 2 3 4 5 6 7}}$$

Teeth unerupted
$$\frac{\text{8} \mid \text{8}}{\text{8} \mid \text{8}}$$

Comments The radiographs of this mummy taken prior to the investigation revealed extensive post-mortem damage to the skull, and advantage was taken of the unwrapping to make a detailed study of the bones of the head.

Maxilla The palatal arch is small but regular and there are sharp wave-like crests of bone lying anteroposteriorly. The right canine is instanding (palatally inclined). Because of the mal-position of this tooth, there is an enlarged area of alveolar bone between it and the lateral incisor. The alveolar bone in the incisor region is pitted whilst that in the buccal area is normal.

Mandible The lower incisors are imbricated and the two centrals are over-erupted. The right canine is out-standing and articulates on the buccal side of the upper one. When in occlusion, the upper lateral incisor is in traumatic occlusion with it. The one remaining condyle (right side) is normal in shape and shows no evidence of any pathological changes.

Facial bones The canine fossa below the left orbit shows a greater depression than on the right side and this suggests a congenital facial hemiatrophy.

Nasal cavity The nasal septum was partially present when first examined but enlarged and deviated (it has since completely fractured, the bone being extremely fragile). The nasal conchae or turbinate bones are all much enlarged and displaced, almost filling the nasal cavity. The nasal spine is absent and the lower border of the anterior nares is rounded.

Sinuses The maxillary and supra-orbital sinuses are normal in shape.

Observations Between the years of twelve and eighteen the evidence for the dental age is derived from the degree of development of the apices of the second molars and the amount of calcification of the cusps of the third molars or wisdom teeth. In this instance the apices are not quite closed and the cusps of the third molars are only partially calcified (radiographic evidence). Thus when death intervened the age was between thirteen and fourteen years.

The most probable cause of the mal-position of the upper right canine was the prolonged retention of the deciduous tooth, a non-pathological abnormality. It could have a genetic origin but usually arises spontaneously.

When two teeth are placed irregularly in the arch, as in the case of the upper right lateral incisor and canine, the interdental space is abnormally shaped and provides a constant trap for food particles which are difficult to remove. This retention quickly results in an inflammation of the gingival crest to be followed by a pathological crater and pitting of the alveolar bone. That no such changes are apparent suggests that there was a total lack of fibrous food in the diet, consequently it must have been a liquid or semi-liquid one. This fact is supported by the absolute absence of attrition on any cusps of the teeth, so characteristic of almost every ancient Egyptian permanent dentition and seen even on deciduous ones.

The pathological changes seen in the bones of the nasal cavity, together with the concomitant oedematous condition of the overlying mucous membrane, would have resulted in an almost complete blockage of the nasal passages. The outward sign of this would have been persistent

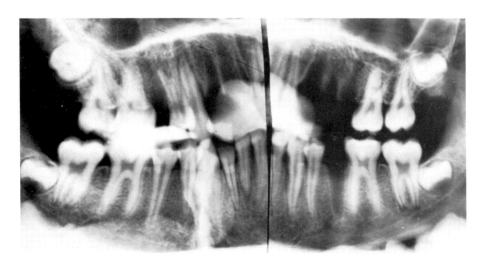

Mummy No. 1770.
The apices of the second molar teeth are not fully calcified and only the crowns of the third molars are developed, thus giving a dental age approx. 13 years. The teeth missing from the dentition became dislodged during the examination.

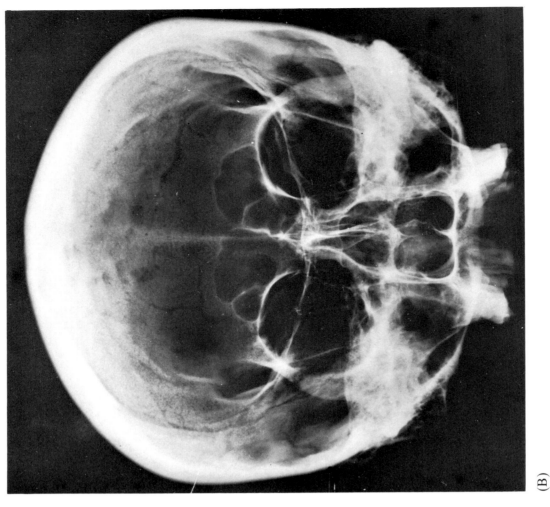

(A)

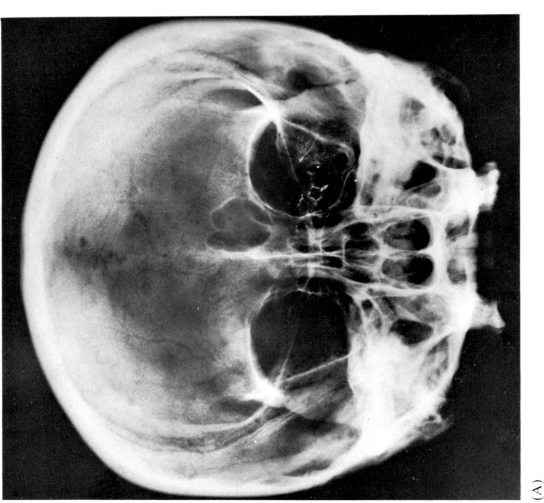

(B)

Radiographs
(A) Nekht-Ankh. Antero-posterior projection of cranium.
(B) Khnum-Nakht. Antero-posterior projection of cranium.
(C) Nekht-Ankh. Baso-superior projection of cranium.
(D) Khnum-Nakht. Baso-superior projection of cranium.

During his examination in 1910, Dr John Cameron recorded many anatomical differences between 'The Two Brothers'. To these can be added size, shape and thickness of calvarium, size of orbits, frontal sinuses, foramen magnum and nasal cavities, size and shape of teeth and palate.

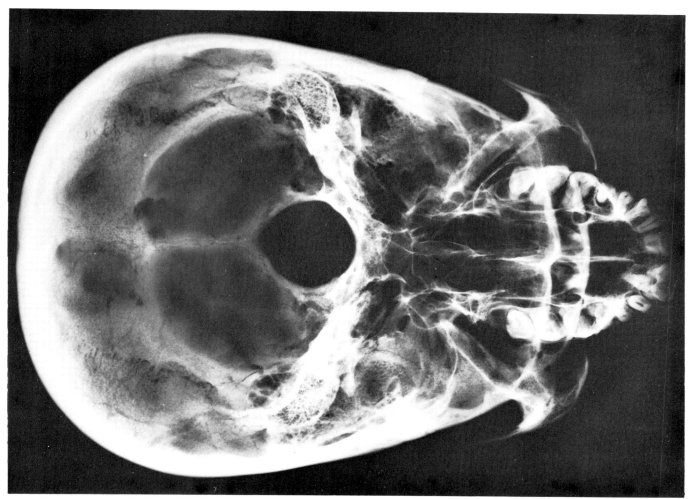

(D)

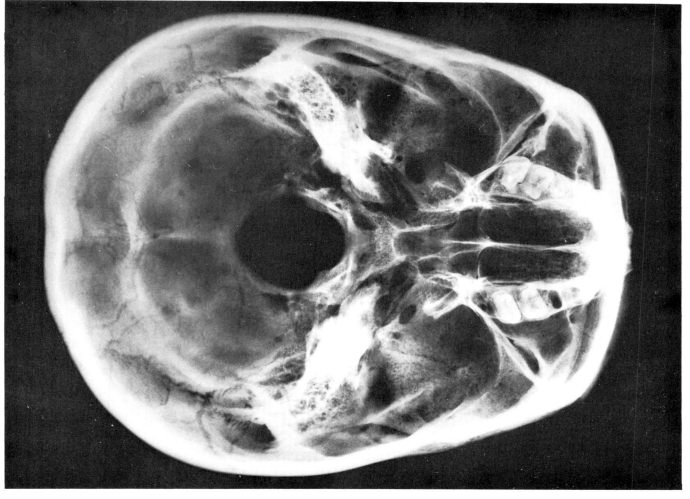

(C)

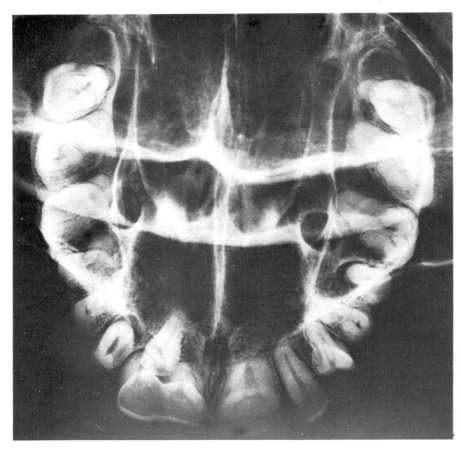

(E) Khnum-Nakht. Maxilla. Both upper central incisors have undergone fusion with supernumary teeth but exhibit morphological differences. The left incisor is instanding because of lack of room within the dental arch.

open lips. This latter appearance was probably aided by a short upper lip pattern. That she did not persistently thumb-suck in her youth is borne out by the fact that the incisor teeth are aligned at their normal angle. A short upper lip pattern together with a thumb-sucking habit usually results in protruding upper teeth.

All these aforementioned factors add up to suggest that during life she was a frail adolescent creature of poor constitution, with a slightly asymmetrical face and her lips constantly open.

During embalming an opening into the cranial cavity was usually made in order to facilitate the removal of the brain. The most usual route was an entrance via one or both nostrils through the cribriform plate of the ethmoid bone. Less frequently, a hole was made through the wall of the orbit. In this instance no such procedures had been followed.

Mummy No. 1775 (Artemidorous)

Maxilla   Only the roots of the incisor teeth with one or more apical abscesses are present and the molar teeth are extruded from their sockets, the latter condition being the result of a longstanding lack of opposing lower teeth.

Mandible   Only the incisor teeth are present. That the posterior teeth had been absent for a long period is revealed by the senile shape of the alveolar bone.

Comments   The conjectural assessment of the dental history of the later years of Artemidorous, as gained by the interpretation of the radiographs and tomographs, is that an overclosure of the mandible took place during mastication. The lower incisors biting on the roots of the upper ones, which at times must have been painful because of apical abscesses, and the upper molar teeth biting on the pad of gum covering the lower jaw.

Mummy No. 1777 (Asru)

Maxilla   Edentulous except for a few incisor teeth; the palate is flat, the result of the complete absorption of the alveolar bone. This is consistent with the earlier involvement of periodical disease and its culminating in periodontosis.

Mandible   Some of the posterior teeth are missing (lost ante-mortem), and those that are present exhibit Class II attrition and marked periodontal infection.

Mummy No. 2109

Teeth present
e d c b a	a b c d e
e d c b a	a b c d e

Comments   All the deciduous teeth have erupted and the cusps of the first permanent molars and the crowns of the incisors have commenced to calcify, thus giving a dental age of between two and three years.

70

Mummy No. 3496

Comments The skull of this infant has suffered severe post-mortem damage, so much so that it is impossible to see in the x-rays any eruption sequence. The degree of calcification of some of the crowns indicate an age of approximately one year at death.

Mummy No. 9319

Teeth present
e d c b a	a b c d e
e d c b a	a b c d e

Comments All the deciduous teeth have erupted and the cusps of the first permanent molars are beginning to calcify. This would indicate an age of between two and three years.

Mummy No. 9354 (Khary)

Teeth present
7 6 5 4 3 2 1	1 2 3 4 5 7
7 6 5 4 3 2 1	1 2 3 4 5 6 7 8

Abscesses
6 5	4 5
6	

Attrition   Class II and III

Comments Attrition is marked on all the incisor teeth and the wear on the buccal ones extends to the pulp chambers. Only the roots of some of the premolar and molar teeth are present, and each of these exhibits an apical abscess. There is marked destruction of the buccal alveolar bone, the result of severe periodontal disease. Three of the third molar teeth are absent and the fourth is represented by its apical third. The appearance of the alveolar bone in these areas points to their loss being the result of advanced periodontosis.

Mummy No. 10881 (Ta-Aath)

Teeth present
6	4 6
7 6 5 3 2	2 3 4 5 6 7 8

Comments The sockets of the missing anterior teeth are clearly defined but bony repair appears to have commenced. This would indicate that their removal had taken place only weeks before death. The upper right canine is unerupted and lying mesially inclined in the palate.

The space for the lower two central incisor teeth appears to be contracted, this suggests their early loss or more probably, the failure of the tooth buds to develop. Anodontia vera is also probably the explanation of the absence of the lower left third molar. The lower left first premolar is also absent from the arch, and whilst the x-ray does not provide a good rendering of the tissues in this area, in all probability its absence is also due to the same reason.

Several cervical vertebrae and the mandible are dislocated, probably the result of post-mortem manhandling of the mummy.

Mummy No. 20638 (Demetria, wife of Icaious)

Teeth present
8 7 6 5 4 3 2 1	1 2 3 4 5 6 7 8
8 7 6 5 4 3 2 1	1 2 3 4 5 7 8

Comments The dental arches are well developed and the teeth are regular and correctly spaced. The four third molar teeth are fully erupted and calcified. The lower first molar is absent from the dentition and the right one is represented only by its abscessed roots. This is probably the result of a successful and an unsuccessful attempt respectively, to extract them. For what reason it is difficult to imagine, as all the other teeth are caries free and with but little attrition on the cusps.

Mummy No. 1976/51a

Teeth present
– – – – – – –	– – – – – – –
7 6 5 4 3 2 1	1 2 3 4 5 6 7

Caries
8 7 6	5 6 7

Abscesses
8 7 6	2 5 7

Attrition   Class II

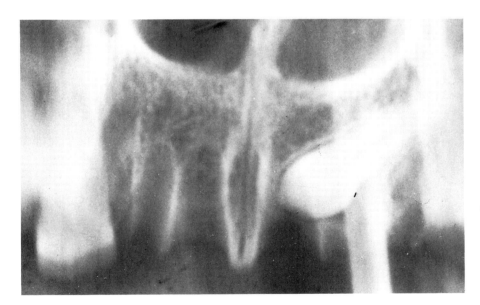

Mummy No. 10881. Ta-Aath. The upper canine lies mesially inclined buried in the palate. The sockets of the missing incisor teeth have begun to be filled with regenerating bone, thus indicating that these teeth were lost only weeks before death.

71

Comments The senile anadontia and the almost flat palate suggests that the maxillary teeth were lost because of advanced periodontal disease, nevertheless he/she almost certainly lived an appreciable time afterwards. The carious cavities are very advanced, the bacterial invasion of the pulp chambers has resulted in at least four apical abscesses and although the radiographs do not give definite confirmation, the remaining carious teeth most probably are similarly affected. The septic foci in the mandible must surely have undermined the well-being of the last years of life.

Mummy Head No. 5275

```
Teeth present        5 4 3 2 1 | 1 2 3 4 5       8
                 7 6 5 4 3 2 1 | 1 2 3 4 5 6 7
Caries                      | 3 4 5
                 7          |
Abscesses                 1 |
                 6          |
```

Comments Whilst there is only slight attrition on the cusps of the molar teeth, the occlusal edges of the anterior teeth are much reduced. There is an apical abscess below the distal root of the lower right first molar. Also one above the root of the upper left central incisor, most probably the result of a blow on the tooth. The carious cavities are in each case small and interstial. Much salivary calculus is present around the lower incisors and there is considerable loss of alveolar bone around all the teeth, a manifestation of advanced periodontal disease.

A molar tooth is lying loose in the cranial vault (in one x-ray it is to be seen lying on the floor of the vault, whilst in another, it resides in the nasal cavity). The movement of this tooth is allowed by the excessive amount of bone removed by the ancient embalmers, in order to extract the brain.

Mummy Head No. 7740

```
Teeth present    8 7 6 5 4 3 2 |     3 4 5     7 8
                 8 7 6 5 4 3 2 | 1 2 3 4 5 6 7 8
Caries               8 7 6     | 4         7 8
                           5   |
Apical Abscesses       7 6     | 4         7
                               | 5 6
Attrition        Class II and III
```

Comments The missing teeth from the maxilla were lost as the result of severe periodontal disease. The remaining teeth of both jaws are similarly involved but to a lesser degree. Caries has invaded the pulps of some six or seven teeth, resulting in apical abscesses. A tooth is lying horizontally buried in the mandible in the pre-molar area.

The orthopantomogram shows a wide interdental space on the right side, whilst those on the left are in occlusion. Also the mandibular teeth on the left side are displaced the width of a whole tooth mesially. Such deformity is consistent with a dislocated mandible. This

diagnosis is confirmed by the tomograph of the temporo-mandibular joint, which in addition reveals arthritic changes and marked lipping of the condylar head. A most unenviable dental history.

Mummy Head No. 21475

```
Teeth present    8 7 6 5 4 3 2 1 | 1 2 3 4 5 6 7
                 8 7     5 4 3 2 1 | 1 2 3 4
Caries           Nil
Abscesses        6 5 4           |
                             1   |
Attrition        Class II and III
```

Comments Each of the abscesses above the apices of the upper right buccal teeth are due to the death of the pulp, the result of attrition. The dentition being completely free from caries. The circumscribed cystic cavity beneath the root of the lower central incisor could also have arisen from the same cause, but more probably was the result of a blow or sudden impact on the tooth. The 6 |6 7 had been removed prior to death but the other teeth missing from the dentition have been shaken from their sockets post-mortem.

The articulation exhibits a Class III skeletal pattern, and this edge to edge articulation resulted in severe attrition to the anterior as well as the buccal teeth. So much so, the stresses involved resulted in inflammation and thickening of the periodontal membrane and whilst details in the radiographs are not distinct, there seems to be abscess formation on several incisor teeth.

A Class III articulation is very infrequently encountered in ancient Egyptian dentitions, it is however not uncommonly observed amongst negroid races. Even in modern times, when only refined and easily masticated foods are eaten, dentitions exhibiting this type of articulation show considerable wear of all the teeth, more especially the incisors.

Mummy Head No. 22940

```
Teeth present    7 6 5 4 3 2 1 | 1 2 3 4 5 6 7
                 7 6 5 4 3 2 1 | 1 2 3 4 5 6 7 8
Caries           7             | 7
Abscesses        7             | 7
                               |
Attrition        11+
```

Comments There is marked absorption of the alveolar bone around all the teeth denoting advanced periodontal disease. The lower left third molar is extruded from its socket, the result of congenital absence or premature loss of its opposing member.

There is a pronounced radiolucent area in the body of the mandible extending from the first premolar to the second molar region. This is not typical of any known pathological abnormality, consequently it is not possible to pronounce on its aetiology or cause.

The periodontal membranes of the upper incisor teeth are thickened and the roots of these teeth are fractured.

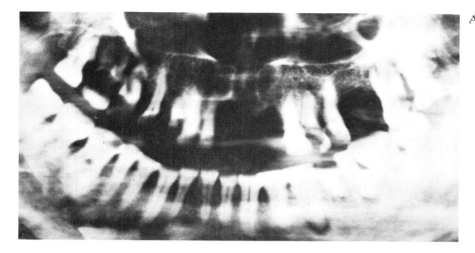

A

Mummy Head No. 7740.

(A)   The alveolar bone around the upper central teeth is diseased; all the teeth display attrition; there are several carious cavities and abscesses also alveolar bone absorption. The mandible is displaced to the left side.

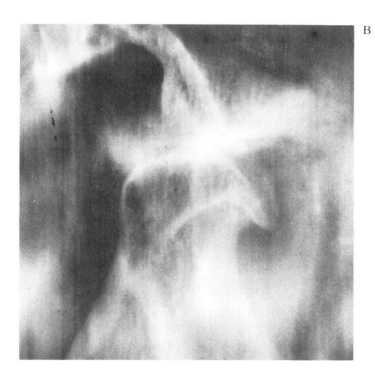

B

(B)   Tomograph shows that the mandibular condyle is disarticulated from the glenoid fossa and that arthritic changes have taken place in the head.

Mummy Head No. 21475
Advanced attrition caused the death of several pulps of the incisor teeth resulting in apical abscesses. Two of the four missing lower teeth were lost ante-mortem.

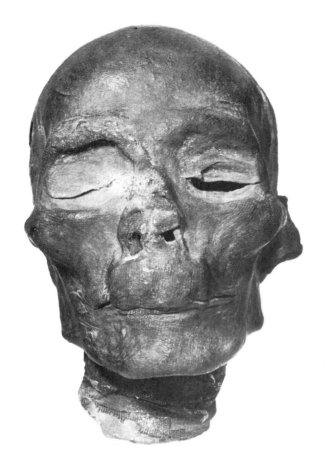

Mummy Head No. 22940.

(A)   The soft tissue of the face is well preserved. Whilst the depression of the cartilaginous part of the nose was probably the result of the pressure of the embalmers bandages, the swollen lip, without doubt, was the result of ante-mortem injury.

(B)   Panoramic zerograph of the dentition shows fracture of the upper incisors, absence of three third molar teeth, attrition and absorption of interdental alveolus.

(C)   Tomograph of the upper incisor teeth reveals fracture of crowns and roots and thickened peridontal membrane.

74

Such damage is consistent with the results following a severe blow on the front of the face. This assumption is confirmed by the appearance of the upper lip, it being morbidly enlarged, which gives the face a particularly repugnant appearance. As the result of these and without doubt, other injuries, consciousness must have been lost almost immediately, otherwise the loose fractured crowns of the teeth would have been ejected. That death was not instantaneous is substantiated by the fact that time is required for the reaction of the periodontal membrane and the swelling of the lip to become manifest. Its intervention, however, could not have been long delayed.

Summary of Abnormalities

Pathological and Traumatic

Caries: Nos. 21470, 1976/51a, 5275, 7740.

Teeth lost ante-mortem: Nos. 21470, 21475, 1775, 9354, 10881, 1976/51a, 7740, 22940.

Attrition: Nos. 21470, 1766, 21475, 9354, 5275, 1976/51a, 21471.

Anodontia senile: No. 1976/51a.

Dislocated mandible: No. 7740.

Fractured teeth: No. 22940.

Abscesses: Nos. 9354, 20638, 1976/51a, 7740, 21475.

Periodontal Disease: Nos. 1777, 9254, 1976/51a, 7740, 22940.

Non-pathological

Anodontia vera: No. 10881.

Unerupted and buried teeth: No. 10881.

Gemination: No. 21471.

Articulation, Skeletal pattern Class III: No. 21475.

Summary

Whilst the collection of human remains in the Manchester Museum is small, the dentitions follow the general pattern as seen in much larger collections. Dentitions of the early Dynastic periods show a remarkable freedom from caries, and the two examples from the Middle Kingdom, namely Nos. 21470 and 21471 reveal only one small pit cavity. This was probably of developmental origin, certainly not one that had arisen because of disintegration of the enamel.

Rampant dental caries is to be seen however, in the dentitions of several adult Ptolemaic mummies, for example Nos. 21470, 1976/51a, 5275 and 7740. Such a plight is so rarely seen in earlier Dynastic skulls, that it gives rise to the speculation that this deterioration in the dental health was the result of an invasion of foreign ideas, leading to an adulteration of foods and a change in eating habits. This era was certainly a period of transformation in Egyptian history and upheavals in the daily way of life must have been constant.

The most common abnormality seen in the dentitions of early man, and those from ancient Egypt in particular, is attrition of the cusps of the teeth. This abnormality is universal throughout the ages and quite positively does not imply that the teeth of those days were deficient in calcium or suffered from hypoplasia. Quite the reverse, for they were all characterized by well developed enamel and dentine. In earlier times, food was generally more fibrous and contaminated by foreign particles, and consequently the cusps of the teeth would wear and become flattened.

Almost more important than the fibrous foods was that flour and consequently bread, principally from the grinding techniques employed, contained many impurities. This is particularly true of Egypt, as examination of bread originating from various sites and from different dynastic periods have shown, that not only were these same impurities from the soil, storage and grinding incorporated into the bread but in addition there was a marked contamination by quartz fragments, that is, wind-blown sand — unfortunately a very heavy contamination. As a result, by adult age not only had the cusps worn down, but in varying degrees the body of the tooth as well. In those cases where the deposition of secondary dentine in the pulp chamber did not proceed faster than the wear, the pulp chamber was exposed, bacteria invaded the root canal causing death of the pulp and eventually producing an apical abscess. This later became a foci of infection, which in minor cases would result in debility and lowered resistance to disease, whilst in more unfortunate instances, it would hasten the termination of life itself. Indeed some investigators are convinced that the death of Ramesses II was the result of dental infection.

The attrition pattern varied greatly, and this inconsistency of pattern has made generalizations and comparisons between individuals and also between different populations very difficult to assess. No system of classification has yet been devised that gives a truly representative picture of a particular dentition, and in this essay recourse has been made to the following general classification which only broadly covers the many types.

Class I   Denotes the flattening of the enamel cusps.
Class II   Denotes exposure of the dentine.
Class III Denotes exposure of the pulp chamber.
Class IV   Denotes advanced wear of the body of the tooth.

One result of the patterns of wear of the dental cusps was that masticatory movements changed and consequently the action of the temporo-mandibular joint became complex. An outcome of which, in many instances, produced progressive or regressive changes in the shape of the head of the mandibular condyle and these in their turn must have produced arthritic syndromes.

Because of the abnormal movements of the temporo-mandibular joint, erratic stresses and strains during mastication were applied to the cusps of the teeth, and these were then transferred down the root or roots to the supporting structures, that is, the alveolar bone. Gradually these tissues were undermined and broken down and sometimes with the addition of faulty hygiene, produced widespread periodontal disease. Many such cases advanced to such a stage that the various components of the dentition could have been dislodged by the application of only finger pressure. The astonishing fact is that many people were allowed to pass their last days in what must have been miserable circumstances only because of failure to perform such a simple operation.

Although many such cases of advanced alveolar disease are to be seen without infected and loose teeth having been extracted, there is a proportion of dentitions in which a tooth or teeth have been removed from strong and well developed arches. It must be accepted therefore, that some method of removal of teeth was known and practiced but no hint of the techniques used nor the instruments employed have as yet been revealed. In fact, although loose teeth and some suggested cures are mentioned in Medical Papyri, there is a reticence on discussions relating to teeth and their diseases. However in a Medical Papyri written during New Kingdom times but thought to have been copied from an even earlier manuscript, a method is described of the operative procedure essential to reduce a dislocated mandible which is almost identical to that practised today. It is more than probable that because of the changes in the shape of the mandibular condyle in so many people as the result of traumatic occlusion, such operative procedures were frequently necessary.

It is most interesting that in a small collection such as this one, that there should be an example of a dislocated mandible, as well as examples of fractured teeth and pathological abnormalities occasioned by accident or violence.

Of the non-pathological abnormalities to be seen in the dentitions, anodontia is one relatively common in ancient times. Whilst the tooth buds of lower premolars sometimes fail to develop, it is the third molar that, most frequently, is missing from the dentitions. Buried, misplaced and supernumary teeth are all common abnormalities, but to have the rare abnormality of the double geminated upper central incisors of Khnum-Nahkt is of such uniqueness that it raises the dental interest of this collection to a point far beyond that which would be normal for one of its size.

Glossary

Anodontia
    Absence of teeth.
Anodontia, senile
    Absence of teeth in the aged because of their earlier removal.
Anodontia, vera
    That due to the failure of the tooth bud to develop.
Attrition
    The wearing away of the cusps of the teeth. In this instance, by chewing foods contaminated by inorganic fragments.
Alveolus
    The bony socket of the tooth, that is, its supporting structures.

Apical Abscess
    A localized collection of pus around the apex of a tooth.
Buccal
    Of the cheek.
Caries
    A localized and progressive molecular destruction of the tooth usually referred to as 'decay'. It begins with the disintegration of the enamel by acids which result from the enzymic action of oral bacteria on carbohydrates.
Dentine
    The calcified tissue which forms the greater part of the tooth. It is covered by enamel over the crown and by cementum over the root. Within it is the pulp chamber and the root canals, which house the nerve and blood vessels.
Gemination
    See page 65 (Khnum-Nakht).
Gingiva
    That part of the gum which covers the alveolar bone and is attached at the junction of the root and crown of the tooth.
Mandible
    The lower jaw bone.
Maxilla
    The upper jaw bone.
Mucosa
    A mucous membrane.
Occlusal surface
    That part of the tooth which is in contact with its opposite number when the jaws are closed.
Periodontal membrane
    An elastic membrane inserted into the cementum and joining the tooth to the alveolar bone.
Periodontitis
    An inflammation of the periodontal membrane which usually extends into the surrounding alveolar bone, resulting in a purulent discharge. Commonly termed 'Pyorrhea'.
Periodontosis
    A later stage of periodontitis, characterized by alveolar bone resorption, epithelial proliferation, pocket formation, migration of teeth, culminating in exfoliation.
Secondary dentine
    That which is deposited by the cells of the pulp on the walls of the pulp chamber in response to stimuli such as produced by attrition or by advancing caries.
Salivary Calculus
    A deposit of mineral salts and organic matter, usually found on the lingual side of mandibular teeth and sometimes on the buccal side of upper ones. In cases of lack of oral hygiene is seen around the necks of all the teeth and when in addition, there is a lack of mastication, it can cover the occlusal surface as well.

Bibliography

Alexanderson, V., *The Pathology of the Jaws and the Tempero-mandibular Joint*, in Brothwell, D. R. and Sanderson, A. T. (eds), *Diseases in Antiquity*, C. Thomas, Illinois, pp. 551–95, 1967.

Batrawi, A., *Report on the Human Remains*, Mission Archeologique de Nubie, 1929–31, Cairo, 1935.

Brothwell, D. R., *Digging Up Bones*, Brit. Mus. (Nat. Hist.), London, 1963.

Elliot Smith, G. and Dawson, W. R., *Egyptian Mummies*, London, 1924.

Elliot Smith, G. and Wood-Jones, F., *Report on the Human Remains*, Arch. Surv. Nubia, Report of 1907–08, Cairo, 1910.

Leek, Filce F., *Observations on the Dental Pathology Seen in Ancient Egyptian Skulls*, J.E.A., pp. 59–64, London, 1966.

——, *A Technique for the Oral Examination of a Mummy*, X-ray Focus, Vol. 9, No. 3, 5–9, London, 1969.

——, *Did a Dental Profession Exist in Ancient Egypt during the 3rd Millennium B.C.*, Med. Hist., Vol. XVI, No. 4, 404–06, London, 1972.

Neilsen, Ole Vagn., *Human Remains*, Scandinavian Univ. Books, Stockholm, 1970.

Qenouille, J. J., *La bouche and les dents dans l'antique egyptienne*, Ph.D. Thesis, 1975.

Ruffer, M. A., *Studies in the Paleopathology of Egypt*, Univ. Chicago Press, 1921.

Harris, J. E. and Weeks, K. R., *X-raying the Pharaohs*, Macdonald, London, 1973.

Acknowledgements

Acknowledgement has been made in a number of articles published during the past twelve years on this and other subjects to those whose inspiration, knowledge and help has encouraged me to undertake them. I know they would not wish for reiteration, but there is always a perpetual feeling of gratitude to them all.

To deal with the present project, the help and consideration given by Dr A. Rosalie David has been outstanding and I also wish to pay tribute to her leadership of 'The Team'. It has been a delightful and interesting experience to work with them all and if I single out Drs A. Curry, D. Dixon, Professor I. Isherwood, Miss H. Jarvis, and Dr E. Tapp for special recognition, the others will know that is only because their work and mine was less closely associated.

I also wish to thank Mr R. Davis, Royal Marsden Hospital; Miss T. Molleson, British Museum (N.H.); and Professor N. J. D. Smith, Kings College Hospital, for their interest and help.

I now come to the point where this list of appreciations should really have started, my wife. Without her help this work would neither have commenced nor reached completion. I am as ever beholden.

The Fingerprint Examination

by

A. FLETCHER

There is plenty of evidence to show that for many centuries man had been interested in the configurations formed by the skin ridges on his fingers and palms, and in many societies a thumbprint has been accepted in place of a signature; potters in Roman times left a print on the base of their work to show it was theirs. As you read this you are holding the book and your prints will be left on the cover and on the pages as you turn over to read on.

If you look at the inner surface of your hand, and touch the soles of your feet, you will find that the skin of these two parts is very different from that covering the rest of your body. It is a hornier type of skin, taking the form of a system of minute skin ridges, roughly parallel with each other, changing direction here and there whilst forming clearly defined patterns, particularly on the last joints of the fingers and thumbs. These ridges are called friction ridges. You will see, if you look again at your own fingers, that these ridges are not continuous; there are frequent interruptions in their flow which are called ridge characteristics. A ridge may end suddenly in any direction or it can fork into two diverse ridges; short independent ridges which lie between two others are a regular occurrence, and there may also be formations resembling lakes. All these are the more common type of characteristics, although there are others. All along the summits of the ridges and characteristics are microscopic pores which, along with others all over the body surface, serve for the discharge of sweat from the body. When an article capable of retaining a finger-mark is touched, an impression of the ridge detail and the characteristics may be left on it, in sweat. We can make this visible by the application of a suitable developer.

Our knowledge and continual research show that the friction ridge surfaces are there from birth and persist throughout life. Although the ridges, patterns and characteristics are common to all hands, no two impressions taken from different skin ridge surfaces, whether they be from the same hand or from different hands, have the same characteristics appearing in the same order relative to each other. Because of this, identity can be established by comparing fingerprints taken from a person with fingerprints left elsewhere. Whilst the task of the fingerprint officer is normally to identify the criminal it is often necessary to fingerprint dead bodies in order to establish their identity. These bodies may have been dead over a long period of time, often having been recovered from water, and as a result the flesh is putrified and fragile. Nevertheless, there remains a certain amount of flexibility in the fingers, and prints can be obtained by conventional methods. In certain circumstances, where the ridge surface is visible, it is possible to record the prints with the use of photography. The technique involves the use of oblique lighting. This casts shadows from the ridges into the depressions, thereby highlighting the ridges in contrast. Similar effects were obtained when photographs were taken of craters on the surface of the moon.

Nobody, of course, was trying to show that Asru had been a burglar, but nevertheless all the knowledge we have outlined was brought into use when we examined the mummy. Asru was not simply an ordinary dead body. This meant that we had to use extreme care because of the delicate rigidity of the flesh. The position of the hands excluded the use of photography to record the prints, as there simply was not enough room to position and manipulate a camera.

Apart from actual fingerprints, the palms of the hand can provide certain information about a person's activities during life. The hands of a man who does manual work, for example, have callouses and thickened skin; alternatively, the hands of a clerk may have a small seg where he holds his pen to write. A man who dresses poultry may have soft but strong hands; the softness will result from the fat in a chicken's inside but the physical strength used in preparing a bird for the oven ensures a firm, well-used hand. Soleprints and toeprints can show not only deformity and fungal infections but also the damage which can arise from constantly walking barefoot. In the Western world few of us walk barefoot but in the past it was not always so.

In the case of Asru there was a very great difference between taking her fingerprints and taking those of a living person. With the latter, one finger at a time is inked and then rolled in a special place on a pre-printed form. However, we were unable to move Asru's fingers in order to apply this technique for fear of damaging the delicate tissue, so yet another method was needed.

Fortunately there is a special and very useful compound now in use in the dental profession. It combines at once a quick-setting quality with easy flexibility. We prepared small quantities of this compound, which looked very much like the grey putty used by a glazier. Then, with one fingerprint officer holding Asru's delicate but rigid hand from the top, another officer carefully applied the grey compound to the surface of each finger, passing it gently upwards in the narrow space available. It was allowed a few moments to set, and then was carefully peeled away. The eight fingers and two thumbs were all treated in this way. Afterwards, several coats of black acrylic paint were applied to each of the moulds, and then peeled away. These acrylic casts were then inked and printed in the manner previously described. The

A mirror is placed beneath the fingers and the reflected image then photographed.

Rubber mould being removed from mummy's left toes.

The first of several coats of acrylic paint being applied to mould to form a cast.

Rubber mould alongside black acrylic cast.

prints are not quite perfect because very small fragments of the mummified flesh are damaged. Nevertheless, their ridge characteristics are very clearly defined. A comparison of these shows that no fundamental change has occurred in the ridge system over the years. If Asru had been suspected of breaking into an Egyptian grocer's and had left tell-tale marks, there is no doubt that suitable evidence could be produced against her.

Most fingerprint work involves comparison of the prints of a suspect, taken in a police station, with the marks found at the scene of a crime. Sometimes the police have only the marks left at the scene of a crime and no trace of similar marks already on record. Then it is a matter of using years of experience to form a judgement. Frequently, this judgement can be surprisingly accurate. For instance, experience can provide a reliable estimate of the age of a person leaving fingerprints. Although body cells are cast from the skin all the time and are replaced at the same rate, the texture of the ridges is affected and the degree of wear and scarring will vary significantly. These features, if interpreted correctly,

may lead to an estimation of age, a guide to the nature of occupation, and an indication of general body structure. One recent example was that of a finger impression left behind at the scene of a murder. The opinion of the experts was that it had been made by a man aged between thirty-five and forty years, who did not do hard manual work and was fairly tall. When interviewed he turned out to be thirty-seven years of age, was a hairdresser, and was five feet eleven inches tall.

The examination of Asru's fingerprints led to the conclusion that she was, at the time of her death, in her early forties. This estimate was later supported by evidence from other sources. It was also fairly clear that she did not do hard manual work. Her fingers had not met with the small accidents commonly encountered by a housewife looking after her home, or by a woman working in the fields. This type of work tends to crease the skin, to lessen the depth of the ridges, and to effect adversely the general condition of the skin.

Asru's toeprints were taken in the same way as her fingerprints. Asru had come from the Temple of Karnak

81

Fingerprint pattern reproduced by inking and rolling acrylic cast.

and she was almost certainly either a dancer or a chantress, that is, one who was concerned with the chanting or singing of accompaniments to various temple rites. Three thousand years ago Egyptian temple dancers performed their ritual dances barefoot, the foot being used as part of the body's expression. The sole was in constant contact with the ground and even on the smoothest of flooring there would be friction and consequent wearing of the ridges on the underside of the toes and ball of the foot. Asru's feet did not show any traces of this constant contact with the floor; the depth of the furrows and the clarity of the characteristics were not consistent with her having been a dancer and the alternative of her being a chantress was much more acceptable.

It is not often that such an unusual opportunity occurs for fingerprint officers to exercise their skills. Most of their working day is concerned with crime and those committing it. Look again at your own hand; the pattern of your fingerprints and the lines on your hand are unique to you. There is nobody quite like you in the whole world. This remains true for the burglar and for Asru, the temple chantress. This individuality can be identified throughout a whole spectrum of activities and has allowed us to explore the annals of history more thoroughly. The skilled tracker can identify the prints of an animal, human or otherwise, from those of another. The essential qualities needed are accurate observation and the application of knowledge, experience, and common sense. Today, we have the benefit of recent scientific development and a great deal of this has been used by the whole investigation team. The sum of knowledge increases all the time and we are glad to have been able to contribute to it.

The Unwrapping of a Mummy

by

E. TAPP

Summary

The unidentified mummy of a child aged about thirteen years was unwrapped. The embalmers appeared to have been uncertain about the sex of the body as they had supplied both gold nipple covers and an artificial phallus. The soft tissues were in a poor state of preservation and the internal organs were missing. There was considerable damage to the tissues in the neck. The lower parts of the legs had been amputated and the embalmers had provided an artificial leg and foot. Carbon dating indicated that the body was from the Twentieth or Twenty-first Dynasty but that rewrapping had occurred some thousand years later.

One of the results of the increasing interest in the history of Ancient Egypt, which arose in the eighteenth and nineteenth centuries was the rather fashionable occupation of unwrapping mummies. At this time the practice was often referred to as unrolling, and prominent amongst the people doing this was Thomas Pettigrew (1791–1865). Pettigrew was a surgeon whose main claim to fame outside Egyptology was that, as Surgeon to the Duke of Kent, he vaccinated Queen Victoria. Despite his medical qualifications however, his unwrappings of Egyptian mummies made little contribution to our knowledge of disease in Ancient Egypt (Pettigrew 1834).

At the beginning of this century, however, the unwrapping and the examination of large numbers of mummies by two distinguished anatomists gave firm basis to the study of what was to become known as palaeopathology (Ruffer 1913). Elliot Smith, who held the Chair in Anatomy in Cairo between 1900 and 1909 and later held similar appointments in Manchester and University College, London, examined mummies from many sites and in particular those found in the archaeological survey of the Nubia. Wood Jones who later held Chairs at a number of universities including that at Manchester from 1938, assisted Elliot Smith in this study and made many valuable contributions to our knowledge of mummification and of disease in Ancient Egypt (Elliot Smith 1907; Wood Jones 1910; Elliot Smith and Dawson 1924).

Meanwhile Marc Armand Ruffer (1859–1917) during his period as Professor of Bacteriology in Cairo, was applying histological techniques to the examination of the tissues from mummies being unwrapped at this time. These studies were extensive and should be recognized as the starting point in the application of scientific techniques to the study of Egyptian mummies (Ruffer 1921).

During the same period, Margaret Alice Murray was Assistant Keeper in Egyptology at Manchester Museum.

It was she who, during the unwrapping of the Two Brothers, appears to have originated the idea of applying a multidisciplinary team to the study of Egyptian mummies, for in addition to an extensive examination of the skeleton by an anatomist, there were chemical studies by a number of eminent scientists (Murray 1910).

After this period the multidisciplinary team approach was allowed to lie fallow for many years. With the advent however, of so many new techniques which can be applied to the study of Egyptian mummies, the concept has been expanded considerably by another Egyptologist in Manchester, Dr Rosalie David, who, in 1972 activated the present project and involved, in addition to Egyptologists, specialists in radiology, dentistry, pathology, electron microscopy, biochemistry, serology, textiles, carbon dating, and fingerprinting. Recently there has been a similar revival of interest in the intensive study of small numbers of mummies in the United States of America (Cockburn, Barraco, Reyman, and Peck 1975), and in Canada (Hart, Cockburn, Millet, and Scott 1977).

In the present study the work done by the many specialists on the collection of mummies in the museum is dealt with in other chapters; here it is proposed to concentrate on a description of the unwrapping of one particular mummy referred to throughout by its museum number '1770'. Mummy '1770' came into the possession of the museum about 1896. Little is known of the source but Sir Flinders Petrie's diary, and a letter he sent to a friend after a visit to Manchester, indicate that '1770' probably came from his excavation site at Hawara in Middle Egypt. An exact date for the mummy is not known but it was thought to be from the Greek or Roman period. X-rays had been taken some years ago and they indicated that the mummy was that of a child aged about thirteen years. In addition, they showed that the lower parts of the legs were missing. However, a much more extensive radiological survey, using the latest techniques, was carried out shortly before the unwrapping and these findings will be described in the appropriate chapter.

The Unwrapping

The unwrapping and autopsy of '1770' was carried out at the New Medical School in Manchester in June 1975. Each stage of the unwrapping and dissection was recorded carefully both by ciné and still photography. In addition, the position of each bandage or layer of bandages was recorded as it was removed and in the same way tissue

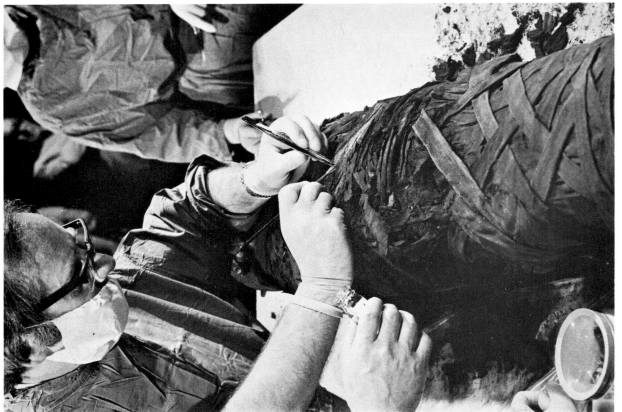

(2) Dead insects amongst the bandages were removed carefully for future study.

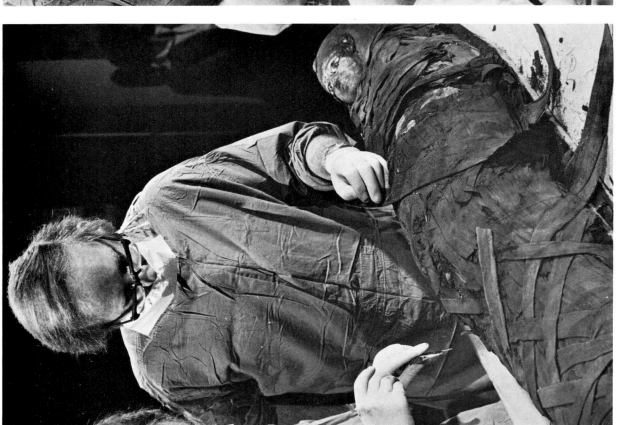

(1) There are wide pieces of material running lengthways beneath the diagonal bandaging.

84

(4) The lower part of the cartonnage mask after preliminary cleaning.

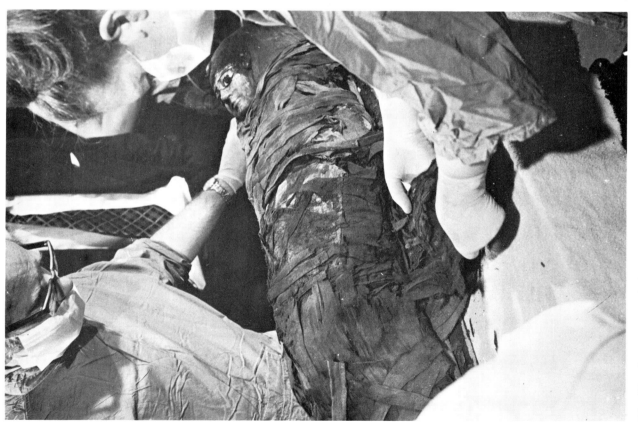

(3) The lower part of the cartonnage mask is now coming into view.

85

fragments were carefully labelled and stored in sealed plastic bags for future reference and examination. This was, of course, a time-consuming exercise which involved a team of at least three people working for some six hours each day for five days before the autopsy was complete. The team, however, felt that this slow systematic approach was essential if nothing was to be missed and the maximum amount of scientific information was to be obtained from the dissection.

The outer layers of bandages were about four inches in width and arranged in a circular or diagonal pattern. When these had been removed much wider pieces of material running lengthways were revealed (1). Very little resin was present in the wrappings, and consequently the bandages were not stuck together and each layer could be removed individually. This aided the examination of the way in which the bandages had been applied and clearly was much more satisfactory than having to use chisels and electric saws to remove multiple layers of resin-infiltrated bandages (Cockburn et al. 1975). At various stages during the unwrapping, dead insects, beetles and larval pupae were seen amongst the bandages

(5) The face and head of the mask has been separated from the lower part.

and these after noting their position, were removed carefully for future study (2).

As the longitudinal bandages were removed the lower part of the cartonnage mask was exposed (3). This, on cleaning, was seen to be an excellent example with most delicately executed designs painted on it (4). That part of the mask covering the head and neck was found to be damaged, the head being completely separated from the lower part (5). When the damaged part of the mask had been removed it was found that the bones of the neck and skull were fragmented and had to be removed piecemeal (6). Some of the pieces of bone from the vault of the skull had red and blue paint on the outer surface. The bones forming the upper jaw were intact and after cleaning, damage to the left side of the nose and the base of the skull was revealed, probably the site at which the embalmers had introduced the iron hook during the removal of the brain (7 and 8).

When the cartonnage mask and the remaining bandages had been removed, it was clear that the body was poorly preserved. All the tissues were extremely dry and separated readily from the bones. The arms were folded across the chest (9). There was some skin on the back of the hands and arms and beneath this tendons and muscles could be identified. There were gold finger stalls on some fingers and further gold leaf was found loose beneath the bandages (10). There was little skin or subcutaneous tissue on the chest wall but amongst the dust close to the ribs were two gold nipple covers. The thoracic cavity was empty, there being no sign of either the heart or lungs. The thoracic spine was intact and showed a peculiar distribution of resin in the intervertebral disc (11). Later similar resin was found in the epiphyseal plates at the ends of long bones and in some joint cavities.

Within the tissues of the anterior abdominal wall there was a hard mass one inch in diameter in a position corresponding with that of a small opaque object that had been seen in radiographs of the trunk. This mass proved to be the remains of a calcified guinea worm and will be described in detail later. The abdominal cavity and pelvis were packed with bandages and mud and despite a careful search no signs of the organs which normally occupy the abdominal and pelvic cavities could be found (12). Just outside the pelvic cavity there was a small roll of bandage which was continuous with the bandages covering the lower part of the anterior abdominal wall (13). Although the possibility was considered that this might be a roll of bandages from the vagina, there was little doubt from its position and relationship to the abdominal wall that it was an artificial phallus.

The legs, as anticipated, had been amputated, the left below the knee (through the tibia), and the right above the knee (through the femur). The right leg had been lengthened by an artificial leg of wood, covered with mud and bandages to make it the same length as the left (14). Removal of the mud from the end of the femur showed pieces of wood splinting the bone to the artificial limb. The bandages on the femur were closely applied to the bone and it was clear that very little flesh had been attached to the bone when the bandages were applied (15). Further examination of the ends of the femur and

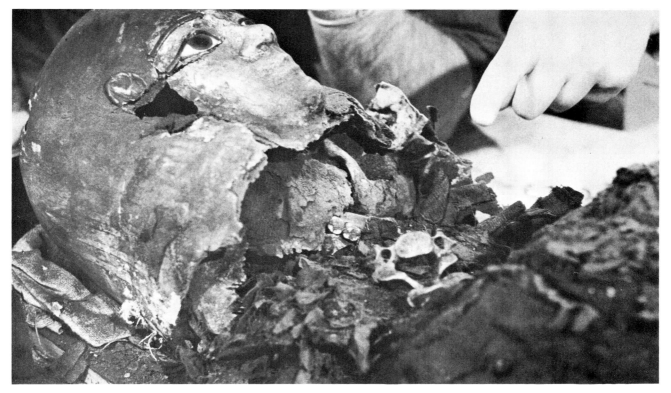

(6) There was considerable damage to the structures in the neck. A cervical vertebra and some teeth can be seen lying free amongst the rubble.

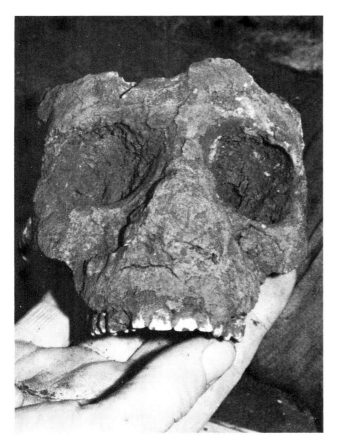

(7) The facial bones, upper jaw, before cleaning.

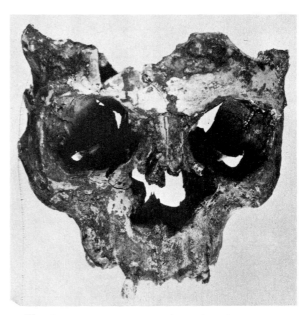

(8) Same bones after cleaning. There is damage to the bones on the left side of the nose.

87

(**9**) The arms are folded across the chest.

(**10**) Gold finger-stalls are present on some of the fingers.

tibia showed that the amputation line was irregular and moreover no evidence of bony callus could be seen.

Beneath the bandages, at the lower end of the tibia and at the end of the artificially lengthened femur were a pair of beautifully decorated slippers (16). Beneath them on the right side was an intricate structure of reeds and mud in the form of an artificial foot, the ends of the reeds representing the toes (17). In a similar position on the left side was merely an irrgular mass of mud and reeds.

Comments

It is clear from the appearance of the tissue that the body was poorly preserved, very little skin, muscle, or soft tissues being present. Such tissue that was detected proved extremely friable and very difficult to prepare for examination under the microscope. In addition to the soft tissue damage the bones were broken in a number of places. It is probable that some of the damage to the head and to the pelvis was due to lack of care in handling the mummy in the past. There is no positive evidence that the bones were broken during the life of '1770'. When bone is broken during life, tissue known as callus forms at the site of the fracture, producing a mass around it and holding the bones together until healing has occurred. Callus is easily recognized in fresh autopsies and indicates that the fracture occurred during life. Unfortunately callus of sufficient density to enable it to be recognized at the fracture site in such a poorly preserved body would take a few weeks to develop. Consequently, it is impossible in this case to exclude the possibility that the fracture had occurred one or two weeks before death. Some of the damage to the head and neck was almost certainly caused at the time that the cartonnage mask was broken, probably by the action of tomb robbers in antiquity. Further evidence for this is seen in the absence of eye covers, amulets or other objects around the neck, whilst gold finger stalls were present on the fingers and gold nipple covers on the chest.

The amputations of the legs are a more difficult problem. There is no evidence of callus at the ends of the bones indicating that if the amputations were ante-mortem then the period that elapsed before death would only be one or two weeks. The appearance of the ends of the bone do not suggest a surgical amputation although it is probable that these were carried out in Ancient Egypt (Moeller-Christensen and Brothwell 1963). The irregular line of the amputations are more like those of accidental trauma such as might occur in a body damaged by falling masonry or even a road traffic accident. It is also known that there was a certain amount of carelessness in the embalmers workshops and it has been suggested that occasionally limbs were accidentally lost from bodies during mummification. This type of loss probably occurred through joints and is an unlikely explanation for the loss of the lower parts of the legs in this case, since it would require considerable force and a deliberate act to amputate the limbs through the bones.

Turning now to the condition of the soft tissue of the body, the poor state of preservation has already been noted. The state of preservation clearly would be deter-

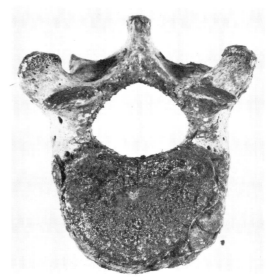

(11) A single vertebra showing the resin in the intervertebral disc.

mined by the method of embalming and there is little doubt that the best preserved bodies are those in which resins have been used liberally to infiltrate the tissues and bandages, and of course in this body little resin was found outside the joints and spine. However, there are a number of features which suggest that the body was in a fairly advanced state of decomposition when mummification took place. Comments have been made on the almost complete absence of soft tissues. Some of this may have been consumed by insects feeding on the body after death but is unlikely to be the full explanation. It is interesting to note that the bandages on the legs close to the amputation sites appear to have been applied directly to the bone indicating the absence of any soft tissues on the limb at the time of bandaging.

The absence of internal organs is also interesting. It was, of course, customary for the embalmers to remove certain organs and for these to be preserved separately either in canopic jars or placed back in the abdomen in separate packages. None of the organs could be found and whilst the thoracic cavity was completely empty, the abdomen and pelvis were packed with mud and bandages. Such complete removal of all the organs would be rare and their absence again suggests decomposition of the body at the time of wrapping. Moreover, the patella and the fibula from the left leg above the level of the amputation were missing. These bones are normally attached firmly to ligaments around the knee and would only be separated if the ligaments had been softened by decomposition.

A further point indicating absence of soft tissues on the head at the time of embalming is the presence of red and blue paint on the skull bones. Clearly for skull bones to be painted in this way, very little of the normal soft tissue of the scalp must have been present. Moreover, it is possible that there was decomposition with possible obliteration of the external genitalia at the time of embalming. This could explain the fact that the embalmers

(12)   Bandages and mud in the abdominal and pelvic cavities.

(13)   A small roll of bandage is seen between the upper ends of the femurs.

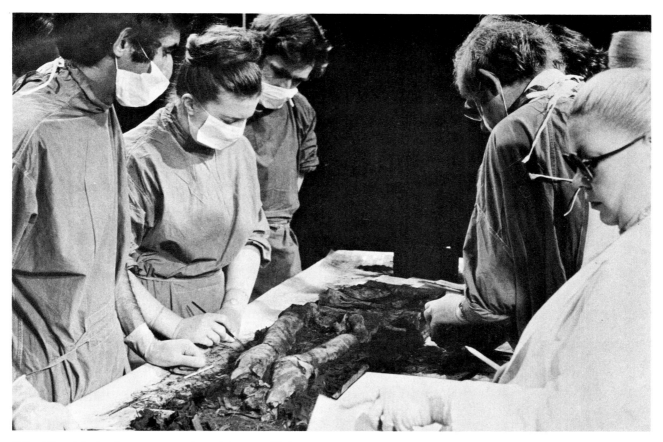

(14) The right leg has been lengthened by an artificial leg of wood covered with mud and bandages.

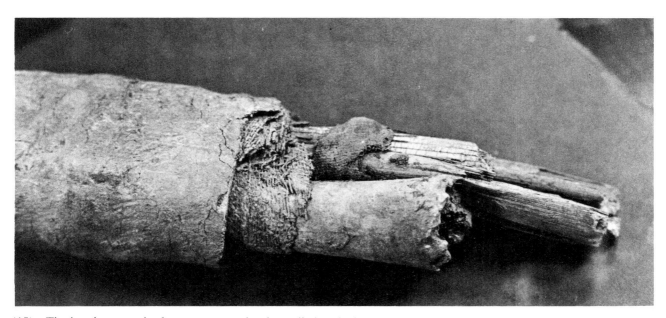

(15) The bandages on the femur are very closely applied to the bone.

91

(16) The decorated slippers.

did not appear to know whether they were embalming a girl or a boy, hence the presence of both nipple covers and an artificial phallus.

Various possibilities were considered as to why the body should be in an advanced state of decomposition before bandaging took place. The practice of leaving girls and young women to putrify for a few days before allowing the embalmers to take the body was considered, but it is difficult to see how a short period of putrefaction would result in such marked decomposition. It was also suggested that the body might have been hidden or lain undiscovered for some time after death and this could have happened if it had been buried under masonry in an accident or possibly left in water after death. Certainly, since water accelerates putrefaction, decomposition would occur much more readily in a body left in water.

A problem which appeared to defy explanation, however, was related to the fact that there was no form of identification on the wrappings of the body or its coffin. Hence it seemed very odd, if the child was an unknown body, that the Ancient Egyptians would have taken such great care in reconstructing the limbs and feet and in fitting the body with gold nipple covers and finger stalls. An explanation for this, however, became apparent when the carbon dating studies revealed that the bones dated from *c*.1000 B.C. whilst the bandages were some 1300 years later. It would appear therefore, that the body dates from the Twentieth or Twenty-first Dynasty and that rewrapping took place at a much later date.

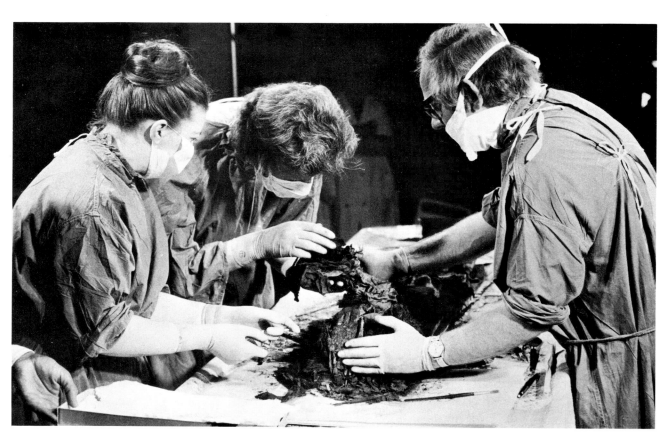

(17) There is an artificial foot made from reeds and mud.

92

There is evidence that some Royal mummies were moved to new tombs and it is possible that '1770' was one of these. The Egyptians, therefore, would not necessarily know whom they were rewrapping, hence the lack of identification. On the other hand, they would know that it was someone of importance and this would explain the careful reconstruction and the gold nipple covers and finger stalls. It is probable that much of the original tissue and wrappings of the body were lost when it was rewrapped accounting for the difficulty in finding any tissue.

The rewrapping also explains the presence of resin in some of the joints and in the epiphyseal plates of the long bones and spine whilst there was very little in the rest of the wrappings. It would appear that a type of resin which produced the discolouration of the cartilage in the bones and spine was used in the original wrapping whilst very little was employed when '1770' was rewrapped some thousand years later.

References

A. Cockburn, R. A. Barraco, T. A. Reyman, and W. H. Peck (1975), *Science*, 187, 1155.

G. Elliot Smith (1907), *Annales du Service des Antiquites de L'Egypte*, 8, 108.

G. Elliot Smith and W. R. Dawson (1924), *Egyptian Mummies*, London.

G. D. Hart, A. Cockburn, N. B. Millet, and J. W. Scott (1977), *Can. Med. Ass. J.*, 117 (5), 1.

V. Moeller-Christensen and D. R. Brothwell (1963), *Man.*, 244, 192.

M. A. Murray (1910), *Tomb of Two Brothers*, Manchester.

T. J. Pettigrew (1834), *A History of Egyptian Mummies*, London.

M. A. Ruffer (1913), *J. Path. Bact.*, 18, 149.

M. A. Ruffer (1921), *Studies in Palaeopathology of Egypt*, Chicago.

F. Wood-Jones (1910), General Pathology, Fractures and Dislocations in Human Remains, *Arch. Survey of Nubia*, Report for 1907–08, Vol. ii, Cairo.

Disease in the Manchester Mummies

by

E. Tapp

Summary

Methods of rehydration and processing of tissue are described which allow the preparation of satisfactory histological sections from Egyptian mummies. A wide range of histological stains proved to be useful, demonstrating the framework and in some cases the cellular detail of the tissue. The mummy of Nekht-ankh showed evidence of sand pneumoconiosis and of pleurisy and pericarditis. Sections from the mummy of '1770' and Asru indicate that they suffered from parasitic worm infestation.

Knowledge of disease in Ancient Egypt has been gained in the past from studies of the medical papyri and from the examination of works of art such as drawings and statues showing malformed persons. However, it was the careful examination of the skeletons and preserved tissue from unwrapped mummies which began early this century that formed the basis for the science of palaeopathology. This term was suggested by Ruffer and defined as 'the science of the diseases which can be demonstrated in human and animal remains of ancient tissues' (Ruffer 1913). The science, therefore, includes the naked eye and histological examination of preserved organs as well as the application of electronmicroscopy and other advanced techniques to the study of ancient tissues.

Although a few early workers including Csermack (1852) had made some drawings of tissue from mummies which had been teased out in sodium hydroxide, it was Ruffer who made the first important observations on histological sections of Egyptian mummies (Ruffer 1911).

Ruffer, who was Professor of Bacteriology at Cairo, published a series of papers on palaeopathology between 1910 and his death at sea in 1917 and these papers have been collected together and published in book form (Ruffer 1921).

Following this basic work by Ruffer there were for many years relatively few histological studies of Egyptian mummies, although those of Simandl (1928) who described histological sections of skin and striated muscle from a 19th or 20th Dynasty Egyptian mummy and Shaw (1938) who carried out a histological study of an 18th Dynasty mummy are worth noting.

More recently Graf (1949) has described histological studies on Egyptian mummies whilst Sandison (1955) has done much to encourage such work. Using Sandison's techniques Rowling (1961) has produced an M.D. Thesis based on his examination of pathological lesions from mummies.

The present studies are based on the collection of Egyptian mummies in the Manchester Museum; they use methods some of which are new whilst others are based on modifications of those described by Ruffer (1911) and Sandison (1955, 1957).

Rehydration

The first stage in the study of mummified material is to re-introduce water into the tissues. This softens it and allows it to regain something of its normal texture. The present workers have found that rehydration occurred satisfactorily in a 5 per cent solution of formol saline but many different methods have been tried in the past. Ruffer (1911) used a mixture of alcohol, sodium carbonate and water, varying the proportions of sodium carbonate and alcohol according to the nature of the original tissue. In general the harder the tissue the more sodium carbonate was used. Other workers have used alcohol alone (Simandl 1928) or merely 1.2 per cent saline (Graf 1949) whilst Sandison (1955) used a modification of Ruffers (1911) solution.

Fixation and Processing

Irrespective of the rehydration procedure, the tissues appear to benefit from 24–48 hours immersion in the commonly used fixative, 10 per cent formol saline.

Processing of the tissue can then be carried out in the usual way preferably by hand although Sandison (1957) has used an automatic tissue processing machine. The present workers used both Gooch crucibles and perforated scintered glass tubes of the Graham Peacock type to help in handling the tissue and to prevent disintegration. A double-embedding technique was also used; after taking the tissue to absolute alcohol it was immersed in 3 per cent low viscosity nitro-cellulose in methyl benzoate followed by toluene to harden the methyl benzoate and to clear the tissue. The tissue was then infiltrated with paraffin wax (melting point 56–58°C). Sections from the blocks were cut on a rocking or rotary microtome in the usual way.

Staining

The following methods have been used:

Haematoxylin and Eosin This stain is used widely in pathology as a routine stain to demonstrate cellular and nuclear detail, but the results with mummified tissue are disappointing. A similar experience has been reported

(1) Cartilage stained with haematoxylin and eosin. The nuclei are clearly seen.

(2) The Verhoff van Gieson Stain for connective tissue and elastic fibres differentiates the various elements in the dermis.

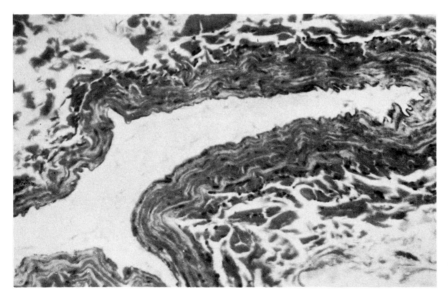

(3) A blood-vessel stained in the same way as (**2**).

previously by Sandison (1963). However, occasionally it may be of value as in the sections of the rib cartilage; here the nuclei are quite clearly stained by the haematoxylin whilst the eosin stains the matrix of the cartilage (1). Cell nuclei have been stained previously in the epidermis by Ruffer (1911) and Sandison (1955) but not in other tissues.

Connective Tissue Stains These have proved most useful, Van Gieson giving good differentiation in most instances between collagen and muscle. When used in conjunction with Verhoff's stain for elastic fibres the structure of the dermis of the skin and of blood vessels can be demonstrated (2 and 3).

These stains may also be of value in demonstrating the overall structure of organs such as the liver where the cellular detail has been lost. In such organs Gordon and Sweet's stain for reticulin or phosphotungstic acid haematoxylin (PTAH) may also be useful, but in the present work the reticulin framework of the liver was demonstrated most satisfactorily by using the Periodic acid Schiff Reagent followed by celestine blue mordanted with iron alum (4).

PTAH was also useful for demonstrating the trabecular structure of bone. Here the osteocyte cannot be seen in the lacunae and the bone marrow has unfortunately disappeared (5).

Striations in voluntary muscle were difficult to demonstrate. Clearly the ease with which this may be done depends on the state of preservation of the tissue and from this point of view the demonstration of muscle striations in naturally preserved pre-dynastic bodies is interesting (Ruffer 1911).

Mucin Stains Metachromasia in the matrix of cartilage could be demonstrated readily with toludene blue. This phenomenon has been studied previously in ancient cartilage and bone (Anderson and Jorgensen 1960).

Alcian blue was useful in demonstrating the particles in the damaged lung tissue which proved to consist of sand. These particles stained metachromatically and would appear to be coated with some mucinous material.

The Periodic acid Schiff Reaction for mucins showed the presence of mucin secretion in the epithelium of the large intestine (6). This is probably the first demonstration of the persistence of epithelial mucin in mummified tissue.

Stains for Pigments Carbon pigment may be seen unstained in the tissue. Other workers have used the Masson Fontana stain for melanin (Sandison 1957) and Perl's stain for iron pigment but in the latter case there is often doubt about the specificity of the staining (Sandison 1963).

Disease in Nekht-ankh

Nekht-ankh was one of the Two Brothers, unwrapped by Margaret Murray at the beginning of the century (Murray 1910). He is believed to be from the Twelfth Dynasty and to be about sixty years of age when he died. The description given by Murray (1910) indicates that at the time of unwrapping, the tissues were moist and in poor condition. However, many of the fragments had been saved and carefully preserved in glass jars. It was material from these jars that the present author re-examined some seventy years after the unwrapping and amongst which he found fragments of rib. Attached to one piece of rib was some soft tissue and this, under the microscope, was seen to be lung. The lung tissue appeared to be damaged and to contain a good deal of scarring with proliferation of both fibrous and elastic tissues. Amongst the fibrous tissue were several aggregations of fine particles. These were brown or black in unstained sections but stained metachromatically with alcian blue (7). This peculiarity of the staining has already received comment.

The study of the lungs was assisted further by the finding of material in two of the canopic jars from Nekht-ankh. One of these the 'Hapi' jar was described by Cameron (1910) as containing a hard brittle mass which he believed was a small piece of intestine. This tissue is seen in its original state (8). After re-hydration the larger airways and vessels can be seen and it is now quite clear that the specimen is one of lung (9). Histological sections again showed damage to the lung and the presence of fine particles. The latter are also seen in the lymphatic channels around large blood vessels in the lungs (10). Examination of the particles under polarized light showed birefringence indicating that they had a crystalline structure and were almost certainly silica particles. The electron microscopic studies described elsewhere confirmed the presence of silica and suggested that the particles were composed of sand. Lesions similar to those in Nekht-ankh's lung have been described recently in the lungs of people living in the Sahara and Negev deserts (Policard and Collet 1952; Bar-Ziv and Goldberg 1974) and the disease has been called sand pneumoconiosis. It is very similar to the condition acquired by coal miners and stone workers who inhaled stone dust and in whom the condition is called silicosis. These workers get massive fibrosis of the lung and it has been suggested that sand particles are probably not as damaging to the lung as freshly broken stone particles encountered by coal miners and stone workers. It is clear, however, that the smoother fragments of stone we call sand are also capable of causing considerable damage to the lung.

The method of his embalming and the inscriptions on the tomb found by Murray (1910) indicate that it is unlikely that Nekht-ankh was a stonemason. There is little doubt, however, that the population of Ancient Egypt would be subjected at intervals to sand-storms of the type that desert populations still have to endure today, and that the mechanism producing Nekht-ankh's disease is similar to that going on in present-day desert populations.

Previous workers (Ruffer 1910; Long 1931) have noted anthracosis (carbon pigment) in the lungs of Egyptian mummies and Shaw (1938) reported anthracosis in association with emphysema and bronchopneumonia. It is only recently, however, that silicotic damage has been described (Cockburn et al. 1975; Tapp et al. 1975). In addition Reyman and his associates (1977) have reported birefringent particles in the lungs of a mummy which analyses have suggested are particles of granite.

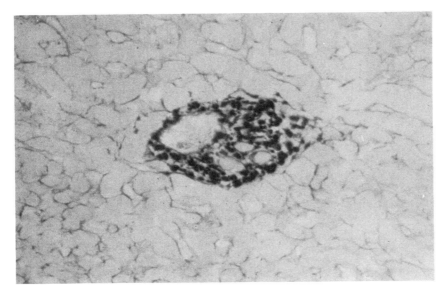

(4) The connective tissue framework of the liver is stained and there is a portal tract in the middle.

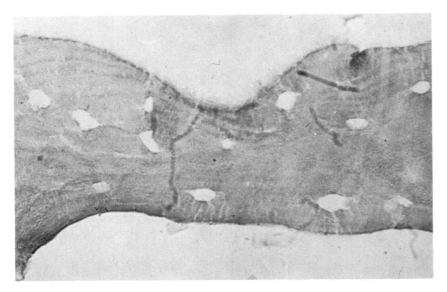

(5) The trabecular structure of the bone is demonstrated with PTAH but the osteocytes have disappeared.

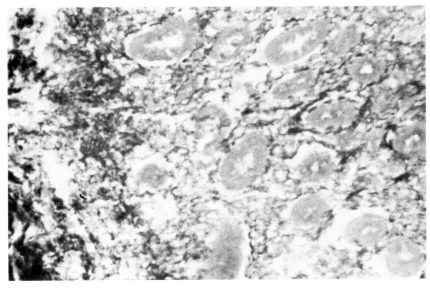

(6) Mucin secretion is seen in the epithelium lining the glands of the large intestine, the mucin being stained with the Periodic acid Scheff reagent.

Further examination of the specimen of lung from the cannopic jar has shown that Nekht-ankh also had disease affecting the heart, for the pale tissue attached to the lung in one area was shown histologically to be part of the wall of the heart. It is clear that when the embalmers attempted to remove the lungs of Nekht-ankh they found that it was impossible to separate the lung from the heart and consequently instead of leaving the heart behind they had to remove part of the wall of the latter along with the lung. The histological sections show fibrous tissue obliterating the pericardial and pleural cavities and it is clear that there must have been inflammation in this area probably associated with pneumonia some time before death had occurred.

Disease in Asru

Asru was a lady who is believed to have lived in the Late Period. The mummy was unwrapped some years ago but the body itself was left undisturbed. However, a mass of material was found between her legs and although this looked most unpromising, histological examination has been worthwhile. The sections showed that the material consisted of intestines and although only the outlines of the muscular walls of the intestine could be identified, in some places clear evidence of parasitic infestation could be seen. Worms were present both in the mucosa and muscular wall of the intestine and appeared to have been causing significant disease (**11**). It is believed that the worm is a Nemotode and is almost certainly of the genus Strongyloides. Further details of its structure will be dealt with in the section dealing with electron-microscopy.

Strongyloides is a parasite that is found in many tropical and subtropical countries as well as in more northerly latitudes. The life cycle is complicated but in man begins when larval forms burrow through the skin of the feet when the latter come into contact with infected water or contaminated soil. From the skin the immature forms pass along the veins to the lungs where they enter the air passages and pass upwards towards the larynx. They are then swallowed and hence gain access to the stomach and intestines. In the intestines they reach maturity and the female lays eggs which are passed in the stools. Eventually the eggs hatch out into larvae in the soil which are ready to start the cycle again. It is clear that infection with this worm will be endemic in conditions where hygiene is poor and where the feet are likely to come into contact with soil contaminated with faeces. Certainly one can understand it being prevalent amongst the lower classes in Ancient Egypt. Asru, however, is believed to be of high rank and consequently it would appear that the disorder occurred at all levels of society.

It is difficult to know whether the worms were responsible for her death, certainly they may have made her anaemic due to blood loss. Occasionally they produce a severe inflammation of the large intestines and from there spread to other parts of the body and under these circumstances may cause death. It has been mentioned already, however, that tissue from the rest of the body was not available for study.

Disease in '1770'

Reference has been made already to the calcified nodule from the anterior abdominal wall of this mummy which on x-ray proved to be the remains of a Guinea worm (*Dracunculus medinensis*). Infection with this worm is still common in some parts of the Near East, Africa and India. It is acquired by man when during the consumption of water infected with a small crustacean containing immature forms of the worm. The latter are liberated from the crustacean by the gastric juices and the immature worms migrate through the wall of the stomach and grow into adult worms in the anterior abdominal wall. The male worm is only a few centimetres in length and dies after fertilizing the much larger, up to one metre in length, female. It would appear that the worm found in '1770' is the male. Calcification often occurs when a worm dies within living tissues and of course it is this calcification which has preserved the outline of the worm for the past three thousand years.

The female worm, after fertilization, wanders through the subcutaneous tissues of the body but usually comes to rest in the legs and feet. Here it causes blistering and later ulceration of the skin (**12**). Eggs are passed through the ulcerated area and if they get into water they are taken up by a crustacean and the life cycle is ready to start again.

Attempts were usually made to remove the worm from the leg and one old method consisted of holding one end of the worm as it emerged from the ulcer in a cleft stick. The worm was then carefully wound on to the stick by turning the latter slowly round so extracting the worm a little at a time each day. If the worm should die before it is removed in this way then severe inflammation occurred in the legs and abscesses were common. It is possible that this happened in '1770' and the child's legs had to be amputated surgically. However, the appearance of the ends of the bones did not support this.

Comments

Previous descriptions of Strongyloides and Dracunculosis in Egyptian mummies have not been found but of course, worm infestations are mentioned in Ancient Egypt writings (Ebbells 1937). Parasitic infestation in Egyptian mummies was first reported by Ruffer who demonstrated the calcified eggs of Bilharzia in the renal tubules of two 20th Dynasty mummies (Ruffer 1910a; 1910b). Ruffer also suggested that some Coptic bodies with enlarged spleens might have malaria but there is no convincing evidence of this (Ruffer 1913). More recently Cockburn and his co-workers (1975) found a single Helminth egg in Pum II which has been identified as Ascaris, whilst Reyman and his associates (1977) have identified calcified bilharzial eggs in the liver of Rom. I. This mummy believed to be a weaver from Thebes was also infected with a flat worm of the species Taenia whilst a cyst of another worm, *Trichinella spiralis*, was found in an intercostal muscle.

It is interesting to note that the most significant disease found in the Manchester mummies may be related to the local environmental and social conditions in Ancient Egypt. The sand pneumoconiosis in Nekht-ankh is a reflection of the dry dusty climate which exists for much of the year and at times the environment is made much

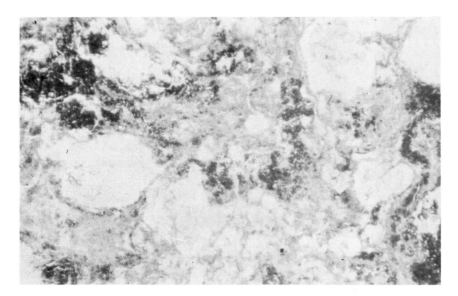

(7) The normal structure of the lung has been destroyed by fibrosis and aggregations of fine particles are seen in the top left and bottom right of the photograph.

(8) A brittle piece of tissue found in the 'Hapi' jar.

(9) A small part of the tissue from (8) rehydrated and magnified in the photograph. A large airway is seen close to the edge of the tissue on the right of the photograph.

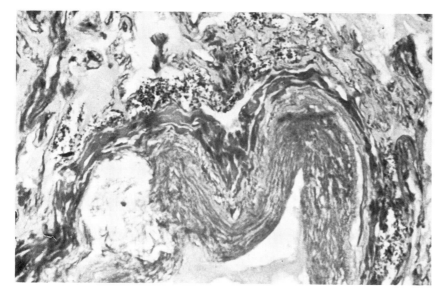

(10) The fine dark particles are seen in the lymphatic channels around a large blood vessel in the lung.

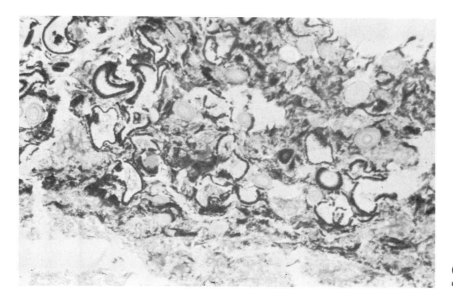

(11) Parasitic infestation in the wall of the intestine, probably Strongyloides.

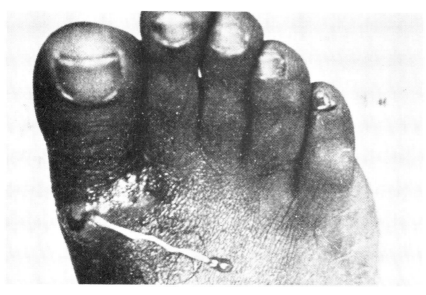

(12) An ulcer is now present and the tip of the worm has appeared through it.

worse by the occurrence of sand-storms. On the other hand the persistance of parasitic infestations such as those found in '1770' and Asru are the result of inadequate sanitation permitting continuous reinfestation of the ground. Flooding of the land for part of the year makes things worse by allowing the development and proliferation of immature forms of the parasites in the wet soil and also results in contamination of the wells from which the people draw their drinking-water. Hence the people are at risk from infections such as Strongyloides and Bilharzia whilst walking barefoot in the infected water and soil and from infestation with Dracunculosis when drinking water from their wells.

References

H. Anderson and J. B. Jorgensen (1960), *Stain Technol.*, 35, 91.
J. Bar-Ziv and G. M. Goldberg (1974), *Arch. Env. Health*, 29, 121.
J. Cameron (1910), in M. A. Murray, *Tomb of Two Brothers*, Manchester.
A. Cockburn, R. A. Barraco, T. A. Reyman and W. H. Peck (1975), *Science*, 187, 1155.
J. N. Csermack (1852), *S. B. Akad, Wiss.*, Wien, 9, 427.
B. Ebbells (1937), *The Papyrus Ebers*; the Greatest Egyptian Medical Document, Copenhagen, Levin and Munksgaad.
W. Graf (1949), *Acta Anat.* (Basel), 8, 236.
A. R. Long (1931), *Arch. Path.*, 12, 92.
M. A. Murray (1910), *Tomb of Two Brothers*, Manchester.
A. Pollicard and A. Collet (1952), *Arch. Ind. Hyg. Occup. Med.*, 5, 527.
T. A. Reyman, M. R. Zimmerman and P. K. Lewin (1977), *Canad. Med. Ass. J.*, 117 (5), 7.
J. T. Rowling (1961), *Disease in Ancient Egypt*; evidence from Pathological Lesions found in Mummies, M.D. Thesis, Univ. of Cambridge.
M. A. Ruffer (1910), *Cairo Sci. J.*, 4, 1.
—— (1910b), *Br. Med. J.*, 1, 16.
—— (1911), *Mem. Inst. Egypte*, 6 (3), 1.
—— (1913), *J. Path. Bact.*, 18, 149.
—— (1921), *Studies in the Palaeopathology of Egypt*, Chicago.
A. T. Sandison (1955), *Stain Technol.*, 30, 277.
—— (1957), *Nature*, 179, 1309.
—— (1963), *The Study of Mummified and Dried Human Tissues*, from Science in Archaeology, ed. Brothwell and Higgs, Thames and Hudson, U.S.A.
A. F. B. Shaw (1938), *J. Path. Bact.*, 47, 115.
I. Simandl (1928), *Anthropologie* (Prague), 6, 56.
E. Tapp, A. Curry and C. Anfield (1975), *Br. Med. J.*, 2, 276.

Electron Microscopy of the Manchester Mummies

by

A. CURRY, C. ANFIELD and E. TAPP

Summary

Transmission electron microscopy (TEM), analytical electron microscopy (AEM) and scanning electron microscopy (SEM) have been used in the examination of various Egyptian mummy tissues. A liver was found to be well preserved with cell membranes and nuclei discernable. Centrioles with typical 9-fold symmetry have been identified in this tissue. Other tissues were found to be poorly preserved. Remains identified as parasites have been identified in the liver and an intestine. Bacteria, bacterial spores and hyphae-like structures were commonly observed in the tissues.

Crystals found surrounded by fibrous tissue in lung contained Si, Fe and Ti. It was concluded that this man suffered from sand pneumoconiosis during life. Heavy metal pollutants were not found in the various tissues examined by AEM.

The hair of two brothers was examined by SEM in an attempt to elucidate their parentage.

Introduction

Electron microscopy comprises of a number of distinct methods, some of which have been applied to the study of Egyptian remains. The transmission electron microscope (TEM) enables scientists to visualize structure finer than that previously accessible. The fineness of detail discernable is referred to as the resolving power and is a function of the wavelength used to illuminate the specimen. The shorter the wavelength the greater the resolving power. Electrons exhibit wave properties and their wavelength is a fraction of that of visible light giving a thousandfold improvement in resolving power.

Analytical electron microscopy is one of the latest developments in electron microscopy This technique utilizes the electron beam as a probe which analyses the elements contained within the area undergoing examination by the collection and analysis of the x-rays produced by interaction of the electrons and the specimen.

The scanning electron microscope (SEM) is used to examine the surfaces of solid objects. A fine beam of electrons is made to scan the specimen and an image is built up sequentially on a cathode ray tube, analogous to the formation of a television picture giving a topographical image with a good depth of field.

These three electron-optical techniques were used in the following study to investigate various tissues from mummified bodies in the Manchester Museum collection. Further details of these techniques can be found in Meek (1976).

Transmission Electron Microscopy (TEM)

The transmission electron microscope has not been extensively employed in the field of palaeopathology even though instruments have been available for well over two decades. Early investigations all concentrated on the study of fossilized and ancient bone, not least of which was that of Ascenzi (1963) who used the electron microscope in the demonstration of the disparity of the Piltdown cranium and jaw. Leeson (1959) published the first study of dried human soft tissues, rehydrated according to Sandison (1955). He described cell membranes, nuclear membranes and chromatin in the skin of an Amerindian dried body from Columbia. These findings were not remarkable, for similar cellular components had been seen at light microscope level by Ruffer as early as 1921. Lewin (1967 and 1968) was the first to investigate with TEM the ultrastructure of ancient Egyptian mummified material. He processed skin and muscle tissue from an Egyptian head, dated at approximately 600 B.C., and published electron micrographs showing nuclear and cytoplasmic membranes, nuclear pores and tonofilaments.

Skeletal muscle and scleral material from two Egyptian mummies, and dermal tissue from a young Peruvian mummy of probable pre-Columbian date were studied by Macadam and Sandison (1969). The results were disappointing in that only vague cellular structure was observed in the skeletal muscle and the dermal tissue had been extensively infiltrated by micro-organisms. Yeatman (1971) described nucleoli and rough endoplasmic reticulum in cartilage tissue from a naturally dessicated Aleutian mummy some two to three hundred years old. He suggested that the cartilaginous matrix supported the cellular components preventing them from undergoing the profound shrinkage which normally occurs in drying soft tissue. Hufnagel (1973) studied several different tissues by TEM, including abdominal wall, aorta and trachea, from an Egyptian mummy 2,700 years old. At the ultrastructural level she described an abundance of fibrous material resembling collagen, trilaminar membranes and myelin-like configurations. Round, dense bodies, comparable in size to nuclei and mitochondria were also observed.

With these promising results in mind, tissues were taken from mummy '1770' which was unwrapped in 1975 at the Manchester Medical School. Unfortunately the tissues were unsuitable for TEM due to the poor state of preservation of the body. Other tissues, however, were available from the extensive collection of Egyptian

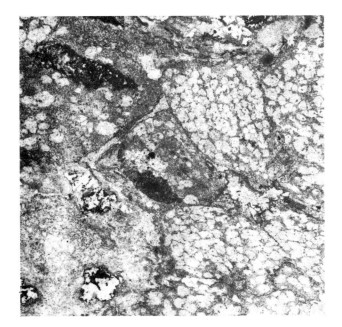

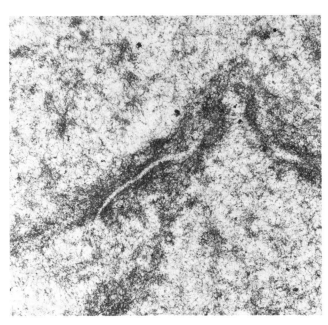

(1) A section of liver showing cell outlines, nuclei and electron lucent areas, interpreted as positions of mitochondria during life. ×2,700.

(2) Remains of two closely apposed cell membranes with an electron dense desmosome from liver. ×50,000.

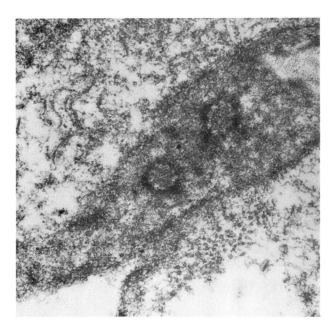

(3) A pair of centrioles from liver. ×38,000.

(4) Liver section showing intercellular space, interpreted as a capillary containing blood cells. ×3,700.

mummies and associated canopic jar material in the Manchester Museum.

Materials and Methods Material for TEM came from three sources: the canopic jars from a tomb of two brothers, Nekht-ankh and Khnum-Nakht of the 12th Dynasty; the mummy of Asru (a female of the Late Period); and an isolated head labelled 'no 7740'. Pieces of tissue approximately 5mm³ were taken from areas adjacent to those removed for histological examination, and placed in a 4 per cent glutaraldehyde solution made up in 0.1M Sorenson's phosphate buffer pH7.4. Twenty-four hours later the rehydrated pieces of tissue were the consistency of firm agar and could be cut into 1mm³ blocks. The blocks were placed in fresh glutaraldehyde solution for four hours, followed by phosphate buffer for

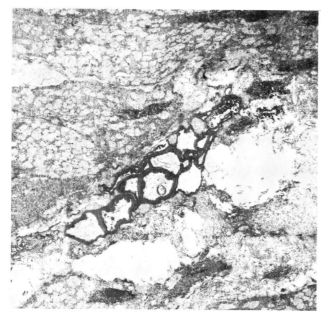

(5) Section of liver containing a group of cells with thickened walls, possibly the remains of a liver fluke. ×2,000.

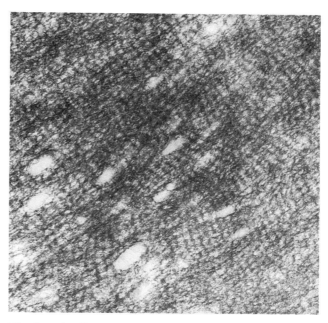

(6) Longitudinally arranged fibrils with a cross-banding pattern from skeletal muscle. ×55,000.

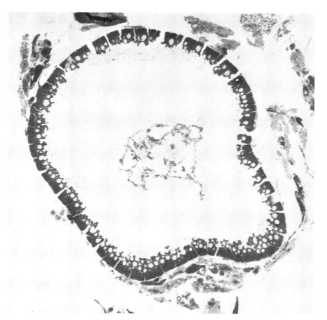

(7) Section through intestinal wall showing remains of a parasitic worm. ×3,000.

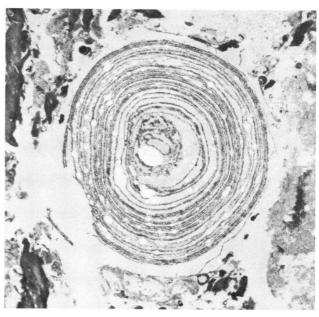

(8) Section through intestinal wall showing a structure composed of concentric layers, interpreted as a parasite cyst. ×5,000.

storage pending the light microscope reports.

Selected tissues were post-fixed with 1 per cent osmium tetroxide in 0.1M Sorenson's phosphate buffer pH7.4, dehydrated in a graded series of alcohols and embedded in an Epon/Araldite mixture. Ultrathin sections were cut on an LKB Ultratome III ultramicrotome using glass or diamond knives, collected on to uncoated copper grids, stained with uranyl acetate and lead citrate and examined in an A.E.I. EM801 transmission electron microscope.

Results The ultrastructure of liver tissue from one of the two brothers was well preserved (**1**). Easily recognizable cell membranes were present with desmosomes at intervals along their length (**2**). Desmosomes are areas of intimate cell contact where cell to cell communication is thought to occur. The cytoplasm showed relatively electron lucent areas of mitochondrial size probably indicating the sites of these organelles prior to their disintegration (1). A cell nucleus of medium electron density with crenated margin was present in most of the cells examined (1). Centrioles were identified in two cells, their typical tubular configuration with walls composed of nine segments being remarkably well preserved (3). Inter-cellular bile canaliculi were present but the expected microvilli were absent (1). Structures resembling red blood cells occurred in an intercellular space that was possibly a small capillary (4). Characteristic bundles of collagen fibres, exhibiting a 64 n.m. periodicity, were in close proximity to this blood vessel and in most other intercellular locations of the tissue examined. After examination of sections of a modern liver fluke and much consultation with parasitologists it was decided that a flattened group of cells with thickened walls (5) were possibly the remains of part of the liver fluke, *Fasciola hepatica*.

Skeletal muscle (6) from the canopic jars of the two brothers exhibited longitudinally arranged fibrils with a cross-banding pattern but did not display the organized regular cross-banding sequences of freshly prepared skeletal muscle tissue. Electron lucent vacuoles were apparent between some of the fibres, possibly indicating the location of mitochondria.

The intestinal tissue remains of Asru were poorly preserved, there being no remnant of cellular organization, only an amorphous ground substance interrupted by collagen fibres. However, Dr Tapp's histological examination had already revealed structures which were obviously not of human origin. Transmission electron microscope examination of this tissue showed two types of structure present, the first was of cylindrical appearance with a thick fenestrated wall (7) and the second was spherical with a wall composed of concentric layers (8). These were interpreted as being worm and cyst remains respectively. Photomicrographs of these remains were sent to Mr P. Gooch at the Commonwealth Institute of Helminthology, who suggested that they may have been the remains of *Strongyloides*, a parasitic worm which invades the intestinal wall, but this identification is by no means conclusive.

Lung tissue, again from the two brothers, was also shown to be largely acellular. The surviving composition was predominantly of bundles of collagen fibres and elastic tissue (9). The collagen, in many areas, consisted of fibrous capsules surrounding numbers of electron dense, crystalline particles (9). These particles were later investigated by analytical electron microscopy.

The brain/dura from the isolated head was disappointing at the ultrastructural level. No cellular organization remained, only amorphous material, large multilaminar bodies, resembling myelin figures, and remains of large numbers of micro-organisms were present (10).

Two types of micro-organism have been identified. Filamentous structures resembling fungal hyphae (11) were present in the brain/dura, lung and intestinal tissues. Almost spherical structures 0.7μm in diameter, indicative of bacterial cocci, were found in most of the tissue samples examined. A wall up to 30 nm thick was easily identifiable surrounding many of these bacteria and on occasion a division septum was apparent. Within the brain/dura, lung and intestines many bacterial spores were readily observed (12). These have a complex envelope composed of many concentric layers.

Discussion Previous transmission electron microscope studies on dried, soft tissues from mummified bodies have not been very successful in demonstrating a wealth of detail at ultrastructural level. The presence of connective tissue components, however, have been consistently documented (Lewin 1967, 1968; Macadam and Sandison 1969; Yeatman 1971; Hufnagel 1973). It seems likely that the rigid, structural organization of collagen and elastic tissues prevent their total decomposition. A similar situation was demonstrated by the skeletal muscle examined, the fibrillar pattern being reasonably well preserved.

Soft body tissues putrefy quite rapidly after death and consequently it was not surprising that little cellular detail was discernable in the intestine, lung and brain/ dura examined. The structural preservation of the liver tissue was therefore quite remarkable. The presence of cell and nuclear membranes are well documented (Leeson 1959) but the finding of desmosomes and centrioles is very interesting. The liver must have been removed from the body very soon after death and dried quickly to preserve the sub-cellular structure to any extent.

Worm infestations in the Ancient World and Egypt have been well documented (Brothwell and Sandison 1967) and appear to have been of common occurrence. Most modern findings of parasitic worm infections in ancient peoples have come from analysis of faecal remains (Gooch 1975). The eggs or cysts of most parasitic worms are extremely resistant to decay and are passed out of the intestine in large numbers. Remains of adult parasitic worms are difficult to identify as these would simply putrefy on the death of the host. However, if the worms become calcified during the life of the host, or if the body organs containing these worms were dried soon after death, then the worms would remain relatively intact.

The calcified remains of the parasite Guinea worm, *Dracunculus*, were discovered by radiology, as discussed by Dr Isherwood. The identification of the two worms discovered by TEM is tentative. *Fasciola* has been identified previously in archaeological deposits (see annotated bibliography of Gooch 1975) from their characteristic eggs. If the remains found in the liver of Nekht-ankh are *Fasciola*, then this was probably an early invasive stage. The second worm, *Strongyloides*, differs from most other nematodes found in the ileum, by living inside the intestinal wall. From here the female worm releases parthenogenetic eggs which pass out of the intestines and hatch. Larvae reinfect humans by burrowing through the skin. After migrating around the body they finally settle in the wall of the ileum. The occurrence of nematode remains within the epithelium of the ileum of Asru suggests that she suffered from an infection of *Strongyloides*, which can cause anaemia in

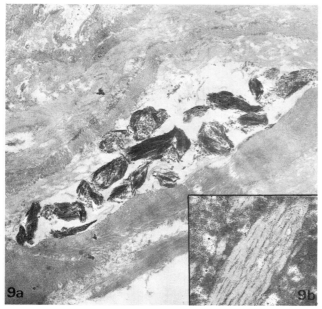

(9) Section through part of a lung containing sand particles. Note that fibrous tissue completely surrounds these particles. ×12,500. (*Inset*) Remains of bundles of elastic tissue from lung. ×17,000.

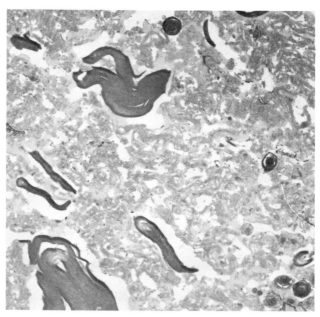

(10) A section of mummified brain showing large myelin bodies and bacterial spores. ×3,700.

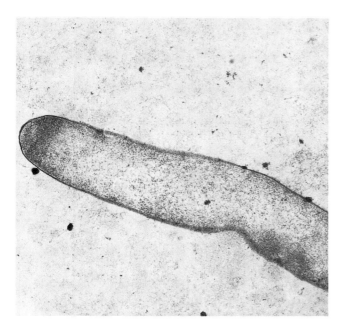

(11) Filamentous structure resembling a fungal hypha. ×25,000.

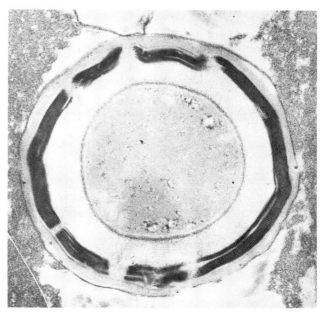

(12) A bacterial spore. Note concentric layers. ×80,000.

life by destroying the intestinal mucosa (Borradaile et el. 1967).

The age of the micro-organisms present in the mummies is problematical. The spores and hyphae-like structures found within the tissues are probably of ancient origin, for they would sporulate as the tissues dried out. The abundance of bacterial spores can give an indication of the state of the tissues when they were mummified. For comparison pieces of fresh brain tissue were allowed to

putrefy over a period of twelve days. Some of the pieces were kept in a humid atmosphere while others were kept dry. The former contained numerous bacterial spores whereas the latter contained very few. The brain/dura from the isolated mummified head contained many bacterial spores indicating that this tissue has been allowed to putrefy. If the brain had been removed soon after death and the body packed with 'natron' the fragments of brain tissue remaining along with the dura would have dried out relatively rapidly and would not have been extensively infiltrated by bacterial spores.

Analytical Electron Microscopy (AEM)

The application of analytical electron microscopy to the study of Egyptology was first reported in 1975 (Tapp, Curry and Anfield 1975). AEM was used to analyse crystalline material found within lung tissue. Since this publication we have used AEM to examine certain mummies for the presence of heavy metals.

Present-day disorders caused by lead, mercury or other metal poisoning are particularly unpleasant. In most cases such poisoning is the result of the inadequate disposal of industrial waste and hence receives much publicity (Hunter 1971). Thus, modern man is exposed to small quantities of certain heavy metals because he lives in an industrial society. We therefore regard such problems as being of fairly recent origin, but did ancient civilizations suffer from cases of metal poisoning and what quantities of such metals occur in Ancient Egyptians? Examination of Egyptian mummy material for chemical poisoning has been previously undertaken by an American group using the neutron activation test and atomic absorption (Cockburn, Borraco, Reyman and Peck 1975) and they have found significantly lower concentrations of lead in bone compared to modern man, although the concentration of mercury was about the same.

Materials and Methods Material was rehydrated (see Materials and Methods, TEM), but was not post-fixed in osmium tetroxide. The small pieces were dehydrated in a graded series of alcohols and embedded in an Epon/ Araldite mixture. Sections were cut on an LKB Ultratome III ultramicrotome using a diamond knife, and coated in carbon in a vacuum coating unit. The sections were examined, unstained, in either an A.E.I. Corinth 275 electron microscope fitted with a Kevex Si (Li) x-ray detector or an A.E.I. Cora analytical electron microscope.

An A.E.I. EM801 was used for the electron micro-diffraction studies.

Results (a) *The examination of diseased lung material* The discovery of diseased lung in Nekht-ankh and its full histological examination has been described in Dr Tapp's earlier chapter. In essence, birefringent particles were seen around blood vessels and in fibrotic areas of the lung indicating disease during life. These particles proved to be of a crystalline nature as they produced an electron diffraction pattern when examined in a transmission electron microscope operating in the electron diffraction mode (13).

The elemental nature of these crystals was examined on three occasions and the surrounding tissues and resin were taken as control areas. A typical result of the crystal analysis is illustrated (14) and the results tabulated (15).

These results indicate that there is a high proportion of silicon, iron and titanium in the crystals with significantly lower levels in the tissue and resin. This would seem to indicate that the crystals are detrital quartz (SiO_2) grains.

(b) *Examination of mummy material for heavy metals* Lung and liver from Nekht-ankh, intestine from Asru and brain/dura from an isolated head were examined in A.E.I. Cora for the presence of heavy metals. No trace was found of any heavy metal in any of these tissues.

Discussion Pulmonary silicosis is common in miners, quarry workers and potters and may produce consider-

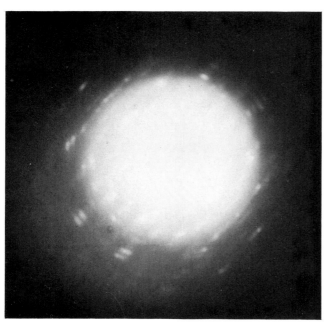

(13) Electron diffraction pattern of crystals found in lung tissue indicating that crystal symmetry is present.

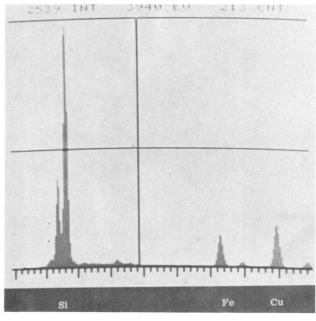

(14) A typical elemental analysis result of the crystals found in lung tissue. Cu peak is from copper specimen grid.

able morbidity and mortality (Cockburn et al. 1975). According to Berry et al. (1976) deposits in lungs of patients with pneumoconiosis were demonstrated to be of crystalline nature by electron diffraction. By contrast, 'normal' patient lung deposits were amorphous in nature; Nekht-ankh undoubtedly had deposits in his lungs and these were of a crystalline nature. The analysis of the deposits suggests that they were sand and thus Nekht-ankh undoubtedly suffered from sand pneumoconiosis. This condition is known in modern Bedouins (Bar-Ziv and Goldberg 1974). Nekht-ankh is unlikely to have been a stone worker and it therefore suggests that his condition was a result of inhalation of sand, silt and/or clay-sized particles during dust-storms. This condition of sand pneumoconiosis in Nekht-ankh is not unique as it is known that Pum II also suffered from this condition (Cockburn et al. 1975).

A.E.I. Cora can detect 10^{-17}–10^{-18} grams of an element if it is present in a sample. Thus, the absence of lead, mercury or other heavy metals in the tissues of the mummies examined is interesting. Perhaps the preparation of the samples for examination eliminated these elements. However, this explanation seems unlikely in view of the low solubility of compounds containing lead or mercury. It seems that heavy metal pollution or conditions caused by exposure to these toxic elements were not common in ancient Egypt. Similar results were obtained by Cockburn et al. (1975) who found that the lead content of two Egyptian mummies examined was

significantly smaller than that of modern man. The mercury level in Pum I and Pum II was, however, found to be the same as that found in modern man. This last result is surprising and is in contrast to the results obtained from the Manchester mummies. It is obvious that this aspect of examination of ancient bodies deserves more attention, and certainly needs to be tackled using several analytical methods. In conclusion it would seem that modern man is exposed to considerable lead pollution compared to Egyptian man.

Scanning Electron Microscopy (SEM)

Scanning electron microscopy was principally used to examine the insect remains found in the mummies, but was also used to examine the surface structure of some mummy hair in the hope of elucidating the race of each of the two brothers, Nekht-ankh and Khnum-Nakht.

The sarcophagi of the two brothers depict one to be negroid and the other of the 'semitic' type. This puzzling situation obviously leads to some interesting speculation as to the parentage of these men. However, was there any race difference between these two brothers? There are pigmentatory and structural differences between the hair of these two races and it was hoped to elucidate any differences by examination of the hair remains from these men whose mummified bodies had been unwrapped earlier this century by Margaret Murray who placed the remains in large storage jars.

FIG. 15 *Major elements found in the crystals of Nekht-ankh's lungs*

Elements: Si, S (small amount), Cl, K, Ca, Fe.
Surrounding tissue (control): Si (small amount), S (small amount), Cl.
Surrounding tissue-free resin (control): Si (small amount), S (small amount), Cl.

Quantitative analysis with reference to the elements Si, Fe, Ti

	crystals	crystals	crystals	crystals	resin (control)
Si peak (P)	3899	3926	14505	11576	1096
background (B)	990	1332	3816	2853	666
P – B	2909	2594	10689	8723	430
$\frac{P-B}{B}$	2.94	2.94	2.80	3.08	0.65
Fe peak	1031	1044	5147	2903	535
B	279	324	1494	1350	405
$\frac{P-B}{B}$	2.69	2.22	2.45	1.15	0.32
Ti peak	546	—	2524	1877	—
B	414	—	1782	1476	—
$\frac{P-B}{B}$	0.32	—	0.42	0.27	—

Quantitative analysis using A.E.I. Cora (no Ti found)

	crystals	tissue (control)	resin (control)
Si peak	1003	88	83
B	165	65	65
$\frac{P-B}{B}$	5.08	0.35	0.27
Fe peak	262	28	—
B	40	23	—
$\frac{P-B}{B}$	5.5	0.21	—

Materials and Methods The dried specimens of hair were attached to SEM stubs by conductive adhesive and coated in gold using either a sputter coater (Edwards) or a vacuum coating unit (A.E.I.). These were examined in either an A.E.I. Corinth 275 electron microscope fitted with an S.E.M. attachment (CESA) or a Cambridge S4–10 Stereoscan. Images were recorded on Ilford FP4 film.

Results All hair samples examined in this study were reddish in colour and examination under the scanning electron microscope showed samples to have an identical structure. The outer surface of the hair is covered by flattened imbricated scales.

Discussion The study of human hair is a much more complex subject than it first appears (Brothwell and Spearman 1963) as micro-organisms, bleaching in life, preparation of the body after death and exposure to atmosphere can alter the colour. Indeed the bodies found preserved in peat in Denmark (Glob 1969) had red hair, as have mammoths recovered from permafrost regions (Carrington 1958). In view of these facts the colour of hair would not appear to be useful. However, as the structure of the hair examined was all found to be identical, two conclusions are possible: The hair of one of the brothers was not preserved or both brothers were of identical race.

Assessment of the application of electron microscope techniques in palaeopathology

The interpretation of the ultrastructural appearance of freshly fixed tissues, under the transmission electron microscope is difficult, to say the least. Tissues, thousands of years old, which were either allowed to dry out naturally or subjected to mummification processes, present an almost overwhelming number of problems in interpretation of TEM results. There are bound to be many artefacts produced by shrinkage, putrefaction or embalming methods.

Subcellular components can be identified from dried soft tissues, as demonstrated by the liver tissue examined in this study. These organelles indicate the success or failure of embalming techniques. Microscopic diagnosis of disease is largely a matter of cellular arrangement and organization rather than the appearance of subcellular components. In this context TEM can only be used as an interesting extension of normal light microscope examinations.

The presence of foreign bodies or material is of diagnostic relevance. The identification of parasitic worm remains and the inference of associated disease is possible, though difficult. The number of micro-organisms present can also be an indication of the state of preservation of tissues prior to mummification.

The analytical electron microscope has been proven to be useful in this study. The structural preservation of the cellular components is not as important in this technique as in transmission electron microscopy and consequently the results are more meaningful. However, leaching of certain salts or addition of salts during embalming must add caution to the interpretation of results. Without the analytical electron microscope, the chemical compositon and therefore the identification of the crystalline deposits in the lung tissue from Nekht-ankh, would have been difficult.

The application of scanning electron microscopy to palaeopathology is limited. In this study it has been used to examine the surface structure of hair and the fragile insect remains.

In summary, it appears that transmission electron microscopy is of limited practical diagnostic use in palaeopathology unless disease is produced by the presence of foreign material. As an extension of routine light microscope investigations, it is interesting from an academic point of view. The analytical electron microscope results indicate a bright future for this relatively new technique in the field of palaeopathology.

Acknowledgements

We are grateful to A.E.I. Scientific Apparatus Ltd (Kratos), Mr P. Gooch and Mr Robin Grayson for their assistance in this project.

References

A. Ascenzi (1963), 'Microscopy and prehistoric bone', in *Science in Archaeology*, ed. D. Brothwell and E. Higgs, London.

J. Bar-Ziv and G. M. Goldberg (1974), *Archives of Environmental Health*, 29, 121.

J. P. Berry, P. Henoc, P. Galle and R. Pariente (1976), 'Pulmonary mineral dust', *American Journal of Pathology*, 83, 427.

L. A. Borradaile, F. A. Potts, L. E. S. Eastham and J. T. Saunders (1967), *The Invertebrata*, Cambridge.

D. Brothwell and A. T. Sandison (1967), *Diseases in Antiquity*, Thomas, Springfield, Illinois.

D. Brothwell and R. Spearman (1963), 'The hair of earlier peoples', in *Science in Archaeology*, ed. D. Brothwell and E. Higgs, London.

R. Carrington (1958), *Elephants, A short account of their natural history, evolution and influence on mankind*, The Scientific Book Club, London.

A. Cockburn, R. A. Barraco, T. A. Reyman and W. H. Peck (1975), 'Autopsy of an Egyptian mummy', *Science*, 187, 1155.

P. V. Glob (1969), *The Bog People*, Faber and Faber Ltd.

P. S. Gooch (1975), *Helminths in archaeological and prehistoric deposits*, Annotated bibliography No. 9, Commonwealth Institute of Helminthology, St Albans, Herts.

L. Hufnagel (1973), Communication in *Paleopathology Newsletter*.

D. Hunter (1971), *The diseases of occupations*, English Universities Press Ltd.

T. S. Leeson (1959), 'Electron microscopy of mummified material', *Stain Technol*, 34, 317.

P. Lewin (1967), 'Paleo-electron microscopy of mummified tissue', *Nature*, 213, 416.

P. Lewin (1968), 'The ultrastructure of mummified skin cells', *Can. Med. Ass. J.*, 98, 1011.

R. F. Macadam and A. T. Sandison (1969), 'The electron microscope in Palaeopathology', *Medical History*, 13, 81.

G. A. Meek (1976), *Practical electron microscopy for biologists*, Wiley-Interscience.

M. A. Ruffer (1921), *Studies in the paleopathology of Egypt*, ed. R. L. Moodie, Chicago.

A. T. Sandison (1955), 'The histological examination of mummified material', *Stain Technol.*, 30, 277.

E. Tapp, A. Curry and C. Anfield (1975), 'Sand pneumoconiosis in an Egyptian Mummy', *B.M.J.*, 3 May.

G. W. Yeatman (1971), 'Preservation of chondrocyte ultrastructure in an Aleutian Mummy', *Bull. N.Y. Acad. Med.*, 47, 104.

111

The Insects Associated with the Manchester Mummies

A. Curry

Summary

The insects found in the Manchester Museum collection of Mummies are described. Various beetles, true flies, and a cockroach have been identified. The feeding habits and the probable time of infestation by these insects is discussed.

Introduction

The ancient Egyptians were well aware of the insects that existed in Egypt. Indeed, a mythology was based on the activities of a dung beetle, *Scarabaeus sacer* (Evans 1975). This sacred beetle's activities were seen by the Egyptians as a reflection of the world around them and was a symbol of rebirth. Likenesses of this beetle were put into tombs to ensure the soul's immortality. Lice and fleas are recorded in Egyptian papyri (Brothwell and Sandison 1967). Some Egyptian plagues were entomological in nature, being composed of flies or locusts (Cloudsley-Thompson 1976). Herodotus (480–425 B.C.) wrote that the ancient Egyptians slept under the protection of mosquito nets (Cloudsley-Thompson 1976). Also, honey from bees was collected by ancient Egyptians (Cloudsley-Thompson 1976).

The Egyptians, unlike many other civilizations in the ancient world, did store food as a safeguard against famine and they effectively stored their dead. There is evidence that ancient Egyptian foodstores suffered infestations by insects (Hinton 1945). It seems likely that insect pests were troublesome to the Egyptians and it was no surprise therefore that several of the mummies and associated canopic jars in the Manchester collection were found to contain insect remains. However, the finding of dead insects with mummies does not necessarily mean that the infestation originated in antiquity. The parasitic worms found in this study of the Manchester mummies must have been present in ancient times as these parasites need living hosts. It is less easy to predict

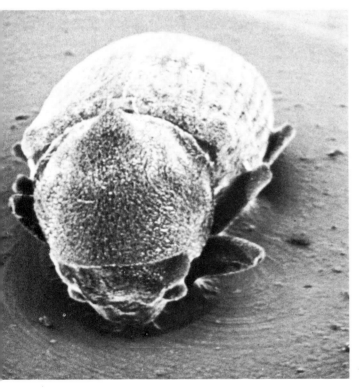

(**1**) An adult woodworm, *Anobium punctatum*, found in a wooden sarcophagus. ×26.

(**2**) Insects found in mummy '1770', *Necrobia rufipes* (*top right*), puparia of common house fly, *Musca domestica* (*top left*), wing case of a carabid beetle (*bottom right*), puparia of the cheese skipper, *Piophila casei* (*bottom left*). All ×6.

113

the time of infestation by insects. Beetles, depending on their habits, could invade a body at the time of death, during its subsequent embalming, in the tomb, during transportation, or on display in a museum. Certain beetles can be serious pests of museum collections if special precautions are not taken. The museum beetle, *Anthrenus museorum*, is a cosmopolitan species and has been found in a mummified fish (Leek 1978), but not in any of the Manchester mummies.

Deducing the time of infestation by flies is easier as their larval stages do require a moist food source. In forensic science estimates can be made of the time of death by the fly larvae present and their stage of development (Smith 1973; Jane 1975). Even here there may be uncertainty as some dipteran flies can infect the human body during life and cause a type of disease called myiasis (Oldroyd 1964; Zumpt 1965).

Insects are identified by the various features found on their exoskeleton and this can be relatively easy if they are adult insects. Larval stages are much less well known scientifically than adult insects and hence are more difficult to identify. Often insects from the mummies are incomplete, because parts of their exoskeletons have broken off and are missing, rendering identification difficult.

Materials and Methods

Most insects were found by carefully examining either the exterior of the mummy wrappings and their sarcophagi or by sorting through the remains of '1770' and the jars containing the remains of Nekht-ankh and Khnum-Nakht, who had been unwrapped earlier this century by Margaret Murray. The insect exoskeletons were very fragile. Examination was undertaken either by viewing under a dissection microscope or in the scanning electron microscope (SEM). SEM specimens were attached to stereoscan stubs with a conductive adhesive and coated in gold, either in an Edwards sputter coater or using a rotator in an A.E.I. vacuum coating unit. These were examined either in an A.E.I. Corinth 275 electron microscope fitted with a scanning attachment (CESA), or in a Cambridge S4–10 Stereoscan.

A novel technique was used to free insects remains from the hardened mass of canopic jar material of Asru. Pieces were immersed in a 10 per cent solution of buffered formalin for several hours. The rehydrated pieces were examined using a dissection microscope and complete larval skins of flies teased out.

Results

The common woodworm, *Anobium punctatum*, was present in the wooden sarcophagi of several of the mummies in the collection (**1**).

'1770', the mummy which was unwrapped, contained within its bandages a multitude of insects. The commonest were a beetle, *Necrobia rufipes* (**2**) and a dipteran fly, *Piophila* probably *P. casei* (**2** and **3**). Adult beetles, but only one adult fly were found, the majority of the fly's remains being puparia. *Piophila* puparia were scarce in the outer bandage layers, but numerous in the inner bandages and body of '1770'. A few puparia of the

(**3**) Empty puparium of *Piophila casei*. ×29.

(**4**) Puparium of *Chrysomyia albiceps*. ×28.

114

common house-fly, *Musca domestica*, were in the inner bandages and bodily remains of '1770' (2). The body also housed a few wing cases (elytra) of a carabid beetle (2).

The remains of the two brothers, Nekht-ankh and Khnum-Nakht, were inundated in insects different to those found in '1770'. Puparia of a dipteran fly *Chrysomyia* probably *C. albiceps*, were common (4). The predominant beetle was an unusual species, *Gibbium psylloides*, unusual because it resembles a giant mite and has the common name of the hump spider beetle (5). Smaller numbers of a second beetle, *Mesostenopa sp.* were also found in the remains of the two brothers (6). Unidentified fragments of a third beetle were also found in the remains of the two brothers (7).

Intact larval skins of *Chrysomyia*, probably *C. albiceps*, were common in the intestinal remains of Asru, found in a canopic jar (8).

An object attached to the outer wrappings of mummy '1767', another mummy in the Manchester collection, proved to be the egg case (ootheca) of a cockroach, *Blatta orientalis* (9). The egg case was firmly attached to the canvas covering of this mummy by the wax used as part of the wrapping process.

The results are summarized in Table I.

Discussion

The woodworm, *Anobium punctatum*, is a highly destructive beetle which has been estimated to be present in up to three-quarters of the buildings in Britain (Hickin 1964). This insect will consume almost all types of wooden structure, so its presence in the sarcophagi of several mummies is not unexpected. The infestation of these wooden sarcophagi with *Anobium* could have occurred at any time in their history.

Piophila is more commonly known as the cheese skipper and is a domestic pest (Oldroyd 1964). It is known to breed in cheese, bacon, ham and similar foodstuffs and, because of these habits, it can be eaten accidentally. The larvae are extremely resistant to gastric juices and consequently can survive to attack the gut wall causing bleeding of the intestine (Zumpt 1965; Oldroyd 1964). Mummy '1770' may have been infected during life but, as *Piophila* is a pest of stored meat, it seems that infestation occurred after death. Some of the extreme deterioration of this mummy was undoubtedly caused by the ravages of this fly and of the beetle, *Necrobia*. *Piophila* puparia were also found in the body cavity of a mummy Pum II unwrapped in Detroit and were covered in resin from the embalming process (Cockburn et al. 1975).

Necrobia rufipes can infest carrion during the fermentation stage when the carcass is drying out, feeding on the skin and ligaments (Evans 1975). In addition to eating some of the flesh of '1770', *Necrobia* would probably have attacked and eaten the larvae of the cheese skipper, as it has been reported to prey on larvae of other species in the same food source (Hinton 1945).

The common house-fly, *Musca domestica*, is probably the most familiar of all insects and has accompanied man everywhere (Oldroyd 1964; Cloudsley-Thompson 1976). It breeds in waste food or faeces if the larval food source is not too dry (Hickin 1964).

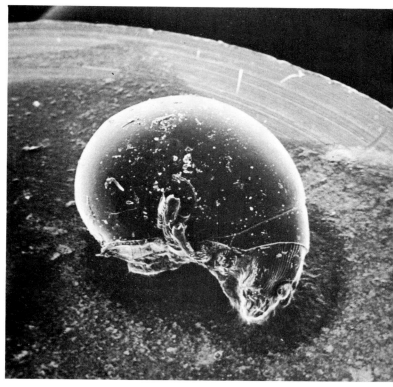

(5) An adult hump spider beetle, *Gibbium psylloides*. ×36.

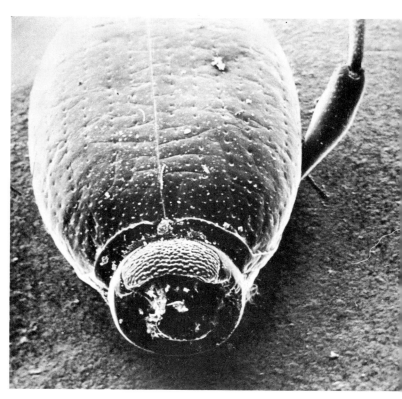

(6) Remains of beetle, *Mesostenopa sp.* from the two brothers. ×30.

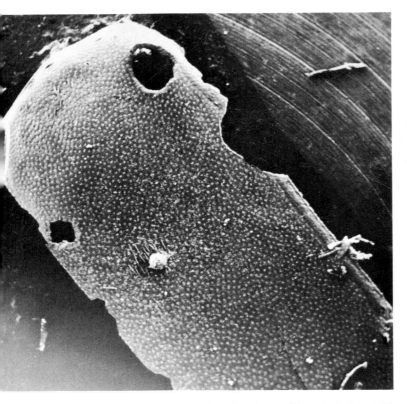

(7) Wing case of an unidentified beetle. Note the holes which have been produced by the feeding activities of other insects. ×24.

If '1770' had been correctly embalmed originally, a few insects in the body would not have been unexpected. Carbon-14 dating (see section by Newton) has shown that the bandages of '1770' are considerably younger than the body. As these 'new' bandages contained many of the insects, it suggests that the body of '1770' was rehydrated, perhaps by flooding of the tomb. This flooding could be the reason why '1770' was rewrapped and perhaps the lower limbs were 'mislaid' at this time.

The many insects living in '1770' did not have an idyllic life surrounded by food, because a carabid beetle was present. Carabids are predaceous beetles (Evans 1975) and were probably feeding on the other insects present in the tissues and wrappings of '1770'.

Chrysomyia found in the two brothers and Asru is known to lay eggs on carrion, which the larvae eat voraciously, but it has predaceous and cannabalistic habits (Oldroyd 1964; Zumpt 1965). As with the cheese skipper, this fly was also found in Pum II, unwrapped in Detroit (Cockburn et al. 1975).

Gibbium psylloides is a serious pest of vegetable products and may therefore have used the bandages of Nekht-ankh and Khnum-Nakht as a food source (Hinton 1945; Hickin 1964). *Gibbium* has long been known to infest grain products and has been reported previously from the tombs of Egyptian Pharaohs (Hinton 1945).

Beetles such as *Mesostenopa* (Tenebrionidae) are pests of stored food and live in sandy, arid environments (Evans 1975).

The ootheca of the cockroach, *Blatta orientalis*, was firmly attached to the bandages of '1767', and was thus of ancient origin. '1767' is a mummy from the Roman period and dates somewhere between A.D. 100–200. This evidence of association with man is, perhaps, not unexpected as *Blatta orientalis* is thought to be a native of North Africa (Cornwell 1968). Cockroaches associated with man attack and consume a wide range of food products and what is not ingested is fouled (Hickin 1964).

The Egyptian art of mummification was to some extent countered by the ravages of insect attack. Insects use a body as a food source and not as a sacred object. Of the two types of insects commonly encountered, the dipteran flies probably infested the bodies prior to or during embalming, unless the bodies were rehydrated at a later period. In contrast, some of the beetles may have infested the mummies at any time during their history. The cockroach's and the house-fly's association with human civilization is demonstrably of ancient origin. Thus the common insect pests of modern man were probably just

(8) Larvae of *Chrysomyia albiceps*, recovered from a piece of rehydrated stomach. ×6.

(9) Egg case of the cockroach, *Blatta orientalis.* ×6.

116

as much a problem to the ancient Egyptians. Life in ancient Egypt was clearly not idyllic. Insects were probably pests around the household, a serious nuisance to the embalmer, and common in food storage buildings.

Acknowledgements

The assistance of Colin Johnson and Alan Brindle (Department of Entomology, Manchester Museum), Ken Smith (British Museum, Natural History), Robin Grayson, John Hutton and A.E.I. Scientific Apparatus Ltd (Kratos) is greatly appreciated.

References

D. Brothwell and A. T. Sandison, 1967, *Diseases in Antiquity*, Thomas Springfield, Illinois.

J. L. Cloudsley-Thompson, 1976, *Insects and History*, Weidenfeld and Nicolson.

A. Cockburn, R. A. Barraco, T. A. Reyman and W. H. Peck, 1975, 'Autopsy of an Egyptian Mummy', *Science*, 187, 1155–60.

P. B. Cornwell, 1968, *The Cockroach* (Vol I), *A Laboratory Insect and an Industrial Pest*, Hutchinson, London.

G. Evans, 1975, *The Life of Beetles*, Hafner Press, New York.

N. E. Hickin, 1964, *Household Insect Pests*, Hutchinson, London.

H. E. Hinton, 1945, *Beetles Associated with Stored Products*, Vol. I, Published by Trustees of British Museum (Natural History).

R. P. Lane, 1975, 'An Investigation into Blowfly Succession on Corpses', *J. Nat. Hist.*, 9, 581–88.

F. Filce Leek, 1978, *Eutropius niloticus, J.E.A.*, 64, 121–22.

H. Oldroyd, 1964, *The Natural History of Flies*, Weidenfeld and Nicolson.

K. G. V. Smith, 1973, *Insects and other Arthropods of Medical Importance*, Trustees of the British Museum (Natural History).

F. Zumpt, 1965, *Myiasis in Man and Animals in the Old World*, Butterworths and Co. Ltd.

Table I

	'1770'	Nekht-ankh/Khnum-nakht	Asru	'1767'	Various Sarcophagi
Coleoptera (beetles)	*Necrobia rufipes* adults +++	*Gibbium psylloides* adults ++++			*Anobium punctatum* adults +++
	Carabid Elytra +	*Mesostenopa sp.* adults ++ + unidentified fragments			
Diptera (true flies)	*Piophila*, probably *P. casei* 1 adult, puparia +++++	*Chrysomyia*, probably *C. albiceps* puparia ++++	*Chrysomyia*, probably *C. albiceps* larvae +++		
	Musca domestica puparia ++				
Dictyoptera (cockroaches)				*Blatta orientalis* ootheca +	

+++++ abundant   ++++ very common   +++ common   ++ occasional   + rare

The Analysis of the Wrappings of Mummy 1770

by

G. G. BENSON, S. R. HEMINGWAY and F. N. LEACH

Introduction

The unwrapping of an Ancient Egyptian mummy is a relatively infrequent event and the opportunities for scientific investigation of such remains have, in consequence, been few; previous reports on the composition of materials used in the mummification process have often been based on methods of analysis of a relatively insensitive or non-specific nature.[12]

The present investigation had three principal objectives: first, to describe and identify both microscopically and macroscopically the nature of the material of the bandages; second, to isolate and characterize the materials which may have been applied to the bandages and third, to compare the results of this investigation with those of previous workers. An empirical approach to the investigation was adopted, influenced partly by previous reports and partly by assumption of the availability of certain plant, animal and mineral products to the Ancient Egyptians.

Bandages used to wrap mummies were almost invariably prepared from the fibres of the flax plant (*Linum usitatissimum* L.).[2,12] The use of gum, rather than glue, to secure the bandages around the corpse was mentioned by Herodotus.[9] The source of such gum would probably have been *Acacia* species, possibly *A. senegal*, indigenous to the Upper Nile region. Glue, the residue obtained by the extraction of animal products such as skin, bone and cartilage with boiling water and evaporation of the solvent, was known in Ancient Egypt and used for a variety of purposes,[12] although its use as a bandage adhesive does not appear to have been documented.

The use of waxes by the Ancient Egyptians seems to have been confined to beeswax which has been found covering the ears, eyes, nose, mouth and embalming incision of a mummy.[12] Plant resins and gum resins, such as colophony, storax, mastiche, myrrh or olibanum were probably available to the embalmer and for application to wrappings.[12]

There has been some debate as to whether bitumen from the Dead Sea was used in mummification. Early references to this include those by Diodorus[3] and Strabo.[18] Abraham[1] quotes a reference to the use of bitumen both in the corpse cavities and to coat wrappings from about 500 B.C. to about 40 B.C. Spielman,[20] using ultra violet radiation and spectrographic analysis of the ash concluded that a series of black mummy materials which he examined occupied positions 'between undoubted bitumen and undoubted resins'. The presence of bitumen in a mummy of the Persian period was claimed by Zaki and Iskander[28] on the basis of detection of vanadium, molybdenum and nickel by spectrographic analysis, these elements being characteristic of bitumen.

The present investigation afforded an opportunity of evaluating the applicability of various current methods of analysis, particularly chromatography, in the identification of natural products used in mummification.

Experimental and Results

Bandages from four depths of the mummy wrapping (ranging from the outer wrapping — 1770/1 to the inner bandages overlying the skeleton — 1770/4) were examined at each stage of the investigation.

A: BANDAGE FABRIC

(a) *Macroscopical description* The bandages from the outer layer (1770/1) were in the form of folded strips of fabric, paler brown and less brittle than the bandages of parts 2, 3 and 4 which were irregularly-shaped pieces of very dark brown, fragile material.

1. Weave description: fabrics of different weave were found as illustrated (**1**). Small samples with either hem-stitched edges or fringing were also included.

2. Weave density: numbers of threads per cm were determined using a linen tester. The values (averages from four determinations) are given in Table 1.

In the absence of selvedges it was not possible to distinguish warp and weft so in each case the lowest number of threads/cm is quoted first.

(b) *Microscopical examination of fibres* Fibres from all four parts of the bandages were examined after solvent extraction and drying (see section C (b)). The fibres were examined in water (after wetting with alcohol) and compared with authentic flax fibres (**2**). The fibres from the bandage were 9–21 μ diameter and those from flax 12–30 μ. It was not possible to measure the length of the fibres because they were broken. The reactions of the bandage fibres with 1 per cent alcoholic phloroglucinol solution and hydrochloric acid, N/50 iodine and sulphuric acid and cuoxam solution indicated that they were of non-lignified cellulose.

B: SURFACE DEPOSITS ON THE BANDAGES

(a) *Fine grey-white deposit* This was present on small areas of some bandages but was difficult to separate from the bandage fibres and therefore analysed *in situ* by x-ray electron microscopy. The results indicated the presence of the elements: Na, Mg, Si, P, S, Cl, K, Ca and Fe with Na, Cl and S predominant.

119

(b) *Adhesive* Several pieces of outer strip bandage bore patches of adhesive, fragments of which were scraped off or removed from the bandage by soaking in water and examined as follows:

1. Hydrolysis and paper chromatography 0.36 g glue was dissolved in water and diluted to 40 ml. 4 ml H_2SO_4 was added and the solution heated under reflux on a boiling water bath for 3 hr. The excess acid was neutralized using $BaCO_3$ and the solution examined by ascending PC on Whatman no. 1 paper. Solvent system: *n* BuOH/HOAC/H_2O 4:1:5.

Visualization of spots: (i) spray with aniline phthalate reagent (see p. 123) and heat at 105° for 2–5 min. (ii) spray with ninhydrin solution (0.1 g in 70 ml EtOH) and warm with a hot air dryer.

The results indicated that amino acids were present but monosaccharides absent. For comparison, a sample of gelatin was hydrolysed in a similar manner to the above and co-chromatographed with the glue from the bandage, together with solutions of L-proline and L-OH proline. The results are given in Table 2.

2. Amino acid analysis The results of automated amino acid analysis are given in Table 3.

C: BANDAGE IMPREGNATION

(a) *Bitumen*

1. Lassaigne Tests were performed on bandage samples from all layers and on samples of Dead Sea bitumen and galbanum. The results are given in Table 4.

2. Tests for Mo, Ni and V were performed using atomic absorption spectroscopy and neutron activation analysis. The results are given in Table 5.

3. Test for Ni was performed on a solution prepared by boiling the ash from approx. 1.8 g bandage with 0.5 ml 10% HCl. A drop of the resulting yellow-green solution was spotted on filter paper, one drop of 1% dimethylglyoxime in EtOH was added and the spot exposed to NH_3 vapour.[25] The resulting precipitate was brown rather than red.

(b) *Solvent extraction of bandages*

Samples from layers 1–4 of the bandages were extracted with a series of solvents of increasing polarity. Each bandage sample was cut into small pieces, weighed and successively extracted with light petroleum (80°–100°), $CHCl_3$, MeOH and H_2O (approximately 1 L each) in a Soxhlet apparatus. Extraction was continued with each solvent until the extract became colourless (6–18 hr).

A

B

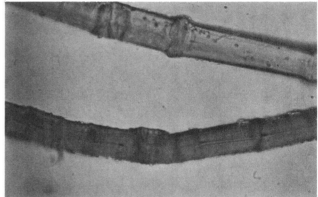

A

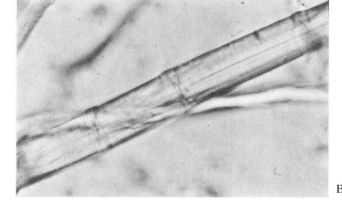

B

(1) Types of fabric weave (texture) found among the bandages wrapping Mummy 1770 (scale in cms).
(A) Coarse plain weave.
(B) Coarse double weave (double threads in both warp and weft).

(2) A. Typical fibre from mummy bandage (×630). Features to note include thickened fibre walls, narrow central cavity and 'beat marks'. Compare with authentic linen (flax) fibres, B.

The petroleum, CHCl₃ and MeOH extracts were evaporated to dryness under reduced pressure and the residues weighed. The aqueous extracts were concentrated to approx. 300 ml each. The residual bandage was dried to constant weight. The extractives of the bandage samples from each of the four parts are summarized in Table 6.

(c) *Chromatographic examination of residues*

1. Light petroleum extracts
    (i) Thin layer chromatography

Stationary phase: silica gel G 0.25 mm, activated at 110°, 30 min.

Mobile phases: A CCl₄[10]
               B C₆H₆/CHCl₃ 7:3[10]
               C *n* hexane/Et₂O/HOAc 90:10:1[21]

Visualization of spots: (a) examine plate in UV light (365 nm); (b) spray with 0.05% aqueous Rhodamine 6G[10] *or* spray with 20% alcoholic phosphomolybdic acid, heat at 105–110° for 5–10 min and examine in daylight.[21]

Reference substances: see Table 7.

The results of the chromatograms are summarized in Table 7.

    (ii) Gas Liquid chromatography
Gas chromatograph: Perkin Elmer F11 equipped with F.I.D., carrier gas (N₂) at 30 ml/min and the following stationary phases packed in 2 mm i.d. × 180 cm columns:
A 15% Carbowax 20 M on Chromosorb P (oven temp. 200°);
B 4% SE 30 on Gas Chrom Q (oven temp. 200°);
C 10% OV 17 on Chromosorb P (oven temp. 280°).

Reference substances: see Table 8.

The results of GLC examination are summarized in Table 8 and (4).

    (iii) Column chromatography: 1 g light petroleum extract from 1770/1 was applied to a column of approx. 100 g silica gel (100–120 mesh) in light petroleum (80°–100°). Elution with 150 ml light petroleum gave the hydrocarbon fraction of the wax (approx. 900 mg) and with CHCl₃ (100 ml) the ester fraction (64 mg).

    (iv) Preparative GLC:
Gas chromatograph: Varian Aerograph Autoprep 705 equipped with F.I.D., N₂ at 30 ml/min, oven temp. 200° and a 4 mm i.d. × 200 cm column packed with 20% Carbowax 20M on Chromosorb P.

Fractions were collected corresponding to the peaks having the following R_t (system A): 12.0, 17.0, 24.4, 35.0, 50.2 and 71.6. Each fraction was examined by mass spectrometry (70 eV, inlet temperature 200°) and the data (presented in Table 9) indicated a series of *n*-alkanes. Fractions corresponding to the peaks with R_t 17.0, 35.0 and 71.6 were also collected from yellow beeswax by a similar procedure. The MS were closely similar to those from the bandage extracts. A graph of log R_t against carbon number plotted for the six *n*-alkanes isolated from the bandage petroleum extract allowed the prediction of carbon numbers for those not isolated (3).

    (v) Preparative TLC of the ester fraction from (iii) resulted in 5.1 mg of the ester fraction free from

n-alkane. The corresponding fraction of yellow beeswax was obtained for comparison, using the same procedure. The MS (conditions as in (iv)) are summarized below:

ester from bandage extract, ions > m/e 200: m/e (% relative abundance) 732 (6), 704 (16), 676 (24), 648 (10), 620 (4), 465 (4), 437 (6), 420 (6), 392 (10), 313 (24), 285 (100), 267 (12), 257 (100), 239 (12);

ester from beeswax: 704 (24), 676 (50), 648 (35), 620 (33), 592 (46), 448 (4), 420 (10), 336 (13), 285 (7), 257 (100), 239 (17).

2: Chloroform extracts
Resins such as those mentioned on page 119 would have their maximum solubility in chloroform so principally the extracts prepared with this solvent were examined for resins but, as shown in (5) and Table 10, the petroleum and methanol extracts were also compared with authentic resins.

    (i) Thin layer chromatography
Stationary phase: silica gel G 0.25 mm, activated at 110°, 30 min.

Mobile phase: C₆H₆/MeOH 95:5, double development using 'S' chamber.[21]

Visualization of spots: (a) examine plate in UV light (365 nm); (b) spray with SbCl₃ in CHCl₃ followed by heating at 100°C for 10 min.

Reference substances: see Table 10.

    (ii) Gas Liquid chromatography

Conditions: Systems A and B as described opposite.

Results: the chromatograms indicated an absence of peaks due to wax hydrocarbons from the CHCl₃ and MeOH extracts and no additional information was obtained, other than that from the chromatograms of the light petroleum extracts.

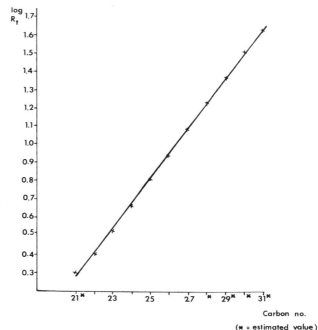

Carbon no.

(✳ = estimated value)

(3) Graph of carbon number against (log R_t) (System B) for *n*-alkanes from light petroleum extract of 1770/1 wrappings.

(iii) Isolation of umbelliferone
A saturated CHCl₃ solution of the CHCl₃ extract of 1770/1 bandages was applied to an alumina column (approx. 7 cm × 0.8 cm) and eluted with approx. 3 ml CHCl₃. The eluate was concentrated and subjected to preparative TLC by the system used in (i) above, except that the mobile phase was C_6H_6/CHCl₃ 95:5. The blue fluorescent band (UV, 365 nm) was eluted with CHCl₃ and the concentrated eluate compared on TLC with umbelliferone and galbanum as follows:

Stationary phase: Systems A and B — silica gel G, 0.25 mm, activated at 110° for 30 min.
System C — cellulose powder 0.3 mm, air dried.

Mobile phases: A C_6H_6/CHCl₃ 95:5 (×2, 'S' chamber)
 B MeOH/CHCl₃ 1:1
 C 10% aq. HOAc.[5]

Visualization of spots: examine plate in UV light (365 nm).

Reference solutions: 3% galbanum in CHCl₃ umbelliferone in EtOH.

Results: see Table 11.

3. Methanol extracts
 (i) Thin layer chromatography: see sections 2 and 4.
4. Aqueous extracts
 (i) Spot tests: a series of spot tests was carried out on aqueous extracts of layers 1, 2, 3 and 4, the methods and results of which are given in Table 12.

 (ii) TLC of plant acids:

Stationary phase: cellulose powder, 0.3 mm, air dried.

Mobile phases: A n BuOH/HCOOH/H₂O 4:1:5
 (upper layer)
 B n PrOH/1M NH₄OH 7:3
 C 95% EtOH/NH₄OH/H₂O 8:1:1[5, 19]

Visualization of spots: (a) 0.04% bromothymol blue in 0.01 M NaOH; (b) equal volumes of 0.1 M AgNO₃ and 0.1 M NH₄OH mixed immediately before spraying.

Reference substances: see Table 13.

Solutions of bandage extracts used: MeOH extracts in MeOH; aqueous extracts after removal of acid-insoluble precipitate by the following method: 10 ml concentrated

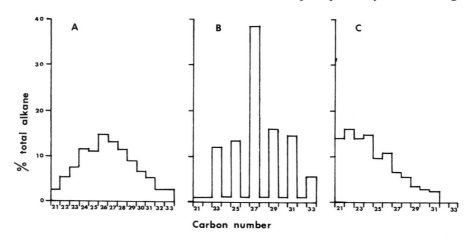

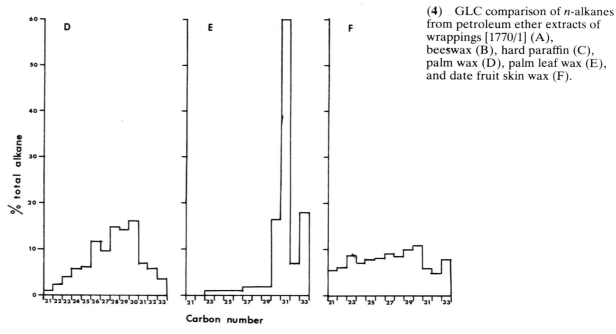

(4) GLC comparison of n-alkanes from petroleum ether extracts of wrappings [1770/1] (A), beeswax (B), hard paraffin (C), palm wax (D), palm leaf wax (E), and date fruit skin wax (F).

122

H₂O extract was mixed with 1 ml HCl and heated in a boiling water bath under reflux for 20 min., cooled and filtered.

The results of the chromatograms are summarized in Table 13. The MeOH and aqueous extracts from all layers gave similar results so only those from one are quoted.

(iii) Paper chromatography of monosaccharides: Descending chromatography on Whatman No. 1 paper.

Mobile phases: A n — BuOH/HOAc/H₂O 4:1:5
      B n — BuOH/EtOH/H₂O 4:1:5
      C PhOH saturated with H₂O.[5]

Visualization of spots: papers sprayed with aniline phthalate reagent (aniline, 1 ml + phthalic acid, 1.66 g in 100 ml n BuOH saturated with water) and heated at 105° for 2–5 min.
Reference substances: see Table 14.

To prepare the hydrolysates 1 g powdered gum or gum resin was heated under reflux with 5 ml H₂O and 1 ml HCl for 30 min. in a boiling water bath. The resulting mixture was filtered and washed with CHCl₃ (for gum resins) to yield an aqueous solution of gum hydrolysate.

Solutions of extracts used: hydrolysed aqueous extracts as in (ii).

The results of the chromatographs are summarized in Table 14. The aqueous extracts from all layers examined gave similar results so only those from one are quoted.

Discussion

A: BANDAGE FIBRES

An assortment of fabrics (1, Table 1) seems to have been used in wrapping the mummy. Near the skeleton quite large sheets of fabric were found, together with smaller pieces with hem-stitched edges or fringes, while strip bandages were used only for the outer layers. This could suggest that the lower layers were not particularly carefully chosen or applied, the uniform folded strips of bandage being reserved for the outer layer.

The only type of fibres which is reliably reported as having been used by the Ancient Egyptians for mummy bandages is flax. Wool, although available was not used in temples or when burying the dead. Of the other natural fibres, cotton, originally from India, and silk (from China) are thought to have been used in fabrics in Roman times or later, but have not yet been found in mummy wrappings; hemp (from an unspecified botanical source), ramie (from *Boehmeria nivea* (L.) Gand., Urticaceae) and kenaf (from *Hibiscus cannabinus* L., Malvaceae) were all indigenous to Egypt but they are coarse fibres and cannot be woven into fine fabrics.[11,12] All these fibres can be distinguished by their microscopical characters.[11,27] The fibres from the bandage fabrics were undoubtedly cellulosic and of plant origin and the diameter (9–21 μ) of the fibres, narrow lumen, pointed apices and cross markings are all strongly indicative of flax (2).

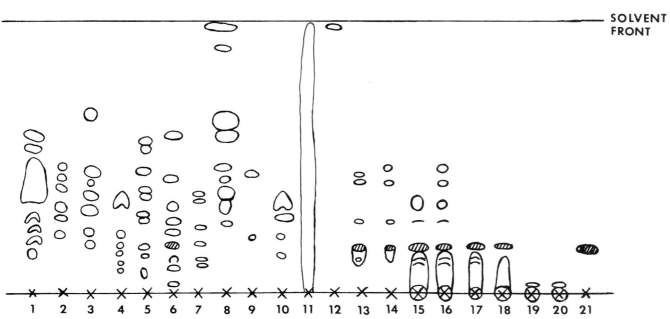

SOLVENT FRONT

(5) Thin layer chromatographic comparison of the petroleum ether, chloroform and methanol extracts of the mummy bandages with reference resins.

1. Colophony	2. Chios turpentine	3. Mastiche	4. Sandarac
5. Olibanum	6. Galbanum	7. Ladanum	8. Myrrh
9. Bdellium	10. Storax	11. Dead Sea asphalt	12. Pet. ether 1
13. Pet. ether 2	14. Pet. ether 3	15. CHCl₃ 1	16. CHCl₃ 2
17. CHCl₃ 3	18. MeOH 1	19. MeOH 2	20. MeOH 3
21. Umbelliferone			

B: SURFACE DEPOSITS

(a) *Grey-white deposit* The identity of the fine greyish-white deposit on parts of the bandage was not conclusively established since there were several elements present. The predominance of Na, K, S and Cl might suggest that it was composed of the chlorides and sulphates of sodium and potassium from a crude mineral source.

(b) *Adhesive* The glue on the surface of some of the outer strip bandages was expected to be a gum of plant origin, e.g. Acacia[9] but hydrolysis and a preliminary paper chromatogram indicated that it was protein rather than polysaccharide. The presence of L-OH proline in the hydrolysate suggested that the gum was a collagen-derived protein since this amino acid is otherwise rare.[13] The results of chromatography and amino acid analysis of the glue hydrolysate (Tables 2 and 3) indicated that the glue was gelatin of very similar amino acid composition to that of the modern product. The presence of gelatin is somewhat surprising in view of the taboo, reported by Herodotus,[9] on the use of animal products in mummification.

C: BANDAGE IMPREGNATION

(a) *Bitumen* Spielman[20] and Zaki and Iskander[28] have suggested that bitumen (asphalt) from the Dead Sea was used in the preparation of mummy wrappings. Bitumen consists of a colloidal suspension of carbon in a hydrocarbon oil which contains about 6–8% sulphur.[26] As such, it has a rather low solubility in any solvent so tests were performed on the whole bandage rather than extracts. The Dead Sea bitumen used for comparison could be dispersed in light petroleum (80–100°) but the resulting suspension gave no useful thin-layer or gas-liquid chromatograms. According to Spielman the presence of the metals molybdenum, nickel and vanadium, as well as sulphur can be used as a means of identification of bitumen in mummies.

Lassaigne tests on the wrappings of 1770 (Table 4) showed that sulphur was absent from the outer layer of the bandages but present in layers 2, 3 and 4 and in the bitumen used for comparison. Galbanum was included in the tests because subsequent results indicated its presence in the bandage. The identification of nitrogen and halogen in all layers of the bandage is not surprising in view of their presence in galbanum.

The results of the analyses for Mo. Ni and V (Table 5) were positive for Mo and V in both the bandage and Dead Sea bitumen although Ni could not be detected in the bandage by any of the methods used. This may be due to the relative insensitivity of the methods but means that the evidence for the presence of bitumen in the wrappings is incomplete, although the detection of S, Mo and V provides a strong indication of its use in the lower layers.

(b) *Solvent extraction* The yields of extractives to various solvents (Table 6) indicate a marked difference between the outer bandages and those nearer the skeleton; 1770/1 bandages gave a higher petroleum extractive than any of the other layers but contained much less water-soluble material. Beneath the outer layers, the amount of petroleum-soluble matter decreased towards the interior but there was no consistent trend in any of the other values.

(c) *Chromatographic examination of extracts* The results of the examination of the petroleum extractive (Table 7) suggested the presence of beeswax in all four layers of the bandage, with spots corresponding to the *n*-alkane and ester fractions being most prominent.[10] Beeswax consists of 70–80% myricyl palmitate ($C_{15}H_{31}COOC_{30}H_{61}$) together with free cerotic acid ($C_{26}H_{53}COOH$) and various minor components,

TABLE 1   Weave densities of mummy bandage fabrics

Bandage from part no.	threads/cm	threads/cm
1770/1 (single weave)	8	18
2 (single weave)	8	18
2 (double weave)*	12	18
3 (single weave)	11	32
3 (single weave)	8	23
3 (double weave)*	14	22
4 (single weave)	13	22
4 (single weave)	16	17
4 (double weave)*	14	22

*numbers quoted are of single threads, e.g. 12 single threads = 6 double threads

TABLE 2   Results of comparison of hydrolysis products of glue from bandages with those of gelatin

hRf	Colour with ninhydrin	Presence (√) or absence (—) in solutions of:			
		L-proline	L–OH proline	glue hydrolysate	gelatin hydrolysate
61	purple	—	—	√	√
46	purple	—	—	√	√
38	yellow	—	—	√	√
31	yellow	√	—	√	√
27	purple	—	—	√	√
23	purple	—	—	√	√
20	yellow	—	√	√	√
14	purple	—	—	√	√

TABLE 3 Results of Amino Acid analysis of glue from bandages and gelatin

Amino Acid	Residues per 1000 total AA residues	
	Bandage Glue	Gelatin
OH-Pro	99.05	101.00
Asp	46.61	47.86
Thr	17.78	19.21
Ser	36.76	35.79
Glu	81.71	80.48
Pro	127.92	125.77
Gly	288.48	305.80
Al	115.30	106.21
Cyst	0.0	0.0
Val	22.76	19.94
Meth	7.20	6.41
Ileu	11.02	10.69
Leu	29.75	26.75
Tyr	3.66	2.46
Phe	14.95	12.88
OH-Lys	11.29	13.08
Lys	28.28	27.86
Hist	8.92	8.10
Arg	48.55	49.70

TABLE 4 Results of Lassaigne tests on Bitumen, Galbanum and the mummy bandages

Material	Presence (√) or absence (—) of		
	S	N	Halogen
Dead Sea Bitumen	√√	?	(√)
Galbanum	—	√	(√)
Bandage 1770/1	—	√√	(√)
2	√	√	(√)
3	√	√	√
4	√	√	√

TABLE 5 Results of tests for Mo, Ni and V in Bitumen, Galbanum and the mummy bandages

Element	Content of Element (ppm) in:		
	Mummy bandage (1770/3)*	Dead Sea Bitumen	Galbanum
Mo	93.8 (AAS)†	219.3 (AAS)	<level of detection (AAS)
Ni	—‡	251.0 (AAS)	<level of detection (AAS)
V	11 ± 1 (NAA)	463.0 (AAS)	<level of detection (AAS)

* Additional elements present in mummy bandage (NAA): Mn 41±3 ppm; Al 1800±40 ppm; Na 0.33±0.04%; Cl 0.45±0.06%.
† Techniques used: AAS = Atomic Absorption Spectroscopy;
NAA = Neutron Activation Analysis.
‡ i.e., below level of detectability.

TABLE 6 Extractives of bandages

Part	Weight bandage (g)	% Extraction*				
		Light Petroleum 80°–100°	CHCl₃	MeOH	H₂O	Total
1770/1	87.745	8.8	4.7	3.4	0.3	17.2
2	101.415	2.8	9.7	15.0	21.6	49.0
3	28.165	1.9	8.6	7.0	30.0	48.0
4	30.040	0.8	4.5	3.1	30.5	39.0

* The light petroleum extracts were coloured as follows: from 1770/1 — pale yellow, layer 2 — orange-yellow, layers 3 and 4 — deep orange. All other extracts were very dark brown in colour.

principally a series of *n*-alkanes including nonacosane (C_{29}) and hentriacontane (D_{31}).[22,23]

In 1770/1 the spot corresponding to the hydrocarbon fraction of the wax was larger relative to the ester than in authentic beeswax, possibly suggesting either the presence of hydrocarbon from another source, or decomposition of the ester on storage. The chromatograms from the extracts of layers 2, 3 and 4 showed a yellow fluorescent streak and the extracts themselves have a bright orange colour, suggesting the presence of resin or other pigmented material in the lower layers. A mixture prepared by melting together galbanum and beeswax gave a similar colour and yellow streak on TLC, although the baseline spot fluoresced blue rather than yellow. The results of GLC of the petroleum extracts of 1770/2, 3 and 4 also suggest that a mixture of beeswax and galbanum may be present (Table 8).

MS of the ester fraction of the wax from the extract indicated clearly the presence of myricyl palmitate ($CH_3(CH_2)_{14}\overset{O}{C}-O(CH_2)_{29}CH_3$) with M^+ at m/e 676 and principal fragment ions at m/e 257 ($[C_{16}H_{33}O_2]^+$), 239 ($[CH_3(CH_2)_{14}C=O]^+$), 420 ($[C_{30}H_{60}]^+$) and 465 ($[CH_3(CH_2)_{29}-O-C=O]^+$). The ions at m/e 257 and 420 are considered to be derived by fission of the alkyl-oxygen bond with rearrangement of 2H from the alkyl group in the former and loss of H from the latter ([17] and references therein). In addition to the myricyl palmitate, there were ions suggesting the presence of higher homologues at M^+ m/e 704 and m/e 732.

The former is most probably due to a small amount of myricyl stearate since the fragments at m/e 285 and 267 would form from a stearate ester, while ions at m/e 448 and 293 which would be expected from a C_{32} alcohol palmitate are absent. The ion m/e 732 probably represents a trace amount of myricyl arachidate ($CH_3(CH_2)_{18}-\overset{O}{C}-O-(CH_2)_{29}-CH_3$) since the corresponding acid fragment at m/e 313 is observed in the spectrum. The esters of the wax are of too high molecular weight to be eluted from GLC columns under the conditions used. The peaks observed (Table 8) were shown by MS to be due to a series of *n*-alkanes of carbon number C_{21}–C_{33} (3). However, the quantitative differences in peak area observed for beeswax, in which the odd carbon number *n*-alkanes predominate, were not observed in the bandage extract. This suggests the presence of hydrocarbon from another source. In plant and insect waxes, odd numbered carbon *n*-alkanes generally predominate probably due to their biogenesis by the decarboxylation of even carbon

TABLE 7   Results of TLC comparison of petroleum ether extracts of mummy bandages with beeswax, beeswax and galbanum, and hard paraffin

hRf	Class of wax constituent[10]	Presence (√) or absence (—) of spot in						
		Beeswax	Beeswax + galbanum	Hard paraffin	Petroleum ether extracts of layers			
					1	2	3	4
System A								
77	*n*-alkanes	√	√	√	√	√	√	?streak
39	*n*-alkyl esters	√	√	—	(√)	√	√	√
11		√	√	—	—	(√)	√	√
6	*n*-secondary alcohols?	—	√	—	—	(√)	√	√
0		√	√*	—	(√)	√†	√†	√†
System B								
80	*n*-alkanes	√	√	√	√	√	√	√
73	*n*-alkyl esters	√	√	—	√	√	√	√
52 }	*n*-secondary alcohols?	(√)	(√)	—	—	—	(√)	(√)
40 }		(√)	(√)	—	—	(√)	(√)	(√)
20 }	*n* 1° alcohol	√	√	—	—	√	√	√
15 }		√	√	—	—	√	√	√
4	*n*-fatty acid	√	√	—	√	√	√	√
0		√	√*	—	√	√†	√†	√†
System C								
75		√	√	√	√	√	√	STREAK
62		√	√	—	√	√	√	
51		√	√	—	—	√	√	
39		√	√	—	—	√	√	
24		√	√	—	—	√	√	
13		√	√	—	—	√	√	
6		√	√	—	√	—	√	
0		√	√*	—	√	√†	√†	†

Footnotes:
* baseline spot fluoresced blue in UV (365 nm), with a yellow fluorescent streak extending from the baseline up the plate.
† yellow UV-fluorescent baseline spot with streak up the plate.

number fatty acids.[4] However, this is not universal and where alkanes form only a minor constituent of plant leaf waxes, as in the genera Pinus and Eucalyptus, alternation between odd and even carbon numbers through the homologous series is almost indiscernible.[6,7]

The leaf wax of Copernicia ceriferae Palmae (Carnuaba wax), shows such a non-alternating pattern as does the stem wax of Ceroxylon spp. Palmae ('Palm wax' of commerce) see (4). As both these plants are indigenous to South America, it is unlikely that their waxes would be available to the Ancient Egyptians. The waxes of two other members of the Palmae, Phoenix reclinata and P. canariensis do not show this anomalous pattern[8] but waxes from the leaves and fruits of P. dactylifera (the Date palm), a plant which was used by the Egyptians to produce wine,[2] were examined. Unlike the leaf wax, the fruit wax from this species did show an anomalous n-alkane pattern (4) but the small amounts of wax which can be extracted suggest that it would be an unlikely material for use in mummification and wrapping procedures. Further, it is reported[24] that the major monoesters of the palm waxes ouricury and carnauba are of

TABLE 8 Results of GLC comparison of petroleum ether extracts of mummy bandage with beeswax, beeswax and galbanum, hard paraffin and other reference waxes

n-alkane carbon no.	21	22	23	24	25	26	27	28	29	30	31	32	33
System A													
Rt. (min)	8.4	12.0	17.0	24.4	35.0	50.2	71.6	98.0	—	—	—	—	—
Beeswax	√	(√)	√	(√)	√	(√)	√	—	—	—	—	—	—
1770/1	√	√	√	√	√	√	√	√	—	—	—	—	—
2*	√	√	√	√	√	√	√	√	—	—	—	—	—
3*	√	√	√	√	√	√	√	√	—	—	—	—	—
4*	√	√	√	√	√	√	√	√	—	—	—	—	—
System B													
Rt.	2.0	2.6	3.4	4.6	6.4	8.6	12.2	17.0	23.4	32.2	43.0		
Beeswax	√	(√)	√	(√)	√	(√)	√	(√)	√	—	√	—	—
1770/1	√	√	√	√	√	√	√	√	√	√	√	—	—
2	√	√	√	√	√	√	√	√	(√	(√)	(√)	—	—
3	(√)	(√)	(√)	(√)	(√)	(√)	(√)	(√)	—	—	—	—	—
4	(√)	(√)	(√)	(√)	—	—	—	—	—	—	—	—	—
System C													
Rt.	3.4	4.4	5.4	6.8	8.6	10.8	13.7	17.4	22.0	28.4	35.4	45.4	57.4
Beeswax	(√)	(√)	√ (12)†	(√)	√ (13.4)	(√)	√ (38.2)	(√)	√ (16)	(√)	√ (14.2)	(√)	√ (5.9)
Hard paraffin	√ (14)	√ (16.1)	√ (14)	√ (14.7)	√ (9.6)	√ (10.5)	√ (6.4)	√ (5.5)	√ (3.3)	√ (2.9)	√ (2.35)	—	—
'Palm' wax	√ (0.7)	√ (2)	√ (3.9)	√ (5.5)	√ (5.9)	√ (11.5)	√ (9.7)	√ (14.9)	√ (14.2)	√ (15.8)	√ (7.0)	√ (5.9)	√ (3.0)
Date palm leaf wax	—	—	(√)	(√)	(√)	(√)	(√)	(√)	(√)	√ (16.0)	√ (60)	√ (6.4)	√ (17.5)
Date fruit skin wax	√ (5.8)	√ (6.0)	√ (8.3)	√ (7.2)	√ (7.7)	√ (8.0)	√ (9.2)	√ (8.4)	√ (10)	√ (10.6)	√ (5.8)	√ (5.0)	√ (8.0)
1770/1	√ (2.4)	√ (5.0)	√ (7.6)	√ (11.4)	√ (11.1)	√ (14.4)	√ (13.1)	√ (10.9)	√ (8.3)	√ (6.1)	√ (4.8)	√ (2.4)	√ (2.4)
2	√	√	√	√	√	√	√	√	√	√	√	√	√
3	√	√	√	√	√	√	√	√	√	√	√	√	√
4	√	√	√	√	√	√	√	√	√	√	√	√	√

Footnotes:
√ = present;   (√) = present (small peak)
* If beeswax is melted with galbanum and a petroleum ether extract subjected to GLC (System A), additional peaks are observed with the following Rt (min):
1.4, 1.8, 2.2, 3.0, 4.6, 5.0, 6.0, 9.6, 13.6, 14.6, 19.6. These peaks were also identified in chromatograms of the petroleum extracts of 1770/2, 3 and 4. The presence of additional peaks in the chromatograms of beeswax + galbanum and of extracts of 1770/2, 3 and 4 caused poor chromatograms in systems B and C. Wool fat, Dead Sea bitumen and olive oil produced no useful chromatograms under the conditions used.
† numbers in brackets indicate % of total n-alkane (area measurement).

TABLE 9   Mass spectral data on *n*-alkanes from a
light petroleum extract of bandage

R_t (min) (System A)	M^+ (m/e)*	$C_n H_{(2n+2)}$ n =
12.0	310	22
17.0	324	23
24.4	338	24
35.0	352	25
50.2	366	26
71.6	380	27

* In each case the MS indicated an $(M-15)^+$ ion and ions representing successive removals of 14 m.u., characteristic of an unbranched saturated alkane.

TABLE 10   Results of the TLC comparison of the petroleum ether, chloroform and methanol extracts with reference resins

hRf and colours of spot

Colophony	58, 54, 43, 29, 24, 20, 14
Chios Turpentine	46, 42, 31, 27, 21
Mastiche	66, 45, 41, 36, 30, 23, 18
Sandarac	35P, 22, 17, 14, 11, 8
Olibanum	56, 53, 45, 38, 35, 29, 26, 16, 13, 7
Galbanum	58, 42, 32GR, 26P, 22.5P, (17), 12P, 9
Ladanum	35P, 34GR, 24P, 18GR, 12P, 10
Myrrh	99MB, 91M, 63MB, 57MB, 46, 42, 37M, 32, 25
Bdellium	44, 20
Storax	34, 28, 21, 13
Dead Sea Asphalt	Black streak
1770 Pet. ether extract (1)	99*
(2)	43.5, 40.5, 26.5, (17), 12
(3)	46, 40, 26, (17)
1770 CHCl₃ extract (1)	33GR, 26, (17), 13, 11
(2)	47, 41, 31.5GR, 26, (17), 13, 11
(3)	(17), 13, 11
1770 MeOH extract (1)	(17)
(2)	3
(3)	3

Key:
( ) = bright blue fluorescence; P = purple, B = black,
GR = green, M = mauve. All other spots grey.
umbelliferone hRf = 17.
* Wax *n*-alkanes, rhodamine positive.

TABLE 11   Identification of Umbelliferone

System	hRf	blue fluorescent compound separated from chloroform extract of 1770/1	Galbanum	Umbelli-ferone
A	14	√	√	√
B	63	√	√	√
C	64	√	√	√

chain length C_{54}–C_{60}, in contrast to those of beeswax in the C_{46}–C_{48} range. The esters in the bandage extract were of similar chain length to those in beeswax and too low for palm wax.

Mineral waxes, which exhibit non-alternating patterns of *n*-alkanes (see **4**, hard paraffin) could have been used. The natural petroleum wax ozokerite, obtained from the shores of the Dead Sea[16] was known to the Ancient Egyptians, beads of this material having been found in some of their graves.[12] Recent GLC analysis shows that ozokerite from the shores of the Dead Sea contains 90% of its *n*-paraffins in the C_{36}–C_{45} range with a maximum at C_{38}.[16] However, in samples from other locations throughout the world, the ranges are lower,[14] therefore it is possible that ozokerite could have been mixed with the beeswax which was applied to the bandages. Other possibilities are that a form of beeswax was used which had a different *n*-alkane content or that paraffin wax was applied to the mummy in modern times.

TLC comparison of the petroleum ether, chloroform and methanol extracts of the wrappings with chloroform solutions of the resins and gum resins previously reported to have been available to the Ancient Egyptians[2,12] failed to give an immediate positive identification of the resin or resins which had been used to impregnate the bandages of 1770 (**5**). This is not entirely unexpected as the volatile compounds present in these products would be lost and others oxidized on storage. However, a blue fluorescent compound (hRf 17, Table 10) present in the petroleum ether and chloroform extracts of the wrappings was also present in the extract of galbanum but not in those of any other resin or gum resin examined. The blue fluorescent component of galbanum is a hydroxy-coumarin, umbelliferone (I).[23]

I

TLC investigation of the fluorescent compound separated from the bandage extracts suggests that it is also umbelliferone (Table 11). A further similarity between the wrapping extract and the galbanum solution is the presence in both of a compound (hRf 32, Table 10) which gives a green colour with the antimony trichloride reagent. Thus it seems possible that the gum resin galbanum which has previously only been reported as an ingredient of Ancient Egyptian toiletries and ointments[12] was used to impregnate the wrappings of this mummy.

The aqueous extracts formed a very high percentage of the total extractive for the lower layers of the bandage but little indication is given by either Lucas[12] or Baumann[2] of water-soluble substances which might have been used in Ancient Egypt, either in mummification and wrapping or in cosmetics and perfumes.

Those suggested include honey, aloes (dried juice of the leaves of *Aloe* spp., Liliaceae), extract of tamarind

128

fruits (*Tamarindus indica*, Leguminosae) and 'extract of Cassia fruits'. It is not clear from the accounts whether 'Cassia' in this context refers to *Cassia* spp. (Leguminosae) or to *Cinnamonum cassia* (Lauraceae), source of an aromatic bark. Since the former are indigenous to the Middle East and the latter to China, it is probable that *Cassia* spp. is intended.

Honey consists principally of invert sugar and water[23] and is considered to be absent from the bandage extract since fructose was not detected among the sugars in the aqueous extracts by paper chromatography (Table 14). Aloes and *Cassia* spp. both contain anthraquinone glycosides, for example, glycosides of aloe-emodin anthrone (II) found in aloes.

II

Glycosides of this type are detectable by Bornträger's reaction[23] but this gave a negative result for the bandage extract (Table 12). It thus seems unlikely that either honey, aloes or extract of *Cassia* fruit are present in any quantity in the extract. The pulp of tamarind pods is characterized by the presence of free organic acids (approximately 10% tartaric, citric and malic) and their salts (approximately 8% potassium hydrogen tartrate).[23] The aqueous extracts of the bandage were acid to litmus, although the tests for both carboxylic acids and phenols were negative (Table 12). The results of TLC examination for tartaric, citric and malic acids were inconclusive

(Table 13): not all the three acids could be detected in aqueous extracts of tamarind in every system used, although in all systems the overall appearance of the chromatograms of the methanol and water extracts of tamarind and those of the bandages was similar.

Galbanum was considered to be a possible constituent of the chloroform and petroleum extracts. Were this to be the case, the gum component would be extracted by water. To check for the presence of gum from galbanum, the aqueous extracts from the bandages and from a sample of galbanum were each hydrolysed and the hydrolysates compared with those of acacia, myrrh and olibanum. The results (Table 14) indicated the presence in the bandage extracts of galactose, arabinose and an unidentified monosaccharide of low hRf, a combination which was found from galbanum but not from acacia (rhamnose present), myrrh or olibanum (unidentified compound giving a bright pink colour with aniline phthalate reagent present in both these extracts). The evidence from PC of the sugars in hydrolysed aqueous extracts of the wrappings thus tends to confirm that galbanum was used to impregnate the bandages.

Gelatin was found as glue on the surface of the outer bandages, therefore it was possible that it had also been used to impregnate the fabric. However, the absence of protein and amino acids from the aqueous extracts (Table 12) shows this not to be the case.

The use of chromatographic analysis has demonstrated that a complex mixture of substances was used to impregnate the bandages and it is likely that in the present study only those have been identified which are:

(a) currently known to have been available to the Ancient Egyptians
(b) used in relatively large quantities
(c) sufficiently chemically stable to have survived storage for 2,000 or more years.

TABLE 12   Spot tests on aqueous extracts of bandages

Test	Results from extract of 1770/			
	1	2	3	4
1. Picric acid (protein)	slight ppt	—	—	—
2. (a) Hydrolysis (HCl) (b) Ninhydrin (amino acids)	—	—	—	—
3. (a) Neutralize by NaOH; (b) Fehlings (free reducing sugars)	+	+	+	+
4. (a) Hydrolysis (HCl) (b) Fehlings (combined reducing sugars)*	+	+	+	+
5. Litmus	H^+	H^+	H^+	H^+
6. (a) ppt in dil. HCl, (b) Sol. in NaOH	+	+	+	+
7. Na_2CO_3 (carboxylic acids)	—	—	—	—
8. $FeCl_3$ soln (phenols)	—	—	—	—
9. Bornträger-test Et_2O extract after hydrolysis (HCl) and oxidation ($FeCl_3$) with dil. NH_4OH (anthraquinone glycosides)				—

* All +ve results here — subjectively judged that more ppt. formed after hydrolysis than before.

TABLE 13 Results of TLC comparison of aqueous and methanolic extracts of mummy bandage with extracts of tamarind and reference plant acids

hRf	Colour with NH₄OH/AgNO₃	Presence (√) or absence (—) in solutions of:						
		Tartaric acid	Malic acid	Citric acid	Tamarind (MeOH)	Tamarind (H₂O)	Bandage (MeOH)	Bandage (H₂O)
System A								
44		√	—	—	√	√	√	√
57		—	—	√	(√)	—	(√)	(√)
61		—	√	—	(√)	—	(√)	(√)
System B								
25		—	—	√	(√)	(√)	(√)	(√)
40		—	√	—	(√)	(√)	(√)	(√)
41		√	—	—	(√)	—	(√)	—
64		—	—	—	√	√	√	√
System C								
14	brown	—	—	√	√	√	(√)	(√)
19	black	√	—	—	√	√	—	(√)
32	pale brown	—	√	—	—	—	—	—
58	grey-white	—	—	—	√	√	√	√

TABLE 14 Results of PC comparison of hydrolysed aqueous extracts of mummy bandage with those of acacia, myrrh, olibanum and galbanum

hRf	Colour with aniline phthalate reagent	Presence (√) or absence (—) in solutions of:						hydrolysates of				
		arabinose	dextrose	galactose	rhamnose	xylose	fructose	acacia	myrrh	olibanum	galbanum	aq. ext. of bandage
System A												
9											√	√
14											√	√
21				√							√	√
27		√									√	√
23			√								—	—
25							√				—	—
System B												
5	brown							√	√	√	√	√
12	brown			√				√	√	√	√	√
20	pink	√						√		√	√	√
14	brown		√					(—)	(—)	(—)	(—)	(—)
33	brown				√			√	—	—	—	—
23	pink/purple					√		—	—	—	—	—
39	bright pink							—	√	√	—	—
44	grey							—	—	√	—	—
System C												
35	brown							—	√	√	√	√
38	brown		√					—	—	—	—	—
40	brown			√				√	√	√	√	√
45	pink/purple					√		—	—	—	—	—
46	bright pink							—	√	√	—	—
53	pink	√						√	√	√	√	√
61	brown				√			√	—	—	—	—

With these reservations, the conclusions from the present investigation are that the bandages were made of linen cloth impregnated with a mixture containing beeswax, bitumen (except the outer layers), galbanum and a water soluble substance or substances, possibly tamarind extract. It is interesting to speculate as to how the bandages were coated with this mixture of substances containing both water insoluble and water soluble components. Perhaps the most likely explanation is that a molten mixture was prepared and used either for dipping the bandages or brushing on to the surface. That the bandages were not matted together and could be separated easily, indicates that they were fairly dry when applied. The final stage of wrapping seems to have been to use strip bandages which were impregnated with a mixture of substances (which apparently excluded bitumen) and to secure these neatly with glue.

Acknowledgements

We gratefully acknowledge the co-operation of the following:
Miss E. McCauley (Pharmacy Department, University of Manchester) for technical assistance; Dr C. A. Shuttleworth and Mrs J. L. Ward (Department of Medical Biochemistry, University of Manchester) for amino acid analyses; Dr G. W. A. Newton (Chemistry Department, University of Mancheser) for atomic absorption and neutron activation analyses; Dr A. Curry (Public Health Laboratory, Withington Hospital, Manchester) for x-ray electron microscopy; Dr O. Amit (The Geological Survey of Israel, Jerusalem) for an authentic sample of Dead Sea bitumen; Mr M. Ashworth (Department of Medicine, University of Manchester) for photography; and Kodak Ltd for a supply of film.

References

[1] H. Abraham, *Asphalts and Allied Substances*, 6th ed., Vol. I, D. van Nostrand and Co. Inc., Princeton, N.J., 1960.
[2] B. Baumann, *Econ. Botany*, 14, 84, 1960.
[3] Diodorus, XIX, 6.
[4] A. G. Douglas and G. Eglinton, in *Comparative Phytochemistry*, Chap. 4, ed. T. Swain, Academic Press, London, 1966.
[5] J. B. Harborne, *Phytochemical Methods*, Chapman and Hall, London, 1973.
[6] G. A. Herbin and P. A. Robins, *Phytochemistry*, 7, 257, 1968.
[7] —— *Phytochemistry*, 7, 1325, 1968.
[8] —— *Phytochemistry*, 8, 1985, 1969.
[9] Herodotus, II, 86.
[10] P. J. Holloway and S. B. Challen, *J. Chromat*, 25, 336, 1966.
[11] R. H. Kirby, *Vegetable Fibres: Botany, Cultivation and Utilisation*, Leonard Hill, London, 1963.
[12] A. Lucas, *Ancient Egyptian Materials and Methods*, 4th ed. (Revised J. R. Harris), Edward Arnold Ltd., London, 1962.
[13] H. R. Mahler and E. H. Cordes, *Biological Chemistry*, Harper and Row, New York, 1971.
[14] R. F. Marschner and J. C. Winters, in *Shale Oil, Tar Sands and Related Fuel Sources*, Chap. 14, ed. Teh Fu Yen, American Chemical Society, Washington, 1976.
[15] M. A. Murray, *The Tomb of the Two Brothers*, Manchester Museum, 1910.
[16] A. Nissenbaum and Z. Aizenshtat, *Chem. Geology*, 16, 121, 1975.
[17] G. Odham and E. Stenhagen, in *Biochemical Applications of Mass Spectrometry*, Chap. 9, ed. G. R. Waller, Wiley Interscience, New York, 1972.
[18] Strabo, XVI, 11, 45.
[19] S. L. Ranson, in *Modern Methods of Plant Analysis*, Vol. II, ed. K. Paech and M. V. Tracey, Springer, Berlin, 1955.
[20] P. E. Spielman, *J. Egyptian Archaeology*, 18, 177, 1932.
[21] E. Stahl (ed.), *Thin Layer Chromatography, A Laboratory Handbook*, Springer, Berlin, 1965 (Academic Press, N.Y.).
[22] P. Tooley, *Fats, Oils and Waxes*, John Murray, London, 1971.
[23] G. E. Trease and W. C. Evans, *Pharmacognosy*, 11th ed., Bailliere Tindall, London, 1978.
[24] A. P. Tulloch, *J. Am. Oil Chem. Soc.*, 50, 367, 1973.
[25] A. I. Vogel, *A Textbook of Macro and Semi-micro Qualitative Inorganic Analysis*, Longmans, London, 1955.
[26] C. G. Wall, in *Materials and Technology*, Vol. IV, Longman, London, 1972.
[27] T. E. Wallis, *Textbook of Pharmacognosy*, 5th ed., J. and A. Churchill, London, 1967.
[28] A. Zaki and Z. Iskander, *Ann. Serv.*, XLII, 223, 1943.

The Textiles from the Mummy 1770

by

J. P. WILD

Introduction

Large quantities of ancient textile material have survived in Egypt, but comparatively little of it has been adequately published.* Understandably perhaps, the lion's share of attention has been paid to the decorated textiles woven by the Copts in late antiquity; for the bulk of earlier material has little artistic appeal and offers, to a superficial observer at least, few points of technical interest.

The importance of the wrappings and padding associated with the Manchester mummy 1770 stems from the fact that they have yielded an average C¹⁴ date of A.D. 380 (see p. 146). The upper and lower limits within which they were woven are A.D. 323 and A.D. 441 — securely within the Roman period.

Examination of the material suggests that only three textiles were used in the wrapping. Since the bandages and layers of padding had to be cut from the body piecemeal, it was impossible to recover any single item intact. Theoretically therefore many separate webs of cloth could have been employed; but the character of the yarns, the count of threads and the weave are so consistent among the fragments which I have assigned to each of the 'fabrics' described below that I feel reasonably confident that only three textiles were used. If the mummy had been re-wrapped during the Roman period, as has been suggested (p. 146), then this would not be unexpected.

Characteristics of the Textiles

(a) *Fabric 1*   The cloth is a fine plain weave (pl. 2 D: warp runs top to bottom):
System (1) warp, S-spun, *c*.32 threads per cm, close set.
System (2) weft, S-spun, *c*.16 threads per cm, well spaced out.

The quality of the yarn is fine and regular and the spin is not hard. The largest surviving piece measures 25 cm in the warp direction, at least 50 cm in the weft direction (1770/447).

Selvedges were found ·in three samples (1770/334: 5 cm long; 1770/335: 10 cm; 1770/447: 5 cm), confirming that the closer-set thread-system is the warp. The selvedges are plain.

In 1770/447 remains of a *hem*, *c*.10 cm long, parallel to the weft, were noted; two identical hems in 1770/335 and 447 were sewn together. Analysis showed that the raw edge of the cloth had been turned over once or possibly twice and neatly tacked down by a series of stitches (*c*.5

* I am grateful to Dr R. David for giving me the opportunity to record this material.

stitches per cm) visible on the outer surface of the cloth (**1**). The hems were brought together and seamed with well concealed running stitches (*c*.4 per cm). The sewing thread was Z-plied from 2 S-spun yarns of the same weight as the yarn in the warp.

The large piece of Fabric 1 in 1770/447 exhibits 4 pairs of self-bands. They are at intervals of 1.5 cm, 9 cm and 5.5 cm, and in each case the bands consist of 5 weft-threads in the same shed. In three of the pairs the bands are in successive sheds, but in one case the two bands were separated by two single shots of weft. Fragments of self-bands were also recorded in 1770/127.

Fabric 1 may be summed up as a fine plain-weave warp-faced (repp) textile with plain selvedges, measuring at least 50 cm wide. Parts of it were decorated with self-bands. Neither starting nor finishing borders survive. When in use the fabric was hemmed and seamed.

(b) *Fabric 2*   The cloth is a medium-fine plain weave (pl. 2 A: warp runs right to left):
System (1) warp, S-spun, *c*.22 threads per cm, close set.
System (2) weft, S-spun, *c*.9 threads per cm, well spaced.

The largest single fragment (1770/441) measures 70 cm in the warp direction, 40 cm in the weft. In 1770/552 the weft survives to a width of 45 cm.

Lengths of plain selvedge (1770/388: 4 cm; 1770/432: 60 cm; 1770/437: fragment) allow the identification of warp and weft.

The large fragment in 1770/432 (64 cm in the warp direction, 44 cm in the weft) carries not only one plain selvedge (the opposite edge is cut), but also a *fringed border* (**2**).

The border consists of 4 groups of weft-threads immediately adjacent to the main body of the cloth. Each group contains 4 separate weft yarns (laid in and not plied) which, to judge by the single preserved selvedge, return into the next shed in a straightforward manner. Each pair of adjacent warp-threads forms a loop (**2**), which projects about 4 mm beyond the edge of the woven cloth. Each loop was Z-twisted two or three times to make a very short fringe.

It is unfortunate that only one corner showing the junction of selvedge and border is preserved. In it the warp was at first crowded together by the weaver who pulled the weft groups through the shed too tightly; but as soon as a single shot of weft was used for the main web, the warp was correctly spaced out at the edge.

A narrow strip of cloth (1770/438), probably cut from Fabric 2, has a fringe — possibly a terminal fringe — in the warp (**3**). It is composed of single loops of adjacent warp-threads, *c*.2.5 cm long: each is Z-twisted together.

The last shot of weft at the edge of the cloth is a pair of threads.

A fringe is also a feature of the large fragment in 1770/441. It is in the warp, but consists of cut ends (not loops), *c*. 9 cm long. A pair of self-bands runs through the weft *c*. 3.5 cm from the base of the fringe; but they do not give any further clue to its character. There is no proof that the fringe represents an original selvedge.

The large fringed fragment in 1770/432 carries a pair of adjacent self-bands, 7 cm from the end of the fringed border (**4**). Each band is a group of 5 individual weft yarns, laid in and not plied. The five may be regarded as the single weft-thread of the ground-weave, plus two extra pairs. In the band nearer to the border it can be

seen at the selvedge that the single weft-thread passes normally from the last shed into the shed of the band, and that the two pairs of extra weft-threads are in fact a single pair, which comes out of the band-shed, round the outermost warp-thread and then back into the same shed to make up the total of 5 threads. The ends of the 4 extra weft-threads can be seen in the second self-band where they approach to within *c*. 1 cm of the selvedge before being eliminated. At this point they seem to form a loop and two loose single ends of thread. It may be that the extra weft is a single yarn, folded double to make a pair and double again round the outer warp-thread in the selvedge to make 4 parallel extra weft-threads running through both self-bands.

Self-bands occur on four more fragments of Fabric 2. In 1770/441 there is a single pair; in the other three 2 pairs of bands are found separated by varying intervals (1770/437: 1.5 cm; 1770/556: 8 cm; 1770/557: 1 cm). In every case the self-band contains 5 weft-threads.

In 1770/437 what may be a fault recurs at irregular intervals. Three weft-threads instead of one are taken into the same shed. The selvedge unfortunately is in a poor condition and the precise course of the weft at that point is not clear. It seems evident, however, that the extra weft yarns are not carried through to the point where the fault next occurs.

Hems, and in one instance a seam between two hems, were noted in several fragments parallel to the weft. The raw edge was rolled back twice to give a hem *c*. 5 mm wide (in 1770/434 31 cm long, in 1770/449 10 cm long). The structure of the seam (1770/449) was identical with that recorded for Fabric 1 above (**1**). The hem showed 2 stitches per cm in thread Z-plied from 2 S-spun yarns.

Fabric 2, in sum, is a moderately fine warp-faced plain weave with plain selvedges and at least one, and probably two, fringed borders in the warp. It measured at least 45 cm wide and its only decoration is several pairs of self-bands. Sections of the cloth were hemmed and seamed.

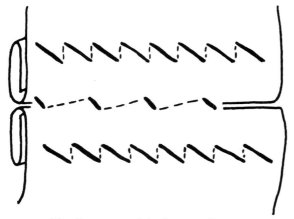

(**1**) Structure of the hems and seams on Fabrics 1 and 2

(**2**) The border on Fabric 2

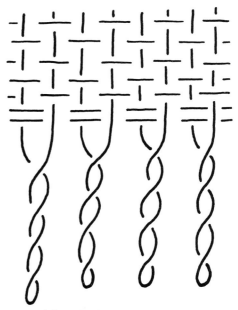

(**3**) The fringe on Fabric 2

(c) *Fabric 3* A basket weave (pl. 2 B: warp runs top to bottom):

System (1) warp, doubles, both S-spun, *c*.18 pairs per cm, close set.

System (2) weft, doubles, both S-spun, *c*. 7–8 pairs per cm, well spaced out.

The main technical details can be established from the largest extant piece (1770/446), which measures 60 cm in the warp direction, 50 cm in the weft direction. The single plain selvedge which it carries (*c*.26 cm long) permits identification of warp and weft.

A curious 'fault' is present in the same fragment. In one shed 8 threads (4 pairs) were introduced, but only for a distance of *c*.6 cm measured from the selvedge. Thereafter the extra threads were progressively eliminated. Damage to the selvedge prevents proper analysis and understanding of this feature.

Fabric 3 may be summarized as a warp-faced basket weave with a plain selvedge and no decorative features.

Discussion

Analysis of the samples by G. G. Benson, S. R. Hemingway and F. N. Leach (p. 131) suggests that all the textiles are linen. Flax was Egypt's leading fibre and was the only fibre ritually acceptable for mummy wrappings, as Herodotus tells us.[1]

The yarns in all the fabrics are spun in the S-direction (left-hand spin). S-spin was almost universal in Egypt and in the eastern Roman provinces and may reflect the fact that bast fibres, when moistened, rotate naturally to the left.[2]

The weaves can be readily paralleled in Egypt and the Levant. Plain weave ('canvas weave' or 'linen weave'), as in Fabrics 1 and 2, was the norm in Egypt. A higher thread-count in warp than in weft was a standard feature throughout the region.[3] Basket weave (Fabric 3), although rarer, is also found throughout the eastern Roman provinces.[4]

The wrappings have no form of decoration except the modest self-bands. These take the form of pairs of raised ribs crossing the cloth in the weft direction. Each band contains 5 weft-threads, and the evidence of Fabric 2 shows how the bands were constructed (4). An extra weft-thread, doubled and then redoubled, was added to the single shot of ground-weft. Self-bands are relatively common in ancient linen, particularly towards the beginning and end of the web; but I cannot find a published parallel to the construction technique noted in Fabric 2.

The simple fringe in 1770/441 may be the remains of another decorative technique in which a few centimetres of bare warp are left by the weaver towards the beginning and end of a fabric.[5]

The selvedges in all Fabrics are plain, in accord with Egyptian linen weavers' normal practice. They do not seem to have regarded reinforced selvedges either in plain weave over warp-groups or with wrapped weft as necessary.[6]

The weaver of Fabric 2 began (or, less plausibly, ended) his work with a border of unusual interest (2). Indications that it is a starting-border are: (1) the long fringe with closed loops in the warp (3), which seems to belong to Fabric 2, is more naturally taken as the finishing border of the cloth web; (2) the technique employed to anchor the extra weft in the self-band nearer the border (4) suggests that this was the first of the two self-bands to be woven and that the border itself was where the weaving began.

This starting-border, however, is not the well-known starting-border associated with the warp-weighted loom. Such borders — almost always with paired warp and often with a cross between the border and the main web — are found in northern Europe and also in the Near East.[7] In fact no exact parallel for its structure can be cited from the published literature, although a number of borders on textiles from the Nile Valley come fairly close to it.[8]

The border has a very short (*c*. 4 mm) fringe with loops through which some form of heading cord might once have passed. The loops were probably too small to admit a wooden rod.[9] While it would be very useful to know on what type of loom Fabric 2 was woven, the structural evidence of the border is far from conclusive. Warp arranged at the start of work on a horizontal ground-loom may have been looped over a heading-cord securing it to the cloth beam;[10] but speculation is probably pointless at present.[11]

It is evident that the textiles in which the mummy 1770 was wrapped were household items in secondary use. This was normal practice in Egypt and in inhumation burials throughout the Roman world.[12] (The re-use of linen towels (*sabana*) was so prevalent that the loanword *sabanum* was taken by the Slavs to mean 'shroud'.)[13] The Fabrics 1 and 2, in view of their hems and seams, may originally have been parts of tunics. The basket weave of Fabric 3 on the other hand, to judge by the parallels outside Egypt, suggests that it may once have been sacking.[14]

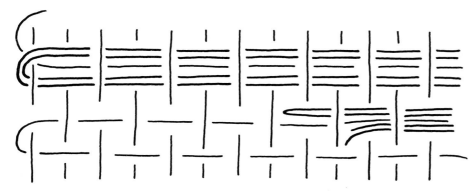

(**4**) Scheme of the self-bands in Fabric 2

The quality of the cloth in general is striking. Spin and weave are good and regular, and few faults can be picked out. The standard of hemming and seaming is first-rate.

There is abundant papyrological evidence for textile technology in Egypt and a matching wealth of surviving remains.[15] The situation is without parallel in antiquity; but full publication of the archaeological evidence is now essential, if we are to understand and appreciate the achievements of the Egyptian spinners and weavers.

References

[1] A. Lucas, *Ancient Egyptian Materials and Industries*, 4th ed., London, 1962, 142 ff.; Herodotus, II, 81, 86.

[2] J. P. Wild, *Textile Manufacture in the Northern Roman Provinces*, Cambridge, 1970, 38; R. Pfister, L. Bellinger, *The Textiles, The Excavations at Dura-Europos: Final Report*, IV, Ann Arbor, 1945, 1 ff.; Y. Yadin, *The Finds from the Bar Kokhba Period in the Cave of Letters*, *Judaean Desert Studies*, Jerusalem, 1963, 177 ff.

[3] G. M. Crowfoot, 'The linen textiles' in D. Barthélemy, J. T. Milik, *Qumran Cave* I, *Discoveries in the Judaean Desert*, I, Oxford, 1955, 19, 22; E. Crowfoot, 'Textiles', in P. W. Lapp, N. L. Lapp, 'Discoveries in the Wâdī ed-Dâliyeh', *Annual of the American Schools of Oriental Research*, XLI, 1974, 64; Yadin (1963), 253 f.; Lucas (1962), 143 f. with literature; M. A. Murray, *The Tomb of Two Brothers*, Manchester, 1910, 68.

[4] Crowfoot (1974), 73; Yadin (1963), 193, 254; Pfister, Bellinger (1945), 4; Wild (1970), 46.

[5] G. M. Crowfoot, 'Linen Textiles from the Cave of Ain Feschka in the Jordan Valley', *Palestine Exploration Quarterly*, 1951, pl. IV, fig. 1.

[6] Yadin (1963), 200, fig. 67. The late Roman textiles from Karanis in Bolton Museum demonstrate the range of reinforced selvedges in both wool and linen.

[7] M. Hoffmann, *The Warp-Weighted Loom*, Oslo, 1964, 151 ff.; 253; Crowfoot (1974), 61; M. Hald, *Olddanske Tekstiler*, Copenhagen, 1950, 160 ff.; M. Hald, 'Ancient Textile Techniques in Egypt and Scandinavia: a Comparative Study', *Acta Archaeologica*, XVII, 1946, 49 ff.

[8] Hald (1946), 57, fig. 5, 6; I. Bergman, *Late Nubian Textiles*, The Scandinavian Joint Expedition to Sudanese Nubia, 8, Lund, 1975, 29, fig. 22, type A3.

[9] As on the sprang from Tegle: Hoffmann (1964), 169, fig. 81; cf. Murray (1910), 68.

[10] H. Ling Roth, *Ancient Egyptian and Greek Looms*, Halifax, 1951, 4, fig. 2 (if this is not merely an inaccurate drawing).

[11] J. P. Wild, 'The tarsikarios, a Roman linen-weaver in Egypt', in C. Préaux (ed.), *Hommages à Marcel Renard*, Brussels, 1969, 816 ff., for an attempt to identify the warp-weighted loom in Egypt; cf. Bergman (1975), 29.

[12] Murray (1910), 67; Wild (1970), 95 f.

[13] *Journal of Roman Studies*, LX, 1970, 130; A. Walde, J. B. Hofmann, *Lateinisches Etymologisches Wörterbuch*, Heidelberg, 1938, s.v. *sabanum*.

[14] Yadin (1963), 259 ff.

[15] E. Wipszycka, *L'Industrie textile dans l'Egypte romaine*, Warsaw, 1965.

Radiocarbon Dating

by

K. C. Hodge and G. W. A. Newton

Summary

Radiocarbon dating is discussed with particular reference to Egyptian Chronology. Details of the technique are given as used to measure the age of bone and bandages from Manchester Mummy 1770. The results obtained were

    Bone: 1000 B.C.   Bandages: A.D. 380

This implies the mummy was wrapped or re-wrapped sometime after death.

Introduction

The unravelling of ancient history is an exciting occupation and in recent years historians have captured the interest and help of scientists in this rewarding task. One important aspect of this work is age determination and the establishment of sequences and chronologies. 'Dating would be a nonsense without radiocarbon dating, and this technique has made a major contribution to archaeology'.[1]

Radiocarbon dating involves many disciplines such as history, physics, chemistry, biology and others. The technique began in 1948 in the University of Chicago under the leadership of Professor W. F. Libby,[2] and in 1960 his excellent research was recognized with the award of the Nobel Prize in Chemistry. From the beginning Egyptian chronology played an important part in the establishment of the technique because, among others, Egyptian samples (usually wood or charcoal from tombs) were used as standards of known 'historical' dates. The comparison of the radiocarbon date with the 'historical' date is important to the scientist and historian. Clearly, the validity of both methods is very significant; Radiocarbon dating is less than thirty years old and is continually being developed and improved. 'Historical' dating has centuries of tradition, but chronologies are still being modified on the basis of new ideas and discoveries. The two approaches will be considered separately. The radiocarbon dating will be considered in general terms first and then with reference to Egyptian chronology, and the 'historical' dating will be discussed in the Egyptian context only.

Radiocarbon Dating

Radiocarbon dating can be carried out mainly on living material that once formed part of the biosphere, and obviously only that part of it which contains carbon. Detailed investigation of this carbon shows that it is present as three isotopes, namely carbon 12, carbon 13 and carbon 14. The ratio of these isotopes in living matter on earth is $100:1:10^{-10}$ respectively. Isotopes contain the same number of protons in their atomic nuclei but can have different masses because they contain different numbers of neutrons in the nucleus. Protons have unit mass and unit positive charge, and in a neutral atom the positive charge is balanced by an equal number of negatively charged electrons outside the nucleus. Neutrons have unit mass and no charge. Carbon atoms always contain six protons in the nucleus, but the three isotopes carbon 12, carbon 13 and carbon 14 also contain 6, 7 and 8 neutrons respectively (12, 13 and 14 refer to the total nuclear mass of each isotope). The isotopes carbon 12 and carbon 13, that is, the bulk of the carbon on earth, are stable and are produced in stars and distributed in space at the end of the stars life, for example when it blows up as a supernova. All the carbon 12 and 13 in our bodies has its origin in some long-dead star.

Carbon 14, the isotope used for dating, is radioactive and has a different source; it is being produced continually in our atmosphere by cosmic radiation. The effects of cosmic rays were noted as early as 1900, but it required daring balloon ascents to heights of 5,000 m by V. F. Hess in 1911 to indicate that this penetrating radiation was of cosmic origin.

Although much is now known about cosmic rays, where they come from in the universe is still in doubt. A detailed understanding of cosmic rays is important to the historian because, as will become apparent, it is imperative to radiocarbon dating that the cosmic ray intensity has remained constant over the past 10,000 years, or that any variations should be known accurately. The present intensity of cosmic radiation is roughly equivalent to that of starlight and 100,000,000 times less intense than sunlight. The maximum energies of cosmic rays are enormous and cannot be produced by man even in the most powerful accelerators; in starlight the average energy is about 2 ev, whereas in cosmic rays energies as high as 1,000,000,000 ev have been observed. The primary particles which have these energies are mainly protons; these protons collide with atoms of the earth's atmosphere, mainly nitrogen, and produce secondary particles. A wide range of secondary particles are produced, and a study of these has been a very rewarding area of research in physics. Of significance to radiocarbon dating are the neutron secondary particles which are knocked out of nuclei in the earth's atmosphere. These secondary neutrons can interact with nitrogen nuclei in the earth's upper atmosphere to produce carbon 14:

$$^{14}_{7}N + ^{1}_{0}n \rightarrow ^{14}_{6}C + ^{1}_{1}p$$

nitrogen + neutron → carbon 14 + proton

The superscript refers to the mass of the atom, that is, the total number of neutrons plus protons; the subscript refers to the number of protons which determines the element (carbon has six protons and nitrogen has seven protons). In the nuclear reaction depicted above, nitrogen is converted to carbon 14 by the secondary neutrons in the earth's atmosphere.

If the cosmic ray intensity was constant with time, then the secondary neutron concentration would be constant also, and if carbon 14 was stable then its concentration would increase with time. However, carbon 14 is not stable, it is radioactive and decays back to nitrogen:

$$^{14}_{6}C \rightarrow {}^{14}_{7}N + {}^{0}_{-1}\beta + \nu$$

carbon 14 → nitrogen 14 + beta particle + neutrino

The notation is the same as before, the −1 on the beta particle (electron) implying a negative charge. This beta particle is emitted from the atom and can be detected by suitable equipment; it is this beta particle which is measured in radiocarbon dating.

Radioactive isotopes decay by first order kinetics and are characterized by a constant time period called the half-life; this is the time in which any radioactivity decays to half its initial value. The measurement of these half-lives requires careful control of instrumentation and errors are involved. In the past twenty years there has been a change in the measured half-life of carbon 14; Libby[2] used a value of 5568 ± 30 years, whereas the current[3] value is 5730 ± 40 years. There is a vast quantity of radiocarbon dates based on the Libby half-life, therefore this value is still used in calculations. It is easy to convert from one to the other; if a radiocarbon age based on the Libby half-life (5568 years) is multiplied by 1.029 this will give a radiocarbon age based on the 5730 year half-life.

Carbon 14 is being continually produced by cosmic radiation and it is continually decaying by beta particle emission, therefore there is the possibility that it will reach some equilibrium in living matter and its concentration will remain constant with time. Let us consider how carbon 14 gets in to living matter.

The bulk of carbon in the atmosphere is present as carbon dioxide and the carbon 14 produced by cosmic rays would be rapidly oxidized to carbon (14) dioxide, and this would mix rapidly with the carbon (12, 13) dioxide in the atmosphere. Carbon is distributed in various compartments in the earth, the whole being in equilibrium; this relationship is known as the carbon cycle and is shown in Figure 1. The four major compartments, the atmosphere, biosphere, oceans and sedimentary rocks are shown in the square boxes. The figure in each box shows the total carbon content of the compartment in grammes. The compartments are linked by arrows which show the direction and mechanism of carbon exchange; the figure on each line shows the rate of exchange in grammes per year. From the diagram it can be seen that it takes about 100 years for the carbon content of the biosphere to be completely replaced once by photosynthesis of atmospheric carbon dioxide. This means that carbon 14 becomes uniformly distributed throughout the biosphere after about 100 years.

The overall mechanism of photosynthesis is:

$$6^{14}CO_2 + 12H_2O \rightarrow {}^{14}C_6H_{12}O_6 + 6O_2 + 6H_2O$$

^{14}carbon dioxide + water → ^{14}C-sugar + oxygen + water

$$^{14}C\text{-sugar} \rightarrow {}^{14}C\text{-cellulose/protein/etc} \ldots$$

In the grazing food chain (there are other food chains in the biosphere) the plants are eaten by herbivores, herbivores by carnivores, and so ^{14}C-proteins become distributed in the biosphere. A similar argument can be applied to the oceans where after about 500 years the carbon 14 from atmospheric carbon dioxide would be uniformly distributed throughout the bicarbonate ions in the oceans. These bicarbonate ions are in equilibrium with carbonate ions which form the shells of marine animals and ultimately become limestone deposits.

$$CO_2 \rightarrow CO_2 + H_2O \rightarrow H_2CO_3 \rightarrow H^+ + HCO_3^-$$
atmosphere   ocean

$$CO_3^{2-}$$
$$+ Ca^{2+}$$
↓
shell deposits
(CaCo₃)
↓
sedimentary rocks
(CaCo₃ etc . . .)

On death the ^{14}C cellulose/protein/etc. is returned to the atmosphere as $^{14}CO_2$ by the process known as respiration:

$$^{14}C_6H_{12}O_6 + 6O_2 + 6H_2O \rightarrow 6{}^{14}CO_2 + 12H_2O.$$

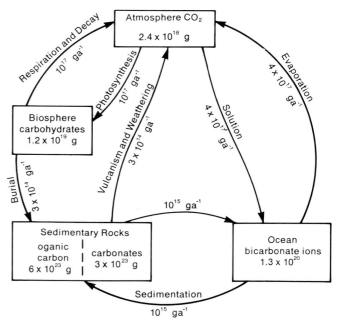

FIG. 1. Carbon Cycle

138

In some cases, example a tree, the process of respiration or decay is long compared with the half-life of ^{14}C. On death the tree no longer takes in $^{14}CO_2$ by photosynthesis, and since decay is slow the ^{14}C content of the tree will decrease by the known half-life of ^{14}C. If the radioactivity of the tree was known at death, and the radioactivity measured sometime later, then the time elapsed since death can be calculated. This is the principle of ^{14}C dating.

Several assumptions are involved in the application of this technique:

1. The ^{14}C content of living matter in antiquity was the same as at present.
2. This implies that cosmic rays had the same intensity in antiquity as now.
3. There is a constant rate of mixing and exchange between ^{14}C in the atmosphere, the biosphere and the oceans.

These concepts, originally proposed by Libby, have been found wanting in view of subsequent research, and it is now clear that there have been fluctuations in the cosmic ray intensity over the past 10,000 years.[4–8] Various reasons have been put forward for these variations, including variations in the geomagnetic dipole,[8] sunspot activity and variations in the mixing of atmosphere and marine reservoirs of ^{14}C. In an attempt to overcome these deficiencies calibration procedures were introduced.

Calibration of Radiocarbon Dates

To overcome the difficulties outlined above, various calibration procedures have been developed, most involving dendro chronology[9–17] and some involving Egyptian 'historical' dates.[18–22] The most popular method is to use tree-rings to establish the age of a piece of wood, and then to measure the ^{14}C content of that same piece of wood.[23] In this way a calibration curve is established as shown in Figs 2–5. Several such curves have been established and they all agree in principle, but differ in detail. It is this detail that disturbs the historian. These differences are discussed in more detail below with reference to Egyptian Dates. However, from the

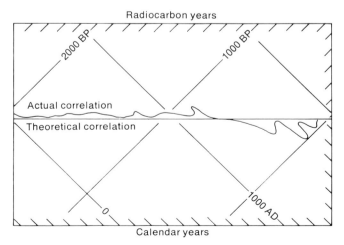

FIG. 2.   Tree Ring Corrective Curve

beginning the results obtained for Egypt in the dynastic period from the radiocarbon method were not of much value in the reconstruction of Egyptian history.[24]

The reverse, that is the use of Egyptian chronology in calibrating radiocarbon dates should be possible and relies on the fact that the sequence should be correct at least. There is an interesting discussion of bristlecone pine corrections and Ancient Egypt by Clark.[25]

Historical Dates

Egyptian chronology has been established by the writings of classical authors, regnal years, astronomical data, and detailed archaeological studies. Psammetichus I was the founder of the 26th Dynasty and his dates were 664–610 B.C. on astronomical, Babylonian and Greek evidence. Since then the facts are taken to be those recorded by classical historians. In the second millenium B.C. astronomical records were used. The Egyptians used three calendars, one the original lunar calendar, one an official 365 day civil calendar, and a modified lunar calendar. The Egyptian contribution to measuring time was the 'Egyptian Year' of a fixed length of 365 days.[26] All other calendaric systems involved religious and political considerations or situations of complex astronomical reckoning. The year was divided into three seasons, akhet, peret and shemu each of agricultural origin (associated with the state of water in the Nile) and nothing to do with astronomy. Each season was divided into 4 months of 30 days, that is, 360 days in all plus five epagomenal days to complete the year.

For fixing time in the Egyptian Middle Kingdom a record of the heliacal rising of the star Sothis (Sirius) was valuable.[18,26,27] The heliacal rising of the star fell one day earlier in the Egyptian civil year every four years, after $4 \times 365 = 1460$ years it would have regained its original position in the civil calendar; this is known as the 'Sothic Cycle'. The Egyptians ignored leap year. According to Neugebauer[26] 'The "Sothic Cycle" of 1460 years can be explained as the result of connecting the agricultural year with a yearly recurring astronomical phenomenon, the heliacal rising of Sirius (Sothis), which roughly coincides with the beginning of the inundation (of the Nile), whereas the beginning of the schematic Egyptian year of 365 days was "wandering" through the course of time through all seasons'.

Censorinus, the Roman author, reports the heliacal rising of Sirius took place on the first day of the first month (1 Thoth) of the Egyptian civil year in A.D. 139, equivalent to 20 July in the Julian calendar.[28] The most ancient Egyptian record was for a heliacal rising of Sirius on the sixteenth day of the eighth month of the seventh year of a King. This King must have been Sesostris III of the XII Dynasty from documents in the same Archive. Thanks to the regular displacement of the civil calendar to the true astronomical year it is possible to count back from A.D. 139 and place the year in question at 1870 ± 6 B.C., with 1872 B.C. being most favoured.[27] Further details of these calculations are described elsewhere.[18] This puts the start of the reign of Sesostris III at 1878 B.C. as quoted.[24]

The Old Kingdom poses different problems. There are no recorded dates of heliacal risings of Sirius, and dates are based on archaeological evidence and information gleaned from the Turin papyrus and the Palermo stone. The Turin document gives 143 years as the duration of the XI Dynasty and Sesostris III's predecessors (from 1870 B.C.) amount to 120 years in the XII Dynasty; the start of the XI Dynasty is about 2133 B.C. A large part of the X Dynasty was contemporaneous with the XI Dynasty and the IX Dynasty was very brief (a few decades), then the end of the Old Kingdom was about 2160 B.C.[24] Further, the Turin Canon of Kings gives the length of the Old Kingdom as 955 regnal years, which places the beginning of the Old Kingdom at about 3114 B.C.

Radiocarbon Dating and Egyptian Chronology

As outlined above the Egyptian chronology has been established with its own uncertainties. Even more difficult is to relate the artefact submitted for radiocarbon dating to that chronology. This in part can account for the disarray in the relationship between Egyptian chronology and C-14 dates. However, the technique is not blameless as inter-laboratory comparisons on the same sample have shown. This is not the place to present detailed arguments about the comparisons of C-14 and historical dates of Egyptian samples, this has been done by others. A very detailed list of Nubian and Egyptian samples has been presented,[22] and the general thesis is that the radiocarbon dates are useless to the historian. One must agree, although the reason is perhaps not as clear-cut as the author would suggest. It is the general view[22] that tree correction curves based on Californian redwoods and New Zealand kauri trees are different and that neither are relevant to Egypt for geographical reasons. This may well be true but the sequence should be valid. That some dates are too old and some too young is a cause for worry. Other authors[20,21] have questioned the provenience of some of the artefacts. In some cases,[24] particularly when wood and reed samples are chosen, the agreement between 'historical' Egyptian dates and 'corrected' radiocarbon dates is quite good. It is clear that there is still scope for a systematic study of artefacts with sound provenience from Egyptian collections. Perhaps this can be achieved with the new techniques which are being developed using a Tandem van de Graaff or a mass spectrometer.[30]

In conclusion, it is a personal view that absolute radiocarbon dates are of little value, but that establishing sequences and contemporaneity should be possible with some precision and both are of considerable value to the historian.

Experimental

The method described below is the one applied to the bones and bandages of Mummy 1770, but it is a general procedure for carbonaceous material. At each stage a discussion will be included giving reasons for the step and the possible sources of error.

Ideally about 5–10 g of carbon are required for each sample, the older the sample the lower the count rate and therefore the larger amounts of carbon are desirable. Clearly, the amount of sample required depends on its

carbon content and for charcoal, wood and cloth weights of about 10 g are adequate. Bone is very different because the organic content can decrease with time, and this will depend very much on how the bone was stored either by the curator or in the archaeological site. It is advisable to determine the carbon content on a small sample before dating, and then the appropriate weight of sample can be taken. As a general rule this can require anything from 200–500 g of bone. In some cases it will be impossible to date bone samples by the radiocarbon method because although the bone has its original skeletal structure there will be no carbon left, the bone will be entirely inorganic, that is apatite (calcium phosphate).

The selection of the appropriate sample for dating is extremely important and requires close co-operation between the historian or archaeologist and the group who are making the measurement. It is essential that the sample be well documented, that is geographical co-ordinates, site of origin, layer (depth below the surface), and other appropriate information be recorded.

The sample is then pretreated, and this is a very critical stage. Ideally, the only carbonaceous material required is the ^{14}C organic material that was present in the sample at death, for example, collagen in bone or cellulose in wood. In Mummy material there is the real possibility that the bones and bandages have been impregnated with carbonaceous material of fossil origin, for example bitumen from the Dead Sea area (possibly used in embalming). Any of this present in the sample would reduce its specific activity and make the sample appear older than it really is. If samples of different origin are to be compared, as in the case of bones and bandages of Mummy 1770 (animal and plant origin), then purification is extremely important. Pretreatment can cause confusion if the sample is very heterogeneous, for example a sample of peat which contains wood, leaves and humic acids each of different origin and age; different pretreatments in different laboratories could select different components and hence give apparently different ages for the peat sample.

The widely used technique and the one adopted here was to soak the samples in dilute hydrochloric acid and sodium hydroxide alternately for several weeks each until no colour was extracted. In the case of the bone specimens the inorganic material was disintegrated by

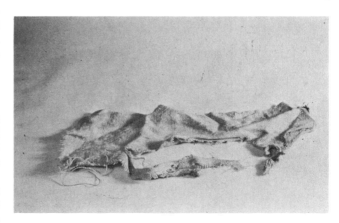

PLATE 1

140

this procedure and the fibrous collagen remained — this was pale brown in colour. With the cloth and bandages, these retained their original form, but they were treated until white in colour. Plate 1. For wood samples cellulose was extracted by a procedure described by Rebello and Wagener.[31] All materials were air dried, and up to this stage required two to three months preparation.

The next stage of the procedure is to convert all the carbon in the air dried sample to benzene. The reaction scheme used by Barker[32] and also by Noakes[33] is the one employed in this project:

$$C + O_2 \rightarrow CO_2 \uparrow \qquad (1)$$

$$2CO_2 + 10Li \rightarrow Li_2C_2 + 4Li_2O \qquad (2)$$

$$Li_2C_2 \rightarrow 2LiOH + C_2H_2 \uparrow \qquad (3)$$

$$\text{excess } Li + 2H_2O \rightarrow 2LiOH + H_2 \uparrow \qquad (4)$$

$$\text{and } Li_2O + H_2O \rightarrow 2LiOH \qquad (5)$$

$$3C_2H_2 \rightarrow C_6H_6 \qquad (6)$$

Apparatus A schematic diagram is shown in Figure 6. It consists of four parts:

1. The carbon dioxide inlet and trapping system,
2. the lithium furnace,
3. the acetylene trapping system, and
4. the benzene synthesis system.

The system is evacuated by a two stage rotary oil pump down to pressures of 10^{-2} mm Hg.

1. *The Carbon Dioxide System* The carbon is converted to CO_2, either by oxidation (with $KMnO_4$ in the case of oxalic acid) or by combustion in a tube furnace. The CO_2 is dried with Analar conc. sulphuric acid and trapped at liquid nitrogen temperature for the oxidation route and in $Ba(OH)_2$ for the combustion route. The $BaCO_3$ product is acidified and the CO_2 trapped at 77°K as above.

2. *The Lithium Furnace* This is shown in Plate 2. The reaction chamber is 2 litres capacity made from 5 mm thick stainless steel. The top one-third is provided with a cooling coil of soft ¼″ copper tubing soldered on. The lower part is shielded with asbestos and heated with a bunsen burner.

3. *The Acetylene Trapping System* This consists of four cold traps, 2 conventional and 2 convoluted (Fig. 6) to prevent loss of solid C_2H_2.

4. *The Benzene Synthesis System* This is shown in Plate 3 and Figure 6. The acetylene is dried by passing through a large U tube containing phosphoric acid on glass beads. The apparatus also comprises a catalysis vessel and a small flask for the collection of the benzene product. Two requirements for the metal catalyst for benzene synthesis emerge from these studies:

1. It must contain cations of charge +5 or greater, and
2. the cations must be combined with a matrix of large surface area, greater than 200 $m^2 g^{-1}$.

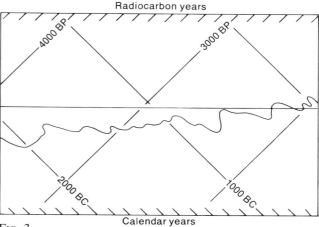

FIG. 3.

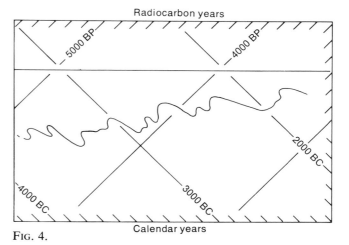

FIG. 4.

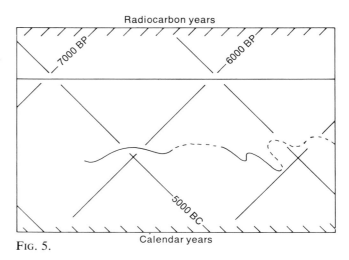

FIG. 5.

141

The postulated mechanism of the reaction is a polarization of acetylene by the cation, and subsequent induced polarization of two other acetylene molecules. Angular rotation then makes the formation of a benzene ring possible.

The catalyst used in this project is based on vanadium in a silica-alumina support. The catalyst base consists of beads of $c.4$ mm diameter, and has the formula $Al_2O_3.Si_{16}O_{32}$. The activation procedure was as follows. The reagents used are: X g catalyst base, X/10 g V_2O_5 (G.P.R.), 2X ml H_2O_2 (100 vol.), and 4X ml distilled water. The vanadium pentoxide was weighed out and mixed with the water in a large beaker which was cooled in ice-water. Hydrogen peroxide was then added in small quantities (10–15 ml) at fifteen minute intervals. An unstable peroxy complex of vanadium (V) was formed and the solution gradually assumed a very intense yellow/red colour. After standing overnight, the solution was decanted into a large crystallising dish

PLATE 2

cooled in ice-water. The catalyst beads were poured in slowly to form a monolayer, and left for several hours. The solution was then poured off, and the beads washed several times with distilled water, and left to dry in air at room temperature for several days. They were then transferred to a screw-top bottle and stored ready for use.

Experimental Procedure

1. Preparation of the apparatus.
2. Combustion of the sample.
3. Formation of lithium carbide.
4. Dehydration of the catalyst.
5. Hydrolysis of lithium carbide.
6. Conversion of acetylene to benzene.
7. Distillation of benzene.
8. Counting procedure.

The whole process takes approximately twelve hours, and is conveniently done by carrying out steps 1–3 on one day, leaving the system overnight, and performing steps 4–7 the following morning.

1. *Preparation of the apparatus* The lithium needed for carbide formation was loaded into the furnace. The lithium used was supplied by BDH Chemicals Ltd. This was packed under liquid paraffin, and was washed five times with sodium-dried diethyl ether. A 50% excess of metal above the stoichiometric amount was used. The metal was spread evenly over the floor of the furnace chamber, and the system mounted and sealed. The entire vacuum system was evacuated and left overnight to check for leaks.

2. *Combustion of the sample* The preweighed sample (about 5 g C) was placed in the furnace and heated in air (purified from CO_2) to 1000°C, the air flow was then changed to oxygen and heating continued for about 80

PLATE 3

PLATE 4

142

minutes. The CO_2 was collected in initially CO_2 free $Ba(OH)_2$. The $Ba(OH)_2$ was acidified with 50% Analar HCl and the resulting CO_2 dried with sulphuric acid and collected in traps at 77°K. The whole process was carried out with a continuous flow of purified white spot N_2.

Carbon dioxide was evolved vigorously, carried into the vacuum system with nitrogen, and trapped out. Reaction was complete in approximately thirty minutes and the acid flow stopped. The reaction mixture was stirred briskly for a few minutes to ensure complete mixing of the sediment and acid, and to purge the mixture of dissolved carbon dioxide, and the cold-traps were then isolated. Nitrogen gas left in the system was slowly pumped off, and the traps isolated from the pump. The Dewar flasks on the second and third traps were removed and the traces of carbon dioxide that had accumulated in them allowed to evaporate into the first, main trap.

3. *Formation of lithium carbide* The lithium furnace was opened to the pump, and a swift flow of water through the cooling coil begun. Heating was commenced with a small flame, which was gradually increased. A considerable amount of gas was given off by the warm lithium. After approximately fifteen minutes the lithium could be seen glowing a very dull red and the pressure in the furnace was 3–4×10^{-2} mm of mercury. Continuing the heating, the furnace was isolated from the pump, and opened, via the 3-way tap, to the carbon dioxide traps. The Dewar flask was removed, and carbon dioxide allowed to evaporate and diffuse over to the hot lithium. After about five minutes, the reaction began and the lithium glowed a bright red

colour. All the carbon dioxide evaporated after about forty-five minutes, and the pressure over the whole system, as monitored by the mercury manometer, had reached 2–3 mm.

After one hour, the furnace was opened to the pump; a brief increase in pressure registered on the Pirani gauge. Pumping was continued for ninety minutes, keeping the furnace at reaction temperature. This was done to remove any radon present which might otherwise contaminate the sample. The furnace was then isolated, heating stopped, and the reaction chamber allowed to cool overnight while still maintaining a flow of water through the cooling coil.

4. *Dehydration of the catalyst* Prior to hydrolysis, the catalyst must be dehydrated and left in vacuo ready for reaction. The quantity used was 5 g activated catalyst per litre of acetylene; this was roughly weighed out and loaded into the catalysis vessel. A vacuum was pulled, and the vessel heated to 350°C with a small tube furnace which can be raised round the lower half of the vessel, controlled by a 2 amp. Variac. Water vapour was pulled off and the Pirani gauge showed a slow decrease in pressure. At $c.10^{-2}$ mm of mercury (usually after one hour), heating was stopped and the catalysis vessel isolated and allowed to cool.

5. *Hydrolysis of lithium carbide* The furnace was opened to the pump via the acetylene traps, and Dewar flasks placed round the second, third and fourth traps. The aspirator was filled with $c. 4$ l. of distilled water, and hydrolysis begun by allowing a very slow trickle of water into the furnace. A very violent reaction proceeded, and

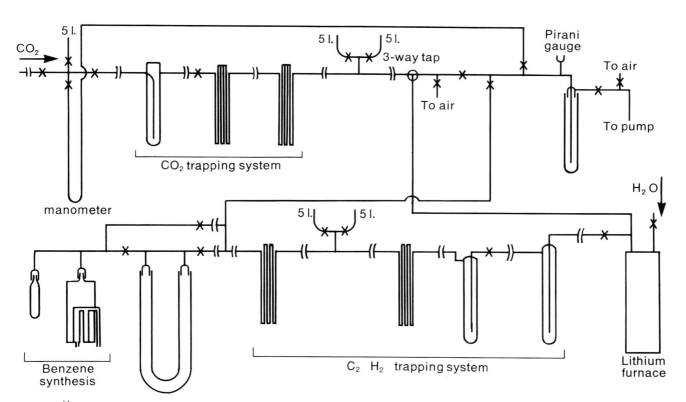

FIG. 6. ^{14}C Vacuum Apparatus

143

excessive frothing could be seen through the viewport. The reaction took about thirty minutes to complete, using c.1.5 l. of water. As the reaction proceeded, the flow of water was gradually increased so as to provide an adequate volume; if a high yield is to be obtained from the reaction, it is necessary to have the solution after hydrolysis as dilute as possible. Throughout the reaction, water was circulated through the cooling coil and the base of the furnace was also cooled with a bath of ice-water.

When gas was either not being evolved, or evolved very slowly, as indicated by the Pirani gauge, the acetylene traps were isolated from the furnace and hydrogen left in the system pumped away. The traps were then isolated from the pump, and all the acetylene distilled into the second trap.

6. *Conversion of acetylene to benzene* The polymerization reaction goes at room temperature but evolves considerable heat; consequently the catalysis vessel was cooled with a swift flow of water through the inner jacket, and also on the outside with a 1.5 l. beaker containing an ice/water mixture.

The catalysis vessel was opened to the acetylene traps via the U-tube containing phosphoric acid by opening the relevant taps on either side of the tube, and the Dewar flask was removed from the second trap. Acetylene evaporated and diffused on to the catalyst through the phosphoric acid column. The phosphoric acid removes water, some of which was always carried over into the acetylene traps during hydrolysis, and ammonia which originated from traces of nitrogen left in the carbon dioxide traps before carbide formation, presumably forming ammonium phosphate.

The reaction was allowed to proceed for one hour, and the catalysis vessel was then isolated.

7. *Distillation of benzene* Benzene produced in the last reaction remains adsorbed on the catalyst. It was distilled off in a similar manner to the catalyst dehydration process, but at a temperature of 150°C, and collected in the small trap adjacent to the catalysis vessel under liquid nitrogen. After one hour, heating was stopped and the system opened up to air. The benzene trap was quickly removed, and any silicone grease round the cone joint taken off with a Kleenex medical wipe.

Difficulties of development of the process Considerable difficulty was encountered during construction of the apparatus and development of the process; most of this was due to the fact that the apparatus was built on a very small scale, and that the chemical reactions involved are extremely vigorous (e.g. the hydrolysis of lithium carbide). This means that the reactions have to be carried out at a carefully controlled rate to avoid problems of excessive pressure. The oxidation ahd hydrolysis stages are examples of this; unless done at the correct rate, there is a danger of carbon dioxide and carrier nitrogen venting through the separating funnel in the former, and similar venting of acetylene and hydrogen through the aspirator in the latter case. If hydrolysis is carried out too quickly, there is also the problem of excessive frothing causing a lithium carbide/water/gas mixture to enter the acetylene trapping system; for this reason the first trap

after the furnace was not provided with a Dewar flask, but left clear to act as an emergency reservoir.

The second major problem was that of a low yield in the reaction

$$3C_2H_2 \rightarrow C_6H_6$$

Vanadium catalysts similar to the one used are known to be highly efficient but yields of only 50% or less were initially realised. This was found to be due to the two 5 litre reservoirs which were originally included in the acetylene system during catalysis; later these were isolated, so that the only residual volume was that formed by the cold-traps and the part of the benzene synthesis system not occupied by the catalyst. Acetylene then evaporates and diffuses on to the catalyst at a much higher pressure. Yields of over 80% were realised once this technique was adopted.

The lifetime of the catalyst was not specifically studied. No deterioration in efficiency was noted when performing subsequent runs with the same batch however, in fact if anything there was a slight increase in efficiency.

8. *Counting Procedure* Immediately the frozen benzene had liquefied it was transferred to a 20 ml polythene low background scintillation vial containing 10 ml scintillator solution ready for counting. The benzene yield was obtained by weight. The scintillator was the commercial preparation 'Lipoluma', manufactured by Lumac Systems A.G., Aeschengraben, 6 CH-4051, Basel.

The samples were counted in a Searle Model 6880 Mark III liquid scintillator counter in the following sequence, Background, NBS oxalic acid, in-house ^{14}C benzene standard, sample 1 . . . sample 6, in-house ^{14}C benzene standard, Background. The samples were counted for 10 min. each and cycled until the appropriate statistics were obtained.

Results and Discussion

The count rates of the various samples and controls are shown in Table 1.

TABLE 1

Count Rates of Samples and Controls

Sample	Count rate (cpm)
NBS oxalic acid 1	13.44 ± 0.16
1770/469 R. Scapula	9.14 ± 0.20
1770 L. Scapula	9.09 ± 0.19
1770 Outer bandage	10.55 ± 0.16
1770 Part 4 bandage	10.40 ± 0.17
NBS oxalic acid 2	13.43 ± 0.16
In-house oxalic acid	13.50 ± 0.16
In-house benzene	13.60 ± 0.16

^{12}C/^{13}C ratios were done on some of the samples, these are given in Table 2.

Table 2
$^{13}C/^{12}C$ Ratios of Samples and Controls

Sample	$^{13}C/^{12}C$ Ratio	$\delta^{13}C°/oo$
NBS oxalic acid	1.107×10^{-8}	-15.1
In-house standard oxalic acid	1.106×10^{-8}	-16.2
1770/469 R. Scapula	1.095×10^{-8}	-26.0
1770 Part 4 bandage	1.096×10^{-8}	-24.3
Belemnite standard (PDB)	1.12372×10^{-8}	—

The results were calculated as follows:

The radioactive law of decay gives

$$\frac{dN}{dt} = -\lambda N \qquad \ldots (1)$$

where N is the no. of radioactive atoms remaining at time t and d is the decay constant for the particular isotope.

$$\lambda = \frac{.693}{t_{1/2}}, \text{ and } \tau = \frac{t_{1/2}}{.693}$$

$$\therefore \frac{1}{\lambda} = \tau$$

In the case of ^{14}C:

$t_{1/2}$	λ yrs.	τ yrs.	
5568 ± 30	1.245×10^{-4}	8035	(Libby)
5730 ± 40	1.210×10^{4}	8267	

On integration of equation 1 and substituting

A (activity) $= \dfrac{dN}{dt}$, then

$$A = A_o \, e^{-\lambda t}$$

A = activity at time t,

A_o = activity at some original time,

$$\therefore \log_e \frac{A_o}{A} = \lambda t.$$

$$\text{and } t = \tau \log_e (A_o/A) \qquad \ldots (2)$$

This enables the age of a sample (t yrs) to be determined from the carbon 14 count rate at death A_o and the carbon 14 count rate at present A.

Initially it is assumed that the radioactivity of the sample at death was the same as modern ^{14}C radioactivity. The widely used reference is NBS oxalic acid, although because it is a recent preparation it contains some activity from weapons testing. The generally accepted[30] ^{14}C radioactivity standard is $0.95 \, A_{ox}$ ($A_{ox} = ^{14}C$ radioactivity of NBS oxalic acid).

Therefore $A_o = 0.950 \, A_{ox}$.

(The factor 0.950 arises because 1890 oak wood — occurring early in the industrial revolution and before weapons testing — has 95% ^{14}C radioactivity of NBS oxalic acid.)

A small correction is applied for the decay of ^{14}C in NBS oxalic acid between the time of preparation

(1 January 1958) and the time of use. In this case this was twenty years and the correction factor is:

$$A_o = 0.950 \, A_{ox} \, e^{\lambda t}$$

$$= 0.950 \, A_{ox} \, e^{1.210 \times 10^{-4} \times 20}$$

$$= 0.950 \, A_{ox} \, 1.00242$$

$$A_o = 0.9523 \, A_{ox} \qquad \ldots (3)$$

Results are often quoted as the difference between the sample activity and the modern reference activity.

$\delta^{14}C$ is defined as $\left\{ \dfrac{A_{sample}}{A_o} - 1 \ 1000 \right\}$ $\ldots (4)$

$$\therefore A_o/A_{sample} = \frac{1000}{\delta^{14}C + 1000}$$

$$\text{and } t = \tau \log_e \frac{1000}{\delta^{14}C + 1000} \qquad \ldots (5)$$

From equations 2, 3 and 5 the ages and ^{14}C values were calculated for the samples using the count rates given in Table 1:

Table 3
Ages of 1770 samples

Sample	$\delta^{14}C$	Age (yrs BP)	Age
1770/469 R. Scapula	-285.6	2780 ± 180	822 BC
1770 L. Scapula	-289.5	2826 ± 173	868 BC
1770 Outer bandage	-175.4	1594 ± 126	364 AD
1770 Part 4 bandage	-187.1	1713 ± 135	245 AD

$$(A_o = 0.9523 \, A_{ox} = 12.794 \text{ cpm})$$

These dates quoted earlier[31] ignore isotope fractionation in the preparation of CO_2 from the sample and oxalic acid. This can be mentioned by using the more abundant ^{13}C isotope measured mass spectrometrically on a sample of the CO_2.

By definition:

$$\delta^{13}C = \left\{ \frac{(^{13}C/^{12}C)_{sample} - (^{13}C/^{12}C)_{std}}{(^{13}C/^{12}C)_{std}} \right\} 1000$$

The enrichment of ^{13}C due to isotope fractionation is only half that of ^{14}C.

$$\left\{ \frac{A_{ox(N)} - A_o}{A_o} \right\} 1000 = -2\delta^{13}C \qquad \ldots (6)$$

Ox(N) = A_o (meaning as before) corrected for isotope fractionation. Factor of 2 for reason above, — sign because ^{14}C activity must be increased due to loss of ^{14}C by fractionation.

The reference standard used is usually PDB calcium carbonate. This is a Cretaceous belemnite (Belemnitella americana) from the Peedee formation of South Carolina. As seen from Table 2 PDB has a $^{13}C/^{12}C$ ratio of 1.12372×10^{-8}. Several measurements of NBS oxalic acid have shown that it has a $^{13}C/^{12}C$ ratio of 1.1015×10^{-8} giving a $\delta^{13}C$ value of $-19.77°/oo$. From equation (6)

$$A_{ox(N)} = A_o \left\{1 - \frac{2(19.77 + \delta^{13}C_{ox})}{1000}\right\}$$

In the present work $\delta^{13}C_{ox} = -15.1°/oo$

$\underline{A_{ox(N)} = 12.675 \text{ cpm.}}$ $(A_o = 12.794 \text{ cpm})$

A new set of ages of 1770 samples are given in Table 4 based on isotope fractionation in oxalic acid alone.

TABLE 4

1770 ages allowing for fractionation in NBS oxalic acid

Sample	Age (BP yrs)	Age
1770/469 R. Scapula	2702	744 BC
1770 L. Scapula	2748	790 BC
1770 outer bandage	1517	441 AD
1770 Part 4 bandage	1635	323 AD

In addition to fractionation in the oxalic acid there is also the possibility of fractionation in the sample.

By definition:

$$\delta_s{}^{13}C°/oo = \left\{\frac{(^{13}C/^{12}C)_{sample}}{(^{13}C/^{12}C)PDB} - 1\right\} 1000$$

$$\Delta^{14}C°/oo = \delta^{14}C - (2\delta^{13}C + 50)(1 + \frac{\delta^{14}C}{1000})$$

(The value of 50 appears because it has been shown that nineteenth-century woods have a $\delta^{13}C$ value around $-25°/oo$. Therefore the $\Delta^{14}C$ will fall close to zero if this constant is included.)

$\Delta^{14}C = \delta^{14}C$ if there is no isotope fractionation.

The age can be calculated from equation (5) if $\Delta^{14}C$ is substituted for $\delta^{14}C$. This has been done in Table 5 where a new set of dates have been calculated allowing for fractionation in both the sample and the oxalic acid.

TABLE 5

1770 Ages allowing for isotope fractionation

Sample	$\delta^{14}C$	$\Delta^{14}C$	Age BP	Age
1770/469 R. Scapula	−278.9	−277.5	2687	729 BC
1770 Part 4 bandage	—179.5	−180.6	1647	311 AD

The radiocarbon ages are shown in Table 6.

TABLE 6

1770 Radiocarbon ages

Sample	No fractiona-tion	Oxalic fractiona-tion	All fractiona-tion
1770/469 R. Scapula	822 BC	744 BC	729 BC
1770 L. Scapula	868 BC	790 BC	—
1770 outer bandage	364 AD	441 AD	—
1770 Part 4 bandage	245 AD	323 AD	311 AD

Finally, it is necessary to consider the variation in ^{14}C activity in the last 2000–3000 years. This can be done with reference to the tree ring correction curve of MASCA[16] shown in Figs 2–5.

The corrected values are shown in Table 7.

TABLE 7

1770 Dates with tree ring corrections[16]

Sample	Corrected for fractionation	Tree-ring Correction
1770/469 R. Scapula	744 BC	900 BC
1770 L. Scapula	790 BC	1100 BC
1770 outer bandage	441 AD	441 AD
1770 Part 4 bandage	323 AD	323 AD
On average bones ∼	770 BC	1000 BC
bandage ∼	380 AD	380 AD

The conclusion is clear that the bones appear older than the bandages, and this conclusion is independent of any corrections. It is possible that the bones contain more organic carbon of fossil origin, example bitumen from the Dead Sea area which could have been used in the mummification process. However, because of the careful pretreatment of the samples we consider this unlikely. The remaining conclusion is that the body was wrapped or rewrapped in bandages some considerable time after death.

References

[1] G. Daniel, BBC Radio 3 broadcast, 2/12/76.
[2] W. F. Libby, *Radiocarbon Dating*, 2nd Edn., 1955, University of Chicago Press.
[3] (i) W. B. Mann, W. F. Marlow and E. E. Hughes, *Int. J. Appl. Radiation Isotopes*, 1961, 11, 57.
(ii) H. Godwin, *Nature*, London, 1962, 195, 984.
[4] H. Suess, *J. Geophysical Research*, 1965, LXX (23), 5937.
[5] E. H. Willis, M. Tauber and K. O. Münnich, *American Journal of Science*, Radiocarbon Supplement, 1960, 2, 3.
[6] H. de Vries, *Kon Neder Akad. van Wet. Proc.*, Ser. B 61, 1958, 94–102.
[7] K. Kigoshi and H. Hasegawa, *J. Geophysical Research*, 1966, LXXI, 1065.
[8] V. Bucha, *Phil. Trans. Roy. Soc.*, London, 1970, A269, 47.
[9] P. E. Damon, A. Long and D. C. Grey, 'Radiocarbon Variations and Absolute Chronology', *Nobel Symposium*, 12, ed. I. U. Olsson, Stockholm, 1970, 617.

[10] J. Vogel, ibid., p. 125.

[11] C. W. Ferguson, ibid., p. 237.

[12] H. Suess, ibid., p. 304.

[13] H. Jansen, ibid., p. 264.

[14] H. Jansen, *New Zealand J. Sci.*, 1962, VI, 78.

[15] H. Tauber, *Archaeologia Austriaca*, 1958, 24, 59.

[16] E. K. Ralph, H. N. Michael, M. C. Han, 1973: *MASCA Newsletter*, 9 (1), 1 (Applied Science Centre for Archaeology, The University Museum, University of Pennsylvania).

[17] J. A. Campbell, M. S. Baxter and D. D. Harkness, *Archaeometry*, 1978, 20, 33.

[18] I. E. S. Edwards, *Phil. Trans. Roy. Soc.*, London, 1970, A269, 11.

[19] H. McKerrell in *Radiocarbon: Calibration and Prehistory*, ed. T. Watkins, Edinburgh University Press, 1975, pp. 47–100 and 110–27.

[20] H. N. Michael and E. K. Ralph, ref. 9, p. 109.

[21] T. Säve-Söderborgh and I. U. Olsson, ref. 9, p. 35.

[22] R. D. Long, *Z. für Ägyptische Sprache*, 1976, 103, 30.

[23] See S. Fleming, in *Dating in Archaeology*, Dent & Sons, London, 1976.

[24] W. C. Hayes, M. B. Rawton and R. H. Stubbings, *The Cambridge Ancient History*, Vol. I and II revised, Fascicle 4, 22–23, 1964.

[25] R. M. Clark, *Archaeometry*, 1978, 20, 5.

[26] O. Neugebauer, *A History of Ancient Mathematical Astronomy*, Springer-Verlag, Heidelberg, 1975, Part Two, p. 559 et seq.

[27] Ref. 20, p. 4.

[28] E. J. Bickerman, *Chronology of the Ancient World*, Thames & Hudson, London, 1968.

[29] W. C. Hayes, *The Cambridge Ancient History*, Vol. I and II revised, Fascicle 3, back cover, 1964.

[30] R. A. Muller, *Science*, 1977, 196, 489.

[31] A. Rebello and K. Wagener, *Environmental Biogeochemistry*, ed. J. O. Nriagu, Vol. I, 1976, 21. Ann Arbor Science, Michigan.

[32] H. Barber, *Nature*, 1953, 172, 631.

[33] J. E. Noakes, S. M. Kim, J. J. Stipp, *Proc. 6th Internat. Conf. ^{14}C and ^{3}H dating*, June 6–11 (1965), p. 68–93.

The Reconstruction of the Heads and Faces of three Ancient Egyptian Mummies

by

R. A. H. Neave

Introduction

The size and shape of a human head is determined largely by the underlying bone structure, as are the facial features, the skull being the matrix upon which the head and face are built. Detailed examination of the skull can generally reveal the age and sex of the individual, and characteristics peculiar to race or ethnic group may also be apparent. The condition of the teeth provides valuable information. The configuration of muscle attachments provides evidence of size and strength, although in the face these are confined mainly to the base of the skull and the lower jaw. It is therefore possible, in principle, to reconstruct the major features of the human head with some degree of accuracy. However, a reconstruction can reveal only the type of face that *may* have existed, the position and general shape of the main features being accurate, but reconstructions of subtle details such as wrinkles and folds being inevitably speculative as there is no factual evidence as to their form or even their existence.

There have been a number of workers in this field, the most notable and often quoted being Kollmann and Büchly[1] who in 1898 published an account of their methods, and listed the thickness of the soft tissues of the head and face at twenty-three points. Table 4 of Kollmann and Büchly's work, in which their data for males are compounded with the earlier figures of His, provides maximum and minimum values for soft tissue thicknesses. It was upon these figures that the reconstruction of a head, thought to be that of Akhenaten, was initiated by Professor Harrison[2] with very positive results. Harrison's method was to mark the measurements off on anterior and lateral photographs of the skull and draw out a profile and anterior configuration. This method differs considerably from that of Kollmann and Büchly who made a three dimensional reconstruction. The three dimensional reconstruction is also the preferred method of both Gerasimov[3] and Krogman[4] when the remains are in an adequate state of preservation, and readily accessible. Because of its wide range of applications it was decided to adopt a similar approach for the reconstruction of the heads of three Egyptian mummies as part of the Manchester Museum Mummy Project.

The objective was to produce drawings and paintings which would enable those who viewed the mummified remains to relate them more easily with living people as they may have appeared. The three dimensional 'busts' of the heads would serve as models upon which such illustrations could be based. It was considered essential that these illustrations be established as far as was possible upon scientific principles to eliminate 'artistic licence', thus ensuring a standardized procedure for all the heads, and enabling comparisons to be made between them.

The first two mummies chosen are in many ways unique. They were unwrapped by Dr Margaret Murray

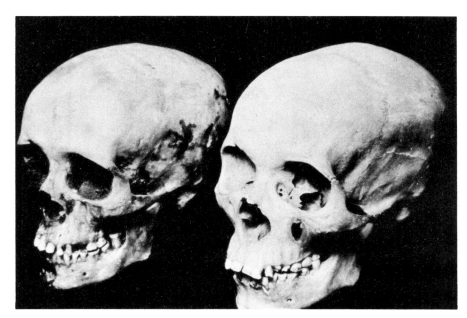

(1) The skulls of the two brothers Khnum-Nakht (*right*) and Nekht-Ankh (*left*)

149

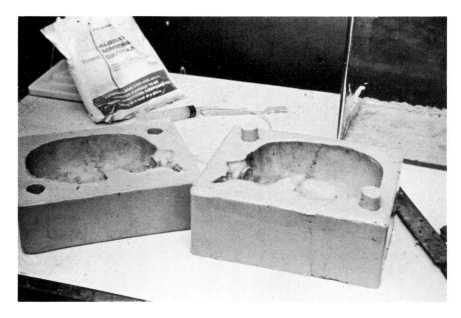

(2) The final appearance of the mould: the location lugs and sockets are clearly shown

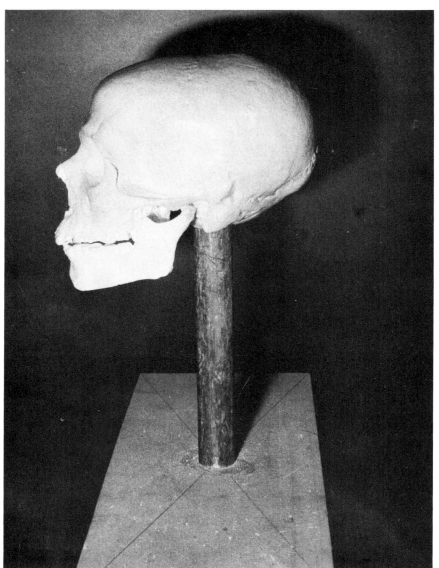

(3) The completed cast of the skull of Khnum-Nakht mounted

150

at Manchester Museum in 1907; all her findings were very carefully documented and a considerable amount of work has been done on them since.[5] It is known that they were buried together in the rock-tombs of Der-Rifeh and date from Dyn. XII. From the hieroglyphs on the coffins it appears that they were half-brothers, sharing a common mother, and all the evidence suggests that the younger of the two, Khnum-Nakht, had a negro father. He is estimated to have been between 40–45 years old at death, and to have suffered from osteo-arthritis which had seriously affected his back. The skull of Khnum-Nakht is in a perfect state of preservation; there are, however, no remains of any soft tissues. The skull is markedly prognathous, powerful in appearance and with a full set of teeth. The two upper left incisor teeth are fused together (geminated) and behind them lies an accessory incisor. The elder brother, Nekht-Ankh, is estimated to have been 60 years old at death. His skull is also in perfect condition, only the upper right incisor being absent. It is very much more delicate in appearance, the zygomatic arches being slender, the mastoid processes small, and the marking of muscle origins and insertions far less distinct than in the younger skull. It has been suggested that he may have been a eunuch, but this has not been substantiated (1).

The third mummy, that of a girl of about 13 years old which was also unwrapped in Manchester in 1975, presented many problems. Labelled '1770' for identification purposes, this mummy, unlike the previous two, was badly damaged; the skull, which had no preserved soft tissue, had been broken into some 30–40 pieces. Fortunately the majority of the bones which form the face were largely undamaged, although covered in a thick layer of mud and packing. The mandible was fractured to the left of the mid line and both mandibula heads were broken. The vault was totally shattered with many pieces missing.

Casting of the Skulls

The conservation of specimens of such antiquity as the skulls of the two brothers was of prime importance. Therefore before any reconstruction work could be started it was necessary to make accurate casts of each, utilising techniques developed in the department for making casts of medical specimens. The skulls were first prepared by lightly filling in all areas which were likely to cause deep undercuts in the mould, for example: the eye sockets, the space between the zygoma and temporal bone, the external auditory meatus, the nasal cavity, the foramen magnum, plus all foramina and openings at the base of the skull. It was felt that these details should be sacrificed rather than risk damaging the skulls when removing them from the moulds.

Each skull was then placed on its side in a glass container supported on three plasticine prongs about one inch high. A thin plastic tube was taped to the side and down to the base of the glass container. A quantity of dental algenate was prepared, one part algenate powder to three parts water. This was poured into the container totally investing the skull up to the mid line. Two 1 in. × 2 in. corks were pushed 1 in. into the wet algenate at each corner of the tank and held in place. The setting

time is approximately two minutes. When the algenate had set the corks were removed and a second mix was poured in filling the holes left by the corks and totally covering the rest of the skull to a depth of 2 in. When the second layer had set, air was forced into the plastic tube releasing the vacuum between the glass container and the mould and allowing the mould to slide gently out. The junction between the first and second layers of algenate was located and the two halves prised gently apart and the skull lifted out. Because of the flexible nature of an algenate mould and its total lack of adhesion it was possible to obtain a perfect 'split mould' without endangering the skull (2). The two halves of the mould were reunited, the lug and the socket, caused by the cork ensuring accurate relocation. The whole mould was then placed back in the glass tank, a small ½ in. opening was cut in the top with a scalpel through which plaster of Paris was poured until the mould was filled. Shortly after

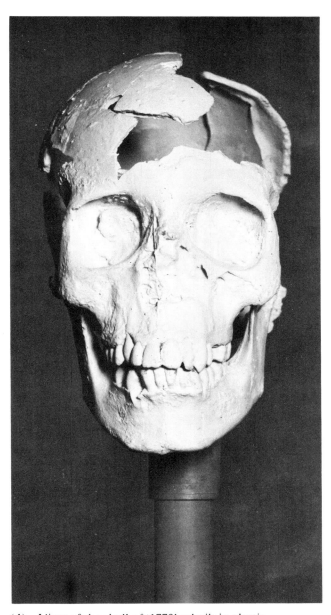

(4) View of the skull of '1770' rebuilt in plastic

151

the plaster had set it was possible to remove a very accurate cast of the original skull. The lower jaw was cast as a separate item using the 'split mould' technique. A bridge of plasticine was fitted across the inside of the mandible with a short pillar in the middle, which protruded through the top of the mould. This provided an opening through which the mould could be filled with plaster after the removal of the mandible. Finally, the plaster mandible was fitted into position on the skull. A hole 1 in. diameter and some 3 in. deep was drilled into the plaster skull at the location of the foramen magnum, the whole then being set on to a stout wooden stand (3). As stated earlier the skull of the 13-year-old girl, '1770', was broken into many pieces a large number of which were missing; fortunately the majority of her teeth were present although some of them were not actually in place. An algenate mould was made of each separate piece of bone. In most cases the fragments had merely to be pressed lightly into a small dish of stiff algenate to provide a very satisfactory mould. The casting of the largest portion which included the maxilla, parts of the

zygomatic bones, and a ridge of the frontal bone providing complete orbital cavities, was less simple. Being extremely fragile only a thin layer of algenate could be applied to the surface; when set, a layer of plaster was added to provide support for the very thin and flexible algenate mould. A quick curing plastic was used to make the casts (N.H.P. plastic), which were then assembled to form the replica skull (4). The missing areas were replaced with wax; this enabled a final cast of the whole skull to be made in plaster of Paris. This cast differed slightly from the previous two in that the lower jaw was in position. Not only did this save time it also provided a much more robust form upon which to do the final reconstruction.

Reconstruction of Soft Tissue

The reconstruction of the soft tissues on the now prepared plaster skulls was started by first 'blocking-in' with soft modelling clay the head, neck and face, allowing the features to develop naturally. It is interesting to note how a skull will start to take on the character of a face at a very early stage. So delicate and fine are the muscles of the face that they leave very few marks on bones to indicate their origins or insertions. The nose is made up largely by cartilage, and fat also is an integral part of the soft tissue of the face. As the controlling factor in this reconstruction was to be tissue thickness there seemed little point in following anatomical structures too closely, the clay being pressed into place in blocks and modelled according to the dictates of the underlying skull.

Measurements were made, the thickness of the clay being increased or decreased as necessary until it corresponded to the mean of the maximum and minimum thickness for soft tissue of the face at twenty-one specific points. These figures based upon Table 4 of Kollmann and Büchly's work are listed below:

Upper forehead	3.56 mm
Lower forehead	4.69
Nasal root	4.93
Mid nasal bone	3.25
Tip of nasal bone	2.12
Root of upper lip	11.57
Phittrum	9.48
Mental sulcus	10.05
Chin pad	10.22
Middle of masseter	17.52
At the angle of the mandible	10.46
Under the chin	6.08
Middle of eyebrow	3.65
Mid infraorbital	4.29
Front of mosseter	8.20
Root of zygomatic arch	6.74
Highest point of zygomatic arch	4.33
Highest point of malar	6.62
Nasal breadth at alae	35.65
Nasal depth from tip to root of lip	23.69
Height of upper lip	21.63

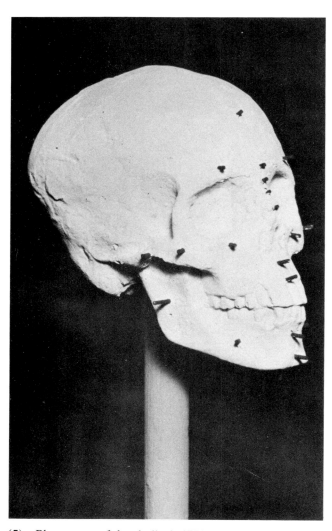

(5) Plaster cast of the skull of '1770' showing the pegs inserted at specific points and of specific lengths

The measurements were taken by passing a thin steel probe through the clay at the specific points, the area was then reduced or increased in thickness to conform to those listed. A slight variation to this system was adapted for the head of the girl '1770' in that pegs cut to the appropriate length were fixed in position on the plaster skull (5). The clay was then built up until it was of the correct thickness. This method was more accurate as it ensured that the measured thickness was in exactly the right place. Adjustments were made at the stage when the clay model was completed, which enabled minor ethnic considerations to be highlighted. These involved the eyes, which in ancient Egyptians were more almond shaped, and the tip of the nose. The measurements for the head of '1770' were based upon those in Table 3 from Kollmann and Büchly. However, considerable licence was allowed in order to avoid the somewhat cadaverous look of the two brothers, and also to try to capture the appearance so peculiar to young adolescents. It is questionable whether the second objective was, in fact, achieved.

The size and shape of the nose, especially the profile, have not unnaturally been the cause of considerable discussion. The width of the nasal cavity can give a reasonable clue to the width of the nose, at a point across the wings, the bony opening being about three-fifths of the overall width (Krogmann). However, although a number of formulae have been suggested, all of which are approximations, the shape and form of the cartilaginous part will always remain a mystery. The anterior nasal spine and the nasal bone, if present, are the key points, for although they do not show us exactly what the shape was, they can give a good indication of the direction and the form that the nose must have taken. This, combined with a knowledge of ethnic group, age, and sex, gives enough information for speculation with a fair degree of accuracy. It does not allow, of course, for the unusual or the bizarre. The width of the mouth is generally recognized as being approximately equal to

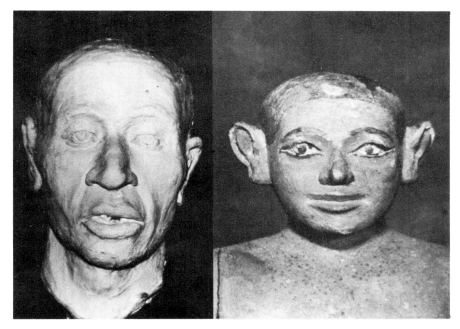

(6) Comparison of reconstruction with carved head of Khnum-Nakht

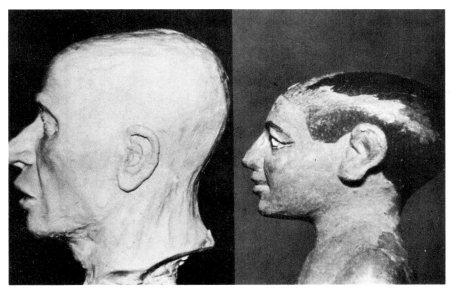

(7) Comparison of reconstruction with carved head of Khnum-Nakht

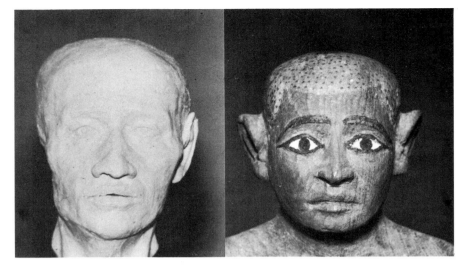

(8) Comparison of reconstruction with carved head of Nekht-Ankh

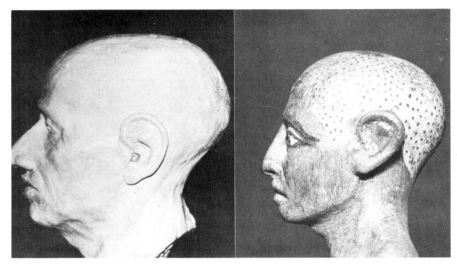

(9) Comparison of reconstruction with carved head of Nekht-Ankh

that of the inter-pupillary distance; again this does not accommodate the unusual forms that the mouth can sometimes take.

Information provided by the remains of '1770' was somewhat limited at the time of making the reconstruction. Both legs appeared to have been amputated, one above and one below the knee, but whether before or after death was not known. There was evidence to indicate some intestinal infection, and an irregularity in the formation of the bone in the region of the nose suggests the probability of nasal congestion, which may have given rise to a slightly adenoidal appearance.

Within the coffins of the two brothers were two small statuettes, 15.5 cm and 25.4 cm high, carved from wood. These represented the deceased as they had been when in full health. There was some apparent confusion as to the identity of these statuettes as the names written on their stands do not seem to correspond. So skilfully were they carved that it was decided to make some comparisons of the heads, which were some 3 cm. long, with the life-size reconstructions. As can be seen from the photographs (6 and 7), the head of the statuette of Khnum-Nakht is powerfully built, with full lips and broad nose,

and compatible with the reconstruction which exhibits the similar features. The head of the second statuette Nekht-Ankh (8 and 9), is quite different, being more lightly formed, possessing a rather more delicate nose and a smaller mouth and chin. Again the similarity, although not striking, is unmistakable. It is unlikely that a very close resemblance between statuettes and reconstruction would occur accidentally as the difference in size is so great.

As stated earlier, the objective was to produce illustrations using the clay busts as models. A sketch of Khnum-Nakht (10) was made from the clay reconstruction (11). The somewhat cadaverous look has gone, caused in the first instance by the fact that the measurements upon which the reconstruction was based were taken from cadavers. Khnum-Nakht would appear to have been a man with strong features somewhat Negroid in appearance. He may well have had quite a handsome face. In this case, we do not know much about his hair, but it would be reasonable to assume that it was black, and that his skin was a swarthy olive colour. The illustration depicts Nekht-Ankh (12) as an older man, about sixty. We know that he had short grey hair as evidence

154

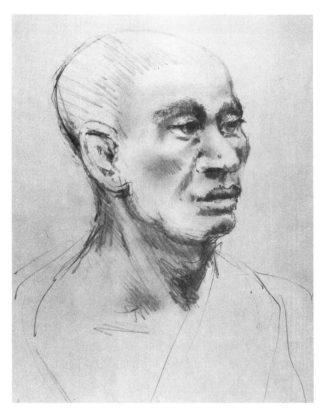

(10) Clay 'bust' of Khnum-Nakht

(11) Chalk drawing of Khnum-Nakht, based on clay reconstruction

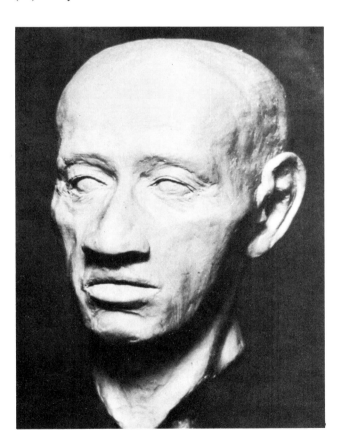

(12) Clay 'bust' of Nekht-Ankh

(13) Painting of Nekht-Ankh based upon the clay reconstruction

155

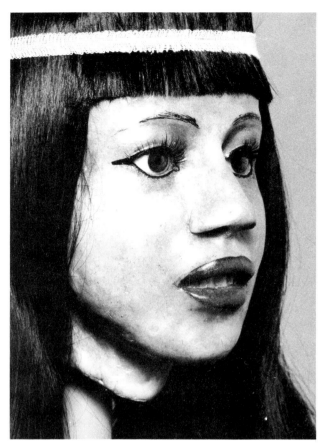

(14) The final wax 'bust' of '1770' complete with hair, eyes and make-up

of this was found during the unwrapping (13). His appearance is less prepossessing than that of his half-brother, with a much weaker face and less well defined features.

The final reconstruction of '1770' (14) is in many ways more satisfactory because we have been able to give some form of identity to a handful of broken bones. This reconstruction was taken further than the previous two because of the rather special circumstances which prevailed at the time. A cast of the clay bust was made in wax, into which it was possible to fit glass eyes and eyelashes. Colour was added to the mouth and skin, together with a limited amount of make-up which would almost certainly have been worn by a girl of this age. The hair, which was added in the form of a wig, was for exhibition purposes only, and is not regarded as a part of the reconstruction work. The results in the case of '1770' were most unexpected and show a young girl, perhaps slightly adenoidal but not unattractive. The bony anamoly of the nose would not have been apparent in life so the contours of the face would hardly have been affected. Her mouth is full and a little fleshy, quite compatible with the skull which is somewhat prognathic. It was felt that to show a finely chiselled mouth as is sometimes seen in Ancient Egyptian paintings and drawings would be too positive a statement from such limited information.

Although the project produced acceptable and useful results, it was impossible to know just how accurate the reconstructed heads were. To check this a very limited study was done in a way that enabled comparisons to be made between an actual head and a reconstruction of the same head. This was achieved in the following manner. Three cadavers were selected from those due to be embalmed in the Department of Anatomy, University of Manchester Medical School, in preparation for anatomical dissection. Before embalming took place photographs were taken of both anterior and lateral views. These pictures were not seen by those involved in the reconstruction work. When the dissection had been completed by the medical students, as part of their studies, the three heads located by their serial numbers were made available for reconstruction. These remains, unlike those of the mummies, had a considerable amount of soft tissue, some of which had to be removed to expose the bone at the required points for the purpose of making measurements. It was, however, not possible to gain any helpful information from the soft tissue, as all the relevant structures had been removed or destroyed during dissection.

The specimens were far from perfect, and thus provided a good test for the method. The top of each skull had been removed, openings had been made to expose both frontal and maxillary sinuses, and in two the mandible had been divided. There were no original teeth present in any of the specimens. Because of the limitations in both time and resources only the anterior portions of the specimens were cast. Measured pegs were fitted into the casts in their prescribed positions and the clay built up as previously described. When completed, photographs were taken and compared with those made of the cadavers prior to embalming. Unfortunately, during the two years which intervened between the embalming and the reconstruction one set of pre-embalming photographs had been lost. Thus only two reconstructions could be properly assessed. The results are useful, demonstrating that the type of face that existed can be roughly reproduced. The reconstruction of the male specimen bore a strong likeness to the original head, although there were details of the nose that did not correspond exactly, and the somewhat fleshy fullness of the face, especially in the region of the lower jaw, was absent. In the female specimen the likeness was even more striking, although here again there was a slight inaccuracy in the nose. It should be stated that, although in both cases the nose did not correspond exactly with those of the original heads, they were approximately the right size and type. The thickness of soft tissue upon the human face can alter considerably during life, some losing and others gaining tissue for one reason or another. An individual will still be easily recognized in spite of these changes. Thus slight variations in a reconstruction are not necessarily critical.

It would be misleading to suggest that this method can recreate an accurate portrait from a skull. There are far too many variations in individual parts of the face that can never be known. However, it would be reasonable to claim that the type of face can be rebuilt to some extent. The size and general configuration can be regarded as accurate and thus provide some idea of the appearance of the individual during life.

Acknowledgements

I should like to thank Mr John Hartshorn, Senior Medical Artist, who worked with me during the reconstruction of The Two Brothers and who produced the bust of Khnum-Nakht; Miss Shian Percy, Medical Artist, who gave so much help, especially with the reconstruction of '1770'; Mr Robert Mitchell and Mr Ronald Murray for recording photographically all the work and producing slides and prints of such fine quality. My thanks are due also to Dr R. W. G. Ollerenshaw and the staff of the University Department of Medical Illustration Manchester without whose support this work would not have been possible.

References

[1] Kollman and Büchly, Arch. f. Anth., 25 (1898).
[2] R. G. Harrison, Pharaonic Remains purported to be Akhenaten.
[3] M. Gerasimov, The Face Finder, 1971.
[4] W. M. Krogman, The Human Skeleton in Forensic Medicine, 1973.
[5] M. A. Murray, The Tomb of the Two Brothers, Manchester Museum, 1910.

157

Conclusion

by

A. ROSALIE DAVID

It has been the main aim of this project to establish a methodology, under near-ideal conditions, for the examination of a group of Egyptian mummified remains, and also to identify disease in the bodies and, whenever possible, to determine the cause of death. Furthermore, information was sought which would either confirm our existing knowledge of funerary and religious beliefs and living conditions in ancient Egypt, or would add to the facts already available. In addition, it was hoped that information would be forthcoming which might contribute to the historical data already on record about certain mummies in the collection.

To fulfil these aims a variety of techniques were used. Radiology provides the most acceptable method of investigation because it is a non-destructive technique, and a complete survey was, therefore, carried out. Conventional radiological techniques were employed, but greater scope existed for thorough investigation than on most previous occasions since, instead of portable equipment, it was possible to use hospital-based equipment. In addition, a new technique (tomography) was utilized and this made it possible to examine sites inaccessible to conventional radiography. The radiological survey aimed at providing information in the two main areas: palaeopathology and archaeology; in addition, it provided assistance with the dental survey.

The presence of disease in the mummified organs was determined and identified by using a variety of techniques; these included rehydration and preparation of the mummified tissue which was then examined by means of light microscopy and electron microscopy. In addition to its role in determining the genus of the worm which caused significant disease in one of the mummies, and the nature of the particles found in the lung tissue of another, electron microscopy was also used to examine certain mummies for the presence of heavy metals in the body tissues. A general survey of the mummified tissue also indicated the level of success achieved by the embalmers in preserving the tissues. The various insects found in the Manchester collection were identified by means of the electron microscope.

The bandages of one of the mummies were investigated by various techniques; from this, the nature of the material could be identified, both microscopically and macroscopically, and the substances applied to the bandages could be isolated and characterized. Additionally, their historical background and significance were examined.

A method was devised to obtain the fingerprints and toeprints of a particularly well-preserved mummy, and these provided an additional indication of the estimated age at death and the lifestyle of the person. Certain human mummies were selected for a controlled experiment in creating three-dimensional 'busts' of the heads, using techniques established on scientific principles, on which further studies and illustrations could be based.

In the wider context, the methods of mummification mentioned in the writings of Herodotus were explored, and a reconstruction of the techniques described there allowed the accuracy of these statements to be assessed.

The unwrapping and dissection of one of the mummies afforded an opportunity to examine a mummy in great detail, using multidisciplinary techniques. It was possible to obtain information which was not provided by the preliminary radiographs, including the presence within the bandages of prosthetic limbs and a phallus, gilded nipple amulets, covers for the finger-nails and toe-nails, and a pair of painted slippers. It also allowed a detailed study to be made of the bones of the head and the tibia. The dating of the bones and the bandages of the mummy by Carbon-14 techniques provided the conclusion that the body was about 1,300 years older than the bandages and therefore must have been re-wrapped at a later period.

In terms of palaeopathology, there were three significant discoveries of disease in the Manchester mummies. These included the calcified nodule in the anterior abdominal wall of Mummy 1770 which was identified by radiological investigation as a Guinea worm, the sand pneumoconiosis discovered in the lung tissue of Nekht-ankh (No. 21470), and the parasitic infestation present in the intestines of Asru (No. 1777). The dental survey showed that, apart from the unusual condition of the teeth of 1770, the teeth of the other human mummies exhibited evidence of the same problems which seem to have afflicted many people in Egypt. The most outstanding dental abnormality was the rare example of double gemination found in the mummy of Khnum-nakht (No. 21471).

In most cases, the cause of death was not apparent, although some of the above conditions may have hastened the death of an individual.

Information relating to religious and funerary customs and to living conditions is less specific but, subject to certain reservations, the experiments in mummification carried out on rats suggest that Herodotus's account of the types of mummification and the length of time involved is probably essentially accurate. Again, the use of tomography in the radiological investigation has enabled the effects of removing the brain to be looked at more closely and, in the wrapped mummies, it has been possible to determine the presence of amulets between the bandages. In the case of the animal mummies, radiology has enabled 'fake' mummies to be detected and, in some cases, it has also helped to establish the species of an animal within a hitherto unidentifiable package.

Re-examination of the bodies of the Two Brothers has confirmed the original report (1910) that the bodies are of such different types that it is difficult, if not impossible, to regard them as close relatives. Although the inscriptional evidence indicates that they are sons of the same mother, anatomical and other factors make it almost impossible to accept such a statement. It has been suggested that they were half-brothers, but it is perhaps more probable that one of the brothers was an adopted son.

It is also noteworthy that the three reconstructed heads belonging to the Two Brothers and to 1770 all bear a marked resemblance to types represented in ancient artforms. The heads of the Two Brothers correspond closely to the wooden statuettes found in their tomb and the type of face shown in the head of 1770 can be frequently seen in reliefs and sculpture.

However, the most interesting information relating to religious and funerary customs has undoubtedly derived from the unwrapping of Mummy 1770. The presence of the slippers, nipple amulets, prostheses, finger-nail and toe-nail covers, and cartonnage head and breast covers, suggests that a considerable degree of care was taken to prepare this body for eternity, despite the fact that the person's gender was apparently unknown to those who were involved in re-wrapping the body. The Carbon-14 dating techniques have provided the answers to a variety of questions resulting from the autopsy of this mummy, but the identity and provenance of the mummy and the cause of death cannot be determined. The date arrived at for the re-wrapping will also have to be considered in connection with the religious and funerary customs of that period.[1]

Although it would be highly undesirable for numbers of human mummies to be unwrapped and investigated to destruction, it is apparent from this experiment that, undertaken under the right conditions, a total investigation of this kind can provide information which is otherwise inaccessible, even using a non-destructive method of examination such as radiology.

In general, the research carried out on the Manchester collection has indicated that the results of such a multi-disciplinary investigation can make a valuable contribution to the existing knowledge of disease, living conditions, and religious practices amongst certain sections of ancient Egyptian society.

An intensive examination, employing mainly non-destructive techniques, of all Egyptian mummified remains and the compilation and co-ordination of the results obtained from such investigations would undoubtedly provide the palaeopathologist and the Egyptologist with a rich source of information relating not only to the history of disease but also to many aspects of ancient Egyptian society.

[1] See forthcoming article.

160